A Shoulder oι

Carol Madeline Graham

A Shoulder on the Hill

by

Carol Madeline Graham

First published November 2020
by
Wagtail Press, Gairshield, Hexham
Northumberland
NE47 0HS

http://www.wagtailpress.uk

email: wagtailpress@yahoo.co.uk

ISBN 978-0-9559395-5-6

This book is dedicated with love to John:
my endlessly patient, constantly encouraging
and extremely talented craftsman husband.
His ability to turn all my ideas, plans and dreams into
solid reality is astonishing and humbling.

CONTENTS

GUESTS

FAMILY

HILLSIDE

I saw upon the hillside, their eyes all black and cold,
The empty farmsteads standing lonely, proud and old;
And all the hill at Spanesfield was covered with gorse bloom,
Giving a gold glow softly to light each empty room.

Where are the bonny children who were born and lived inside?
Where are the old and tired ones, sat by their fireside?
The kennels are all empty now, the byres house just straw;
Shadows of a lapwing fall on a closed front door.

Where have they gone from Lark Seat, Hill Top and Throstle Nest?
Sweet Wells, Warm Wells and Harrow Bank?
When will they leave the rest?
A fire glowed inside that range, the flags were whitest stone;
An oil lamp in the window to guide the workers home.

I saw upon the hillside, their eyes all black and cold,
The empty farmsteads standing lonely, proud and old;
And all the hill at Spanesfield was covered with gorse bloom,
Giving a gold glow softly to light each empty room.

Carol Madeline Graham   Eastgate in Weardale
                                                    1972

OPENIN' THE GATE...

A woman leant on her scythe, pausing from slicing it through long grass stalks on the verge by a farm gate.

"It's just up there; go along to the crossroad and up the hill; on your left. There's a bit of a shoulder on the hill – the house sits right on it."

It was thus that we first found Hill House East.

And now it has been our home for nearly twenty years and there is nowhere else on God's good earth where l would want, or need, to be.

The word 'shoulder' has many meanings which perfectly describe the many roles the house has performed over those years:

Something to lean and rest on.

Something to depend on for comfort.

Something broad and strength giving.

Something to snuggle into lovingly.

Something to weep on.

What follows is a true account of incidents, places, people and animals that have formed the many rich layers of our life here.

There is nothing earth shattering or heroic about these tales, but they are, I hope, insightful into the nature and true value of a life shared with genuine, generous neighbours, animals with eccentric characters and people who have come to spend just a day or two under our old stone roof, arriving as total strangers and leaving as lifelong friends. The tales are interwoven around the central themes of our life, which are the same as those of any family:

Homemaking, marriage, births, deaths.

And of course, getting older.

I have been scribbling down notes about people, animals, family and guests for probably fifteen years or more. Recently I realised that my husband John and I were both aged around fifty when we moved here; we were 'middle aged' I suppose but filled with energy, enthusiasm and dreams. Now we are both aged around seventy; we still have the enthusiasm and the dreams, but the energy levels are dropping and, no matter how we try to ignore it or resent it, we *are* getting 'old' and the process is unlikely to reverse. On the plus side, we now have twenty years of memories, so I feel the time has come to draw from those memories all the tales of the setbacks and blessings, of the hard work and the rich rewards, of the sheer privilege of living in a place like Weardale, which remains at heart, a rural and even wild place. And, having done this, I would like to share our tales with you, in the hope that they might make you smile, or be touched, or even be surprised at what unfolds.

Whilst trying to organise my copious collection of notes and scribblings into something cohesive, I realised that they more naturally fell into sections that looked at the different facets of our life at Hill House East rather than into some sort of chronological account - and so that is how they are presented.

Upper Weardale is within the North Pennines Area of Outstanding Natural Beauty and is also within a UNESCO Global Geopark. It has a rich and fascinating history; the Romans hunted wild boar and mined lead and possibly silver here, the mediaeval Prince Bishops of Durham built Westgate Castle as a base from which to hunt the abundant local wild game and the population here exploded and then dwindled with the fortunes of the lead industry.

It is also one of the last upland sanctuaries for species of birds that are becoming increasingly scarce – the lapwing, the black grouse, the snipe and the glorious curlew.
It has been described as England's Last Wilderness. Yet many people have no idea it even exists.

So open the gate onto our world: Let me take you there, let me introduce you. Come and share a view of Weardale from our Shoulder on the Hill for a little while.

Carol Madeline Graham

FOREWORD

A Shoulder on the Hill

Carol Graham takes us with her on a journey, narrated with humour, discernment and, above all, love through 'twenty years of memories' of life in Weardale.

Her love for the Dale, its people, landscape, history, wildlife and even the weather illuminates, but never sentimentalises, the story she has to tell.

Acutely observed and compellingly written, A Shoulder on the Hill is essential reading for anybody who knows, or spends time in, the North Pennines.

Chris Powell

NorthPens Writers

The Incomers

1

RETURN OF THE INCOMER

It had taken me fifty years to find home; my soul-home, my never-want-to-leave-home. That's half a century. When I did find myself there, it was love at first sight - if it is possible to fall in love with a place rather than a person. Certainly all the pulse quickening, stomach fluttering, irrational, yearning ingredients were there; in which case it *was* love at first sight on that sunlit day in May. I stood knee deep in the grass of a once-lawn, gazed over the weeds of a once-garden to the far hillside with its chequerboard of grey stone walls running down to the valley bottom and my heart sang, 'This is where I want to be. This is where I actually need to be.'

Perhaps longing was a better word to use than love; an unexpected and overwhelming longing, not so much to possess as to *belong*. The Welsh have a word for this feeling, which cannot be exactly translated; 'Hiraeth'. It means a lot more than just feeling homesick or missing a place, it implies a longing for a place or time in your life that is ingrained in your very soul and being; a place or time that may in fact no longer exist and may have to remain forever a yearning. My incredibly longsuffering husband John, who had devoted most of the last five years to single-handedly creating our current most perfect and beautiful house from the very unpromising remains of some old stable buildings, received the news with quiet fortitude. We were both just into our fifties, our respective offspring from respective previous marriages were fledged and flown. We thought ourselves embarked upon a comfortable, uneventful journey through the next decade – one without sharp bends, hard inclines or rapid descents. A journey that would lead to that most desired of destinations; retirement. I truly subscribed to this plan. The two decades of my life prior to meeting John had been plagued by bad health, bad judgement, wrecked relationships and financial hardship. The decade subsequent to meeting him had been the most secure, happy and settled I had known and that was not something I wanted to prejudice. As well as my wonderful husband I had a fulfilling job and a daughter, my only child, who was doing well at university. Surely, to have wanted anything more than my very benign lot in life, would have been sheer greed?

And yet… there was one longing left unfulfilled.

I had once lived in Weardale in the early 1970s, in the first house I had ever owned. I had never known Weardale even existed until, searching for a cheap home within a ten mile radius of the school I was about to start work in, I found a dilapidated and long unlived in station master's house on the side of a railway line, then only used to transport cement trucks from the local factory. In fact, much of the adjacent area was dotted with old stone buildings in a dilapidated and derelict state; houses and farm buildings long deserted and mournful, settling quietly back into the hillsides. I was much moved by these and wrote the poem 'Hillside' which begins this book in 1972. My first husband and I put in a sealed bid of £4,066 for the station master's house which was accepted (probably we offered far too much) and we moved in joyfully to a property that had no useable electricity, a bucket on a rope down a well for water, a chemical toilet and dry rot in the hall. We were, as the locals put it, 'Incomers', having no birth right or family ties there in Weardale. And in the 1970s it took a very, very long time to lose the label 'Incomer' in Weardale. Not having a driving licence in those days, I took the little local bus into the nearest large village of Stanhope to do my shopping on a Saturday morning. Sat quietly at the back of the bus one day I could not help overhearing two elderly gentlemen in the seats in front of me:

"Ah hear he's dead then. Fred"

"Aye."

"He were a good age."

"Aye; eighty fower."

"Aye."

"Are ye goin' t'funeral?"

"No, ah think not. Ah mean, it's not as if he were local; he were fower years auld when they moved here."

"Aye."

I had shrunk into my seat thinking that there was no hope whatsoever for me or mine.

We would be Incomers forever!

In actual fact, we were accepted warmly by our neighbours in the Dale and I found that, as long as you were willing to put something back into the community rather than just take the privilege of living there for granted, then you were welcome – although you were, and always would be, an Incomer. And it was a privilege to live in Weardale. The river, from which it took its name, carved its way along the valley bottom with the villages strung out along its sides like beads on a necklace at roughly three mile intervals. The villages had names that were heavy with history; Stanhope, the main settlement, meant 'stone valley' from the Norse 'stane' (stone) and 'hope' (valley); a fitting description of Weardale with its quarrying and mining heritage stretching back to Roman times. Also with a Norse lineage came 'Ireshopeburn', which translated literally as 'The stream in the valley of the Irish' – by which was meant the Viking settlers who had come here via their territories in Ireland. Most people in Weardale shortened the pronunciation to 'Iyers-up-bun', though I heard truly vernacular speakers called it 'Arse-up'. Then there were the villages of Eastgate and Westgate, named for the entrances into the walled deer park that was once the private hunting ground for the Prince

3

Bishops of Durham in the heart of Upper Weardale in mediaeval times. The wall and the Bishop's castle at Westgate that he used as a hunting lodge were long gone by the twentieth century. But the village names remained, as did St John's Chapel; where the Bishop kept his own chapel of ease, dedicated to St John the Baptist, about a mile outside his hunting park walls. The 'ease' in this case presumably meant that he did not have to disturb his hunting activities by having to return to Durham to attend to his bishoply duties too often.

With its long history of hill farming and lead mining, Weardale was a unique environment. Livelihoods had been hard won. Tiny smallholdings had been carved out, higher and higher up its valley walls, nearly to the tops of the fells. All this achieved by people who had to be both miners and farmers if they wanted to make even the simplest of livings. Conditions in the mines and quarries had been brutal and life expectancy was short. When the lead mining industry crashed many families were forced to emigrate to unimaginably distant parts as their only chance of finding new work. And it must have been unimaginable for people, who had maybe never been further than Stanhope in their whole life, to set off for the other side of the world knowing their journey would be one way, with little hope of ever seeing familiar people or places again. Weardale began to empty and the stone houses and farm buildings, that drew the eye in every direction up the fell sides, were left to the weather and the wildlife; piles of stone slowly returning to the ground from which they had been hewn. The raw wounds of the quarries, mine spoil heaps and hushes had softened and healed over with vegetation through the years since they were last worked so that, by the 1970s, they too were fading and merging back into the hillsides where they had been formed and had just become another part of the undulating landscape. But Weardale was not, and never had been, a soft Dale, a pretty Dale. It was beautiful and challenging and wild; a place of hard work and hard livings but a place that its peoples were fiercely loyal to, fiercely proud of. Nor was it on a well frequented tourist route, like the Yorkshire Dales or the Lake District. But those who went there to walk or cycle or just to gaze upon its fells and valleys came away mystified that more people did not do the same.

First moving there in my early twenties, everything about Weardale was intoxicating; the river Wear that flowed fifty yards from my new home, the paths and lanes that rose steeply from it up to the fell tops where the trees and even the stone walls finally petered out and heather, sedge and boggy coarse grass took over. A kingdom of curlew, snipe, the rare black grouse and the hardy, wary Swaledale sheep. That life, and my introduction to Weardale, lasted only about four years before shattering around me like a breaking mirror. My first marriage ended very painfully. With that shattering went my job, my life as I had known it and my home. I found myself an exile from Weardale, still living within easy reach but unable to even travel down its length without eyes tightly closed, so painful was the loss of all that had been, so raw were the wounds. Although I was never to move more than twenty miles away from it for the next fifteen years, it became to me the promised land that I had loved, lost and mourned for. And then, aged forty one, I met John and I began to truly live again. On our agenda for some fairytale time in the future when I had retired, was a retreat to the hills of Weardale. One of the important synchronicities I had found with John was our shared love of Weardale. And most importantly his ties were formed by blood; a not insignificant advantage to an Incomer considering a comeback. His mother's family were called Westgarth, a well known name in Weardale; John's full name was in fact John Westgarth Graham. He proudly told me that his twice and thrice grandfathers had lived in Stanhope, were stonemasons who had lived at Jollyboddy Farm and were buried in Stanhope Churchyard. Further research found that even further back, as far as 1600, a John Westgarth had owned the manor of Unthank Hall in Stanhope and the family continued to do so until the 1730s when the Westgarths merged with the Hilyard family of Horsley Hall - the incumbent Westgarth at Unthank Hall having produced only three daughters. Maybe this was a sign to lead us back? I was a firm believer in signs and portents. It began to dawn on us (well, me really) that perhaps we should start making a move well prior to my retirement, so that any hard work on a new home could be done while we were still fit in wind and limb, and then we could enjoy living there awhile before we both needed walking frames. There was of course no rush, no panic but there would be no harm in just having a look around, seeing the sort of places that might be available. Surely picking up a few leaflets from local estate agents would be an interesting way to spend the odd Saturday afternoon? Of course, we would look no further west up the Dale than Stanhope, otherwise the drive to my school in Durham would be too long and the winter roads too difficult for me to get to work.

"But that house is in Westgate - that's seven miles west of Stanhope!" was John's response to me saying, 'Ooh, that's interesting!' when I looked in the very first brochure I had picked up.

"I know. But we are just looking aren't we? And it's only another ten minutes – and we're not doing anything else this afternoon are we?"

We followed the directions in the brochure, drove along the back lane from Daddryshield where the cow parsley was in full bloom in front of the hedgerows, bobbing up and down like ladies in creamy lace caps. Two women were cutting grass along the roadside; the younger, tall and strapping, was expertly wielding a scythe and the older was raking the herbage into piles with a wooden hay rake.

"Hello; we are looking for Hill House East. I wonder if you could tell us where it is?"

The younger woman leant on her scythe and brushed her hair back with her hand.

"It's just up there; go along to the crossroad and up the hill. On your left there's a bit of a shoulder on the hill – the house sits right on it."

My eyes followed the direction of her finger pointing to a place where the valley side, plunging headlong down towards the river at its foot, seemed to have paused briefly to catch its breath before making its final descent. There was indeed a shoulder on the hill and on it sat two stone houses. Anticipating my next question she volunteered, "They are both Hill Houses actually; you'll find Hill House East on your left of the hill.

It's empty, has been for over two years now. The people in the pub in the village own it. The one on the right is Hill House West."

Having said our thanks, it took less than a minute to drive to the crossroads, swing right up the steep hill and pull up on the flat shoulder beside the house on the left. The first impression was that it was a typical traditional stone built Weardale smallholder's house, probably around a hundred and fifty to two hundred years old, solid and thick walled. It still had its original heavy stone slab roof, which was a joy as so many of the old houses had had them replaced with modern roof tiles. What was unusual was that the house was orientated east and west, although the main entrance seemed to be through a recent porch extension along the south side. Most the other houses in the area were north and south facing, including the house opposite. What was incongruous about it, in fact verging on the ugly, was the second storey extension on the western side. In the 1960s and 1970s, when grants were as abundant as the number of empty properties in the Dale, everyone was encouraged to buy and modernise; planning requirements then were much more lax. The traditional homes tended to be only one or two rooms downstairs with a matching one or two rooms upstairs and then a single storey along one side, which housed the kitchen and scullery. This single storey was connected to the main part of the house by a long, steeply sloping 'cat-slide' roof on that side of the building. Modern home seekers required, quite reasonably, more than one or two bedrooms and considered indoor plumbing a necessity. The cheapest and easiest way to achieve this with a traditional property was to take off the cat-slide roof, build another storey on top of the kitchen area and then top off this extension with a flat, felted roof; a quick but ungainly solution that never looked in harmony with the original house. This had obviously been the fate of Hill House East and it had not added anything to it other than space.

"It's empty; shall we take a peek while we are here?"

"Do you think we should? I mean we haven't made an appointment or anything."

John was far more into proper procedure than I was.

"Oh come on! No one will mind - if it has been on the market for two years I should think they would be glad!"

We pushed open a rather rusty iron gate at the end of the drive and the first sight to greet our eyes was a partially decomposed rabbit lying on the tarmac; not the most promising of starts but I am by far the more curious - well, downright nosier - of the two of us and soon I was pressing my nose to the porch windows and gazing upon wall to ceiling, varnished pine panelling and red quarry tile floor set off by a large, scarlet, Spanish fan pinned to the wall; classic 1970s. Round the corner I peered into what was obviously the living room, a big room that covered the whole of the original two storey ground floor area. It had obviously also undergone 'modernisation' some decades ago and had a varnished pine, open tread staircase at one end - again classic 1970s - and a wooden pseudo-Adam fireplace surrounding a gas log-effect fire at the other. The decor was interesting; the two deep recessed alcoves were painted in billiard-table green gloss paint, and there were lots of imitation ships' brass wall lights. But the room was big and, mercifully, the original wooden ceiling beams were still in place, although they had been painted a most depressing brown colour. I retraced my steps, carefully avoiding the dead rabbit, and peer into the roadside window of the house. I saw a kitchen that was obviously very recently installed with uniform ranked kitchen units and cupboards, all with white PVC doors. Any hopes of an old Rayburn or Aga, a Belfast sink or any glimmer of character faded instantly. I thought of my lovely kitchen at home, so carefully crafted by John with handmade wooden cupboards, beech worktops, a walk-in shelved pantry and my large range cooker; it would take an awful lot to make this bland space a place that would make me as happy. John followed me on this inspection tour at a discrete distance and without making a comment, though I could pick up his thoughts on wife-radar; they were along the lines of, 'You must be joking.'

"Shall we look in the garden?" I asked brightly, not quite ready to give up on the place. John nodded in polite agreement and, pushing open an even rustier iron gate, we walked along an overgrown path and there it was: the View!

As I stood there on that glorious May day, what drew my eye and my heart was not the house behind me, nor the overgrown garden, but the view. It was sublime; no other word would suffice to describe it for me. Straight opposite, the south facing side of the Dale flowed down to the river banks in a series of fields that were separated by a chequer board of dry stone walls. The vertical walls did seem to literally flow down the hillside in streams of stone towards the river and the horizontal walls glowed in the afternoon sun, like the curtain walls of some ancient castle. Between the walls the hayfields and the pasture fields were every shade of green and yellow imaginable and the overall effect was like looking at some vast piece of quilting. To the west the high, conical peak of Burnhope Fell stood dark and commanding at the head of the Dale. Never before, nor since, have I come to such a strong and impetuous decision that seemed to override all common sense.

"This is it John, this is where I want to live. Forever if possible."

He cleared his throat. "But, this is the first house we have looked at in Weardale, and, um, we haven't actually been inside the house yet."

"I know. But it doesn't matter; I know you will make it wonderful, whatever state it is in. Look at that view John, just *look* at it. Can you honestly tell me if you have ever seen a more glorious view than that? It's, well… it's what I've been searching for, longing for, for twenty seven years. I feel I've finally come home John – to my soul home I suppose; it's where I need to be. Can you understand? I just feel, *know*, that for me this place is really it.'

I don't think he really did but he could tell that I was being serious, that I was, in some genuine way, deeply affected by the place where I stood.

"So it will be down the pub to ask for the key, will it?"

The inside of the house did not have quite the same transformational effect on me as the outside. Although the house appeared basically sound and in terms of space offered all we needed, there was not a single room we came out of without a discussion of what it would need to put it right. The main problem was that the house had been modernised in around the 1970s in a way that disguised or altered its inherent, simple character

9

and, thirty odd years on, those features were neither modern nor original. Flush doors, brown diamond leaded windows and liberal daubings of Artex swirling over all the ceilings were simply out of keeping, as were the log effect gas fire and the open tread staircase that was more like a fire escape. The two rooms that had obviously been recently upgraded, the bathroom and the kitchen, had been installed with fittings that, whilst clean and shiny, were just not sympathetic with the house. Even the original beams in the upstairs rooms had been boxed in with plywood. But we both had enough experience of old houses to know that all these issues were superficial and mostly cosmetic. With effort, time, expense and above all love, the true character of the house could be restored; nothing had been done internally to actually destroy it. And the views from the windows were as glorious as the views from the garden.

Having put so much effort into creating our existing home John had declared, when it was finally finished, that he would never take on such a physically challenging project again. But I knew that actually, a couple of years on from its completion he was often seeking for a job to do, itching for a project. Unlike the old stables, Hill House East did not actually need rebuilding, it just needed, well, alterations and it was perfectly sound enough to live in while these were done and these could be done at as leisurely a pace as we wanted.

I decided to play my trump card.

Whilst my long time unfulfilled dream was simply to return to Weardale, John's had always been a hankering to run a little bed and breakfast business. By profession he was neither a builder nor a joiner, but a printer and as the twenty first century began small printers were going out of business every week as personal computers took over a lot of the bread and butter work of their trade. The writing had been on the wall for a while that John's business was becoming increasingly unviable and we had had discussions on the need to get out while he could and to do something else. But what? I had a good teaching job that I enjoyed; I was responsible for the sixth form in a special school for young people with learning difficulties. We were lucky in that we could without doubt

10

manage to live on my salary. John had kept on with his business mainly to provide him with some income of his own – though this was increasingly diminishing – but also because, at fifty one and never having done anything other than printing, he was doubtful he would get any other sort of employment.

I slid my arm through his as we both gazed eastwards right up the Dale through the main bedroom window.

"Just think about this seriously for a moment. This house has got everything you could ever look for in a little country B&B; the location in an Area of Outstanding Natural Beauty, the views, lovely walks in all directions and a layout that would lend itself to providing a couple of guest bedrooms, whilst still allowing us the space and privacy of our own home when people stayed. "What if," and I took a deep breath at this point, "What if we could manage to buy it and you gave up printing and worked here instead, doing all the alterations, steady away, not in a mad rush? In a couple of years or so we could be putting up a B&B sign and welcoming the first guests. This house could fulfil both our dreams John; do you not think we should give it a chance to do so?"

The following six months were not ones I would wish to live through again. We put our current home on the market the next day and then just lived on our nerves waiting for someone to buy it. The sellers on the other hand were in no rush to sell; Hill House East, they announced, would go to the first person that came along ready to meet the full asking price with no complications or delays. We braced ourselves against the possibility of someone else snapping it up. We travelled far and wide looking at other properties for sale that were as desirable as Hill House East, but none came even close. We took our nearest and dearest to see it to gauge their opinion on it. My best friend thought it was absolutely perfect. My daughter burst into tears and said what sort of social life would she have when she returned from uni, stuck out in the hills with a load of sheep? John's father said he wouldn't give ten grand for it as a holiday bolthole and we must be mad. As so often happens, just when you give up on something and reluctantly box your dreams away for another time, we got a knock on the door from a couple who lived less than a mile away who said they had always liked the look of our cottage. Their aunt had just died and had left a healthy bequest; they had a neighbour who had always said she would buy their house if they moved, and who had the cash to do so. And, unbelievable as it sounded, that was completely true, despite the day being Friday 13th October. Legal wheels went clashing into gear and the completion date for our respective moves was set for sometime in mid December.

The Incomer was about to return…

2

IN THE BLEAK MIDWINTER

The move took place approaching the end of the first year of the new millennium; eleven days before Christmas, five days before my birthday and seven days before the Winter Solstice, the darkest, bleakest point in the year; the Celtic festival of Yule. Schools actually allowing such things in those days, I was granted a day's leave of absence for the move. Early in the morning, having spent a sleepless night on a mattress on the floor of our otherwise packed bedroom, I put an indignant cat into a travelling box and then put her and our rolled up bedding into the back of my car. We then watched as two very big furniture vans rolled into our yard. We needed two; one for the house contents and one for John's large and well equipped workshop.

The cunningly dovetailed plan was for our new buyers to be loading up at the same time as us so that, when we rolled off our drive, they would roll off theirs and we'd drive to our respective new homes where, at 11.00 am on the dot, we would be phoned by our respective solicitors to be told the sale was now complete, the cash was in the right hands and we could collect our respective keys from the respective people. Idiot proof, surely? Mind you, I had always wondered why it was necessary to play this cat and mouse game of not exchanging contracts till the clients were actually waiting on their new doorstep with a freezer full of thawing food! But it was not my place to question the sanctity of the British legal system. We sat outside Hill House East gazing longingly at the locked door when, bang on time, the phone rang.

"Mrs Graham? Um, good morning, um..."

'Um' is never an encouraging word to hear from a solicitor, so I braced myself.

"There appears to be a bit of a problem."

"Go on." I said, though I did not want to know.

"There would appear to be a problem with a previous mortgage on your new property, so I'm afraid we are not in a position to exchange contracts."

"And you find this out *NOW*, when we are actually sitting on the doorstep!"

"Well, it's not quite as bad as it sounds. The mortgage has been paid off..."

"So what is the problem?"

"Well, it has not been recorded as such on the deeds."

"Can't you get in touch with the people that made the loan and sort it out?"

"Well, um, yes, we are trying to... but it is a bank in Ireland."

"Ireland?"

"Ireland."

"Do you know it will be pitch dark here in just over four hours? Do you know that there are people sitting on our old drive wondering what the hell is going on? Do you know my cat has been in a box in the car since seven this morning?"

"We are doing everything we can, Mrs Graham, but as your solicitors we cannot advise exchange of contracts till this is resolved, nor the handing over of keys."

"Look, whatever it is do something and do it quickly."

Nauseous with disbelief, I reported back to John and the removal men, who lifted their eyes heavenward in a 'now I've heard it all' glance. At midday, in an attempt to raise morale, I went to Stanhope for fish and chips all round. The day, which had not started out warm, was now cooling rapidly and we were chilly, frustrated and hungry. I tried to offer the wailing cat a tempting morsel of fish in her box in my car but she just hissed at me and then continued her wailing.

By one o'clock I was a nervous wreck every time the phone rang; could it be our solicitor with encouraging news? Was it our purchasers venting another tirade about why they couldn't have our keys? Usually it was the latter and I ran out of platitudes and apologies, pointed out we were in the same boat and suggested they ring our solicitor and put a bomb under her.

By two o'clock the light was starting to fade and the removal men were getting mutinous; they might not be able to get into the house but, they pointed out, the workshop was a large building and they could easily get the padlock off that and pile everything into there. I discouraged them, not wanting to add a charge of breaking and entering onto a list of the day's woes. I felt sick with fear and fury, my fish and chips lying in my stomach like stones. At three o'clock, as a winter evening spread over the hillside and the temperature dropped still further, I reluctantly answered the phone again; all the fight was going out of me.

"Mrs Graham? Good news. We have managed to get the charge removed from the deeds so we can now exchange contracts. But.."

"*But?* No, no, no – tell me there isn't a 'but'."

"Well, the problem is that it is now too late to actually exchange the funds across; but I assure you that will be done first thing tomorrow morning."

I was trying to compose an answer in my mind that would best express a response to that statement, when a car pulled up and out got the lady from the pub; our vendor.

"Right, enough of this nonsense," she said, "Is that your solicitor? Give me that phone!"

I nodded.

"Now listen to me, I am not having these people sitting freezing on this hill a minute longer. I am giving them the keys to the house and if that's not correct legal procedure then you should have done your job right in the first place. And see you sort out this mess, *sharpish*, in the morning!"

My soul, and my fish and chips, felt suddenly lighter.

15

"Thank you! Thank you!" I said rather deliriously, clutching the bunch of keys.

"Bloody ridiculous!" she fumed and slammed her car door and drove off.

"Hello? Hello – Mrs Graham?" It was my solicitor sounding frantic now.

"Yes. Now listen very carefully; as my solicitor I am instructing you to send our keys round at once to our buyers. Do you understand? At once!"

"But.."

"No buts!"

I switched the phone off and waved the keys at the removal men; "We're in!"

At three thirty in the afternoon, at 1,150 feet in the North Pennines, one week before the shortest day, night comes swiftly. But the removal men were trying to outrun it. They should have been long gone by now, instead of which they were just beginning to heave and haul everything out of the two big vans as rapidly as they could. I am a very organised person and I like forward planning. On this occasion, it had meant carefully colour coding every box so that I knew, not only whether it was for upstairs or downstairs, but also for which room.

"Sorry missus," the removal man grunted when I made squeaking noises about the random heaps of multicoloured boxes that were growing on the kitchen and living room floors. "There's no time to sort it, the best we can do is to just get it in. We'll put the furniture upstairs for you though."

Ah well, at least there was some hope of a bed for the night!

With my organiser's hat on I had arranged the switch over of the electricity, water and phone to our name, so at least we had all lights blazing to speed the work. The heating was a different matter. Heating at Hill House East was solely by LPG gas; no mains gas in the country. The gas was stored in a huge, very ugly green tank that resembled a submarine in dry dock, just outside the back door. Now the house had been empty for over two years but the vendors assured us that they had always kept a bit of gas in the tank so that they could keep the frost-stat on in the house to prevent things freezing up if it got really cold. As the evening wore on and the temperature continued to drop I began to wonder just how cold it would have to get before the boiler kicked in! But there was no time to investigate as I tried to channel the constant stream of all our worldly goods into vaguely the right directions. In any case, the outside doors were all wide open. By about five thirty, the last items were in, the big doors on the vans were shut, the men climbed in, I suspect very thankfully, and they rolled away down the hill.

It was pitch black outside.

We shut the front and back doors and were truly in possession of Hill House East for the first time. It should have been a lovely moment of elation. But we were too exhausted and cold and almost overwhelmed by the haphazard piles of boxes to feel elation; I certainly didn't feel like getting the carefully stowed bottle of bubbly and glasses out of my car, but sheer necessity demanded I rescue the cat.

"John! Go up and see if you can get the heating on full blast while I get Holly out of my car. Thanks!"

Holly was beyond howling and complaining. She seemed just as miserable and overwhelmed as I felt but I gave her a cuddle, got her bed, supper and litter tray out of the boot and, feeling rather guilty, shut her in the porch. There was just too much to do before bed without worrying about losing her.

"There's no gas."

"Sorry?" – a stupid thing to say when I had heard John perfectly well.

"There's no gas; the boiler won't come on nor will the gas fire in the living room. There is no gas."

"Oh."

"So there is no heating and no hot water – the boiler does both."

"Oh."

Five years as a Girl Guide and three years training at the Yorkshire College of Housecraft had prepared me for just such moments.

"Right; well you can order some more tomorrow. I'm just going to get the Emergency Survival Box out of your car and you look round for the electric convector heater – I'm sure I saw it in the living room somewhere."

The Emergency Survival Box provided us with a kettle, milk, sugar, tea, biscuits, fruit cake, cheese and apples. Oh, and mugs, plates, knives, a teaspoon, a towel and a toilet roll. With a hot drink and sweet food inside us and hands warmed over the rising hot air of the convector, things did not seem quite as bad.

"Right, I think we should get our bedroom organised now. I'll go out and get our bedclothes out of my car and you go and put that convector in the bedroom. I also need to get clothes organised for school tomorrow somehow."

"Remind me why you are going to work tomorrow? Remind me why we couldn't have had the move tomorrow and then the weekend ahead of us to get sorted out?"

I shook my head firmly, "Oh no, we couldn't have done that, not move on a Friday; my mother would think we were mad!"

"Because...?"

"It's one of her little sayings; 'Friday flitting, short time sitting.'"

"Oh, of course," John muttered sarcastically, "Well we don't want that, do we?"

"Certainly not! Once we are settled in here I've no intention of moving for a very long time."

As I went to open the kitchen door I noticed that a thin blade of icy air was blowing right down one side, probably because the door did not quite fill the frame. Moving to the front door I discovered where the icy air was coming from; down a similar sized gap to the outer world. Bracing myself I stepped out into the freezing, inky blackness beyond. No street lights, no sound, just intense cold and a moonless sky, that showed no delineation from the rising hillside, spangled with stars. This was my first experience of Hill House East at night and it was powerful, beautiful and just a little scary. I gathered the bedclothes from the back seat of the car where I had dumped them what seemed like days ago, but was, in reality, only twelve hours. I headed back for the house where light spilled out from the windows for the first time in more than two years. I felt a small surge of pleasure; this was the first step to bringing it back to life.

"The phone is dead."

"Sorry?"

I was doing it again; I had heard perfectly well.

"The phone is off. It doesn't work"

"Oh. Well... I'll contact the phone people from school tomorrow while you contact the gas people."

"But there is no phone"

"Oh. Well... I'll do both shall I? Look, it's been a long day and we are both shattered. Let's go up and get the bed sorted out. Tell you what, I'll make another hot drink and then I'll bring a kettle of hot water up and we can have a nice warm wash."

John merely grunted assent. What I knew he really wanted, and what he knew I really wanted was a nice, long, hot bath. But there was no hot water. A long, hot shower would have been equally good, but there was only a bathtub. So it was a splash about in a frigid bathroom sink with a kettle of hot water. Then we closed the bedroom door, switched off the convector heater and I opened the bedroom window a crack, as I did every single night, and we climbed wearily beneath the bed clothes, switched off the light and drifted off to sleep embraced in each other and the utter darkness and stillness of the hillside night.

I was dragged out of sleep by the cold.

I don't think I have ever been so cold in bed in my life. I had drifted away from John and, when I tentatively moved a hand or foot a few inches away from the exact outline of where I was lying, there was no warmth in the bed at all. My feet and hands were too unbearably cold to place on warmer parts of my body and my jaw was beginning to chatter with shivering. As I leaned up to look at the clock I would not have been surprised if what was left of the warm air in the bed had risen, condensed, frozen and fallen back on us as tiny snowflakes. It was two thirty in the morning and I was utterly miserable. I pulled the quilt round my head, rolled towards the certain heat that always radiated from John and, placing my freezing nose in between his shoulder blades and my freezing feet on the back of his legs, I began to sob. One, or all, of these actions brought him quickly awake.

"Hey? What's the matter? Are you crying? God, your feet are cold!"

"What have we done?" I wailed and sniffed. I thought of our previous immaculate, well insulated cottage, the mains gas central heating, our hot powerful shower, my range cooker nurturing a slow cooking stew and then realised that none of those things were ours anymore; we had sold them to someone else - to come and freeze in this draughty, Artexed, stone relic.

Then I wailed some more.

"What have we done? It's my fault! I made you come here! What have I done?"

Life is always at its most unbearable around two o'clock in the morning.

"Hey, shush, shush; it's not that bad, though there is an arctic blast coming in through that window!"

"You know I always sleep with the window open."

"Fresh air is one thing, hypothermia another," John slid out of bed, dashed to the window, shut it and dived back in again. "Snuggle in and get warm; go back to sleep. You'll have to get up for school soon."

The man was a saint.

I found out later that the temperature had dropped to minus five that night.

The 6.30 am morning alarm clock sounded cruelly in the still pitch black and frigid bedroom and once again I wanted to moan 'What have I done?' but I already knew exactly what I had done; moved us into an unheated, long unlived in, very old stone house above 1,000 feet in the North Pennines. And I had also nearly trebled my journey to work from ten miles to twenty seven miles, a lot of it over high moorland. And I would have to make this journey for at least the next ten years. So, the alarm clock would going to go off at 6.30 am weekdays, winter and summer, for the next decade and I had better get used to it because I had only myself to blame. Washing in the little bit of hot water left over in the kettle from our morning tea, made me realise just how much we take for granted; all the comforts and conveniences in our modern homes. When I was a little girl I used to stay with an elderly great aunt who was crippled with her 'rheumatics' yet called home the ground floor of a 'Tyneside Flat' in Blaydon with appalling damp, no bathroom, no running hot water, an outside toilet and a coal fire to relight every morning. So when I stayed with her, when we got up in the morning, before the fire was lit and in the interests of speed and the economy of 'saving the gas', I had to tip out the contents of my hot water bottle into an enamel bowl in the scullery to have my morning wash, the just tepid water redolent of perishing rubber with small, red, gritty lumps floating on the surface. I could evoke the sensation and the smell for ever after.

The journey to school seemed endless but as I headed towards Durham at least light was gradually returning to the sky. The day passed over somehow, though I am not sure how I managed to teach feeling so utterly exhausted and wretched.

"How did the move go?" my teaching assistants asked cheerily.

"Don't ask. Please just don't ask." I tanked up on as much tea, coffee, snacks and hot food as I could throughout the day and found enough energy to ring the gas and phone companies at lunch time.

"Gas delivery? Mmm, not over the weekend. Monday at the earliest; it is getting very near Christmas, we are very busy".

"Engineer to check the phone line? Mmm, not over the weekend. Monday at the earliest; it is getting very near Christmas, we are very busy."

Determined to be more proactive about our situation, I gave myself a good talking to. So what if we had no central heating, no hot water, no shower and no phone? Good God, I was a Queen's Guide, I had been trained by Miss Millington in Home Management at the Yorkshire College of Housecraft; I knew how to survive! We had a kettle, a microwave, an electric toaster and a convector heater; what more did we need? On my way home I stocked up on good bread, plenty of butter and lots of things that could be easily heated up. I cheered myself with the thought that, by the time I got home, John would have brought some order to the chaos and soon he would hitch up our lovely gas range cooker so we could have some real food. The journey home seemed to take even longer than the journey to school, the light fading rapidly with each mile, the unfamiliar bends and twists in the narrow road up the Dale getting more tiring to drive with each mile. But at last I was back safely - I couldn't bring myself to say '*home*' yet – with the shopping and a whole weekend ahead. John seemed cheery enough, which was encouraging. Many of the stacks of boxes had been dispersed, hopefully to their correct destinations and he had the convector heater going full blast in the kitchen, so it actually felt quite habitable. Holly the cat glowered maliciously at me, glued into her basket next to the heater as if to say, *"I won't forgive you for this. Not for a very long time."*

"Good day?" he enquired.

"It's over and it's Friday, those are the main things and..." I opened a carrier bag with a flourish, "I've resorted to a microwave meal and a bottle of red wine to wash it down. Let's eat! Just think, by Monday we'll have a proper cooker again."

"Um..."

It was that word again!

"Oh no! No, no, no! Don't say they aren't bringing the gas!"

"Actually, that's the least of our problems. You know how I made enquiries about our cooker and whether it would work on bottled gas as well as on mains gas and was assured it would?"

"I don't think I want you to tell me."

But, of course, he had to.

"Well, reading all the small print in the handbook it would appear that it won't. Nor can it be converted to use LPG"

"Therefore?"

I knew the answer to the question but asked it anyway out of sheer masochism.

"Well, it's no good; we'll have to offload it, buy a new one. Of course, I would have phoned the firm again if I could have done..."

"...but we have no phone" I finished for him.

My spirits plummeted to a level that was as soggy and flaccid as our food was going to be once it had been heated in the microwave. Was this some sort of trial by the fates, the divine- or both - to test my resolve over the move? I grabbed the wine bottle and twisted its neck; "Wine?"

"Lovely!" smiled John; he truly was a saint.

The wine had just begun to glug into two mugs – the glasses were yet to be unpacked – when a car drew up slowly outside, its door slammed and there was a knock on our front door; our first visitor! The very thought was cheering and, when I opened the door, there stood Jessie Pickering with a basket on her arm.

"Oh, I've found you at last!" she said with obvious relief.

Jessie was the last person I had imagined to find standing there. She was a retired college lecturer, a cookery teacher of the old school like myself, who had been my boss for several years when I had first gone back to teaching out of sheer, desperate financial need after many years out of the profession. She had guided, supported and helped me and later become a good friend. She lived in the Lower Dale at Wolsingham and was a pillar of the local church and choir. She was a very private person and a reluctant driver who disliked new journeys or driving in the dark. Yet there she was on the doorstep, framed in blackness, with a steaming basket on her arm.

"Jessie! What a lovely surprise! Come in, come in; you are our first visitor!"

"No, thank you, I won't come in," she said emphatically, "I've just come to give you this. I know how upside down things are when you have just moved and I thought you could do with a good hot meal without the bother of cooking. That is if it is still hot; I wasn't sure where you lived exactly - I have had to knock on a fair few doors in Westgate to find you!"

"Oh Jessie, how very kind of you. I don't know what to say. Look, do please come in; at least let me offer you a cup of tea?"

The basket was thrust into my hands.

"No, I must go; I am worried the roads will freeze up and you will have lots to do. Don't let it get cold!"

"Don't worry Jessie, we won't. And thank you *so* much."

She found her way back to her car, did a very cautious twelve point turn and rolled slowly away. I watched till the red dots of her tail lights had disappeared down the hill and then turned, amazed, into the kitchen. Opening the basket we found, carefully insulated with towels, a tasty stew with mashed potato and carrots and a hot treacle tart with a pot of custard. Underneath, wrapped in foil, there was a selection of home baked biscuits, flapjack and fruit cake – presumably just to keep us going. Food had rarely been so welcome or tasted so good. But it wasn't just the warmth and comfort of the meal that made us feel so happy and grateful, it was that this good, kind person should drive out on a dark December night to an unsure address and persevere to find us and bring us cheer in our new home.

Home!

I had actually said the word; home. For better or worse, for richer or poorer, Hill House East was indeed now our home and, for the first time, thanks to such astonishing true Weardale kindness, it felt like the right place to be.

3

IT CAME UPON A MIDNIGHT CLEAR...

The second night, thanks to an extra quilt, a closed window and a long flannelette nightie, we slept as snug as two hibernating dormice. Next morning, which was bright though bitterly cold, we consumed large quantities of tea and hot toast and then set about sorting out our new home in earnest. A little later in the morning, when we were outside the front door trampling on emptied boxes, we heard the steady throb of a quad bike coming down the hill. How little did we guess that that noise and tempo was to become part of the daily pulse of our life on the Hill. The bike pulled up and a broad, stockily built man with very close cropped sandy hair and apparently only one front tooth, wearing wellies with turned down tops and a warm jacket that had seen better days, swung his leg across the quad bike and greeted us.

"Mornin."

"Good morning."

"Ah see yer in then?

"Well," I laughed, "After a fashion."

"Aye, I heard ye had a bit of bother like."

I looked at him quizzically and he looked back at me - or at least one eye looked at me; the other was roving somewhere over the other side of the Dale, as if scanning for a lost sheep.

"Small village, small village; nowt's a secret here for long. Any road, ah just came down to introduce mesel' and see if ye needed any help. Ah'm

Ian Dent by the way, from Glenwhelt - the farm just up the hill there – close enough to mak' us neighbours I think."

We made our own introductions and then I made the customary offer of a cup of tea.

"By, ah won't say no; it's got a bite to it up on't fell this morning. Not as cold as night before; d'ye know it went down to minus five on Thursday night?"

"I know it did," I told him, "It was our first night here and I nearly froze to death in bed!"

"Canna be havin' that! Howway John, de ye not know how to keep yer missus warm in the night?"

John shuffled his feet a bit awkwardly. Ian took my arm and led me gently to one side, one eye staring earnestly at me, the other wandering off on a journey of its own. He lowered his voice and drew close to my ear; "Seriously, is he, well, much trouble to ye in the night?"

I was completely stumped as to what to say; was he joking? Was he serious?

"Well, I, er... well, no – not usually."

Ian nodded sagely, "If he ever is then, you just let me know; ah've got just the thing to sort him."

He put his hand in his pocket, fumbled around, withdrew something and placed it solemnly in my hand. It was an orange, rubber castrating ring for a lamb. Then he burst out laughing and clapped us both on the back. "Ee, ah'm sorry; couldn't resist it! Ye'll get used to it – me sense of humour that is. Now, did someone say tea, cos' ah'm claggin!"

So I led the way into the kitchen and tea was taken with Ian Dent and, had I but known it, that was to be the first occasion of something that was to become an almost daily part of our life.

And one of the richest.

It took Ian Dent the best part of an hour to have his tea, during which time he pretty well managed to fill us in with his life story. He lived at Glenwhelt, a hill farm of about 3,000 acres that filled the vast, bowl-like valley of Swinhope that rose above our house to an altitude of nearly

2,000 feet. The road up was a single track road punctuated with five gates across it. At its summit, (where Weardale ended and Teesdale began) it was the highest minor road in England. Glenwhelt was owned by the Vickers family, whose home farm was at Thornley, some fifteen miles away at the lower end of Weardale. Ian was employed as shepherd at Glenwhelt, a position held by his father before him and his grandfather before that. Incredibly, he worked that vast acreage and flock alone on a quad bike, whereas in his grandfather's day, there had been at least four men, lots of dogs and several fell ponies. Ian had worked alongside his father Ray until he finally retired and now he worked alone. Ian had been born in Swinhope, raised in Swinhope, had worked in Swinhope since he left school at fifteen and had never ventured much outside of County Durham in the fifty something years of his life. Swinhope was one of the ancient Weardale names that echoed back a thousand years or more to the game rich forests that once filled it. 'Hope' was the Anglo Saxon for a valley and 'Swin' derived from swine – in this case the wild boar that once roamed there. So, literally, Boar Valley. The next valley up to the west was Harthope, presumably because it was a rich hunting ground for deer. I knew there had once been wild boar in Weardale because at Eastgate, some three miles away, a stone Roman altar had been found giving thanks for a very fine specimen killed by a centurion hunting there. Two thousand years on and the boar had gone, the forests that they had lived in changed by man and sheep into open, upland fell. But the name and the memory lingered and so we found ourselves living at the foot of Swinhope.

On the Monday evening I drove back from school in high spirits; central heating, a gas fire to sit in front of, hot water and contact with the outside world. It was the 18th December and there were only two days till the end of term and then we could really begin to get into the mood for our first Weardale Christmas!

John's face however, looked less than festive when I pulled up in the car. My spirits sank yet again.

"Don't tell me; no phone and no gas?"

27

"No, no" he said cautiously, "We have both; gas tanker has been, phone engineer has been and phone is on; the cable had frayed and filled with water."

"But..." I ventured.

"No heat and no hot water; I have been working on it all afternoon and it would appear that the boiler is broken."

I omitted the expletives and just said "Oh," before adding, 'Well, if the phone is on I'll just call the insurance people! We've got one of those 24/7 policies where they promise to be out within a day. Remember?"

By the time I came off the phone my warm glow of hope had been replaced by cold disbelief.

"What's the problem?"

"Well, I forgot to tell them that we were moving, that's the first problem – although it is not a big problem as the policy is transferable. But, the policy covers every conceivable make and model of boiler - except LPG. They don't insure, or repair, LPG boilers."

"What! Why not?" John spluttered indignantly, but all I could do was shrug my shoulders miserably.

"Tell you what," it was John's turn to come up with a bright idea, "I've just realised we have the gas –so we can now use the gas fire in the living room! You make us a bite to eat and pour a couple of glasses of wine, I'll light the gas fire and we can toast our toes while we have supper. Good idea?"

So while I put together yet another meal heated up in the microwave, John sat down on the hearth with a box of matches and began fiddling about and turning knobs. Soon there was an encouraging '*woomph*' sound and gas flames began to flicker around the pseudo logs. I took the wine glasses through and we chinked them with a toast to the heat to come.

"Thank God." I sighed.

But it was not heat that began to radiate from the fireplace; it was a wave of horrible smelling fumes and smoke that made us cough and splutter.

"Turn it off!" I yelled, "We are going to be poisoned! Or blown up!"

John quickly switched the fire off and opened all the windows, which allowed gusts of icy air into the room. I retreated into the kitchen, once more on the verge of tears and wondering if anything, ever, was going to go right for us in our new house or were we simply cursed.

"It's Christmas next weekend and Megan's coming home from university; some Christmas it's going to be! Microwaved turkey and all sharing a convector heater and a kettle of water to wash with. And," I wailed, "It's my birthday tomorrow!"

"There, there. I'll sort something out; I promise." I had complete faith in John as an ingenious fixer of all things practical, but how he was going to sort things out I had no idea and went to bed, again cold, miserable and disheartened.

"Getting very near Christmas pet and we're all pulled out; funny how everyone's boiler goes on the blink with the first big freeze isn't it?" said the first man I eventually found who would even entertain looking at an LPG central heating boiler. I personally didn't think it was very funny at all but I moved swiftly on.

"We are honestly absolutely desperate," I pleaded, "Five days now since we moved in and we have no heat and no hot water. We just so want to celebrate Christmas in our new home but, if things don't improve, we might be warmer moving into a farm building with the animals, like Mary and Joseph. I admit I am not just about to give birth to the Messiah, but, today *IS* my birthday; and that's the honest truth – six days before Christmas – that's why I am called Carol you see! Please try and help us; we'll pay you double for coming all the way out here, just *please come*!"

"Tell you what pet, I really can't do anything today or tomorrow but I think I could squeeze you in on Wednesday. How about that?"

"Oh thank you, thank you! That's the best birthday present I could have!"

Wednesday 21st December acquired a new importance. It was no longer just the shortest day, the Winter Solstice, the old Celtic festival of 'Yule' when our hemisphere began to turn back into the light of the sun again. Nor was it the just the day when the long, hard school term ended for me: it was the day that the boiler man came!

I drove home optimistically. I was beginning to get to know all the twists and bends in my journey now, even in the dark. By the time I went back to school in the New Year, the days would already be just that little bit longer and lighter and each week would see the light increase. I had a bag full of Christmas cards and gifts from my colleagues and students and hope in my heart. When I pulled up outside the front door there was a curious pile of rubble to one side of it but I couldn't make it out what it was in the dark. I passed quickly through the porch, which was still perishing cold but, when I opened the kitchen door, a wave of warm air rushed towards me.

"He came!" I shrieked, "The boiler man came! The radiators are hot!"

"And," John walked over to the kitchen sink and turned a tap on; steam was actually rising from the sink as water gurgled down the drain. Hot water!

"Thank you God! Thank you gas man!"

"Oh, there's one more thing," John smirked as he propelled me across the kitchen and opened the living room door.

When I had left that morning the fireplace had surrounded a cold, dead and lethal gas fire. Now the fireplace surrounded a hearth where a hot, cheerful coal fire burned in a grate.

"But... how?"

"Well, I just had to get that gas fire out, it was dangerous; no wonder it didn't work, it was all corroded and rusted away behind. But, once it was out, there was a perfectly serviceable chimney and hearth behind it, so I went out and bought a grate and some coal – and a fireguard! – and well: belated happy birthday!"

"It certainly is! What a wonderful, wonderful present! I think it is time to finally open that bottle of bubbly; I think things are coming right at last."

That evening we sat bathed in firelight, watching the flames and soaking up the heat while we drank our champagne.

"Here's to us and here's to Hill House East; may we share many happy, healthy years together."

"I'll drink to that." John chinked my glass.

"Do you know what would make the best possible end to the day?"

"Go on."

"A long, deep, hot bath!"

Within ten minutes I had the tub as full as I dared with water as hot as I dared and I sank beneath the fragrant, bubbly water with an audible 'Aahh!' as I immersed myself up to my neck. I had dreamed of this moment all week. My bliss was short lived however as John pounded up the stairs and burst unceremoniously into the bathroom.

"What are you doing!"

"What do you mean?" I replied indignantly "I'm just trying to enjoy my bath!"

"Have you forgotten to turn the tap off and let the bath run over?"

"No! Why?"

"Because there is water pouring through the kitchen ceiling, that's *why*!"

Thus ended the bliss of my first bath and, after the water was emptied and John got the side panel off, the reason for the leak was clear; a brand spanking new bathroom suite might have been installed but a connection for the overflow from the bath had not, so when I got in and the water level rose it had flowed straight out of the overflow onto the floor beneath the bath then through into the kitchen.

"Sorry to spoil your first bath."

John looked quite crestfallen.

"Don't be silly; you haven't – you couldn't! I think it's quite funny actually. There's us getting cocky about all our troubles being over but the old house had to have the last say. I think it is trying to test us."

"What? Sorry?"

John did not share my more eccentric beliefs, such as places and buildings having a sort of soul, a spirit of their own – a type of memory that reflected what had happened there, who had lived there over time. He did however humour me in this as it was so much easier than arguing.

"Well, think about it. This house has been knocked about a lot over the centuries and recently it's been badly neglected. Abandoned actually, for over two years. Cold, damp and unloved. If you were this house, before you embarked on another long term relationship, wouldn't you want to make sure that the new people who wanted to call you home were really committed? Ready to see you, warts and all, and still want you? Not going to give up easily on you?"

"Well, yes, I suppose so." John conceded.

What he really meant was 'how much of that bubbly did she drink?'

I am sure we did in fact turn a corner that night because next day my oldest and dearest friend Maria drove up in her estate car with the rear seats folded down and a large, blanket shrouded shape in the back.

"I've got something for you; call it a housewarming present!"

She opened the boot and pulled off the blanket to reveal a full size cooker lying on its back.

"I really don't know why I didn't think of this sooner; it's the cooker out of that old caravan we had. When we scrapped the van it seemed too good to throw away, so it's been stuck in the back of the garage for ages. It should still work; it's worth a try at least. Oh! And there's half a bottle of propane gas to go with it."

We squealed and hugged, as if we were both still eight year old school girls.

"You angel! Let's get it in!"

"Steady on," John's sounded a voice of caution, "I'd better check it all out in the garage first; you know what happened when we tried to light the gas fire."

So there was a delay until, after a thorough MOT and safety checks, John declared the cooker perfectly safe, installed it in the kitchen and hitched it up to the gas bottle. Maria and I held our breath till, with a plop, the gas jet lit and clear blue flames danced on the hob. I was deliriously happy at the thought of real meals, real food and a real Christmas dinner; being a cookery teacher without a proper oven had felt like being a racing driver reduced to using a bicycle. But now that we had a phone, central heating, hot water, a coal fire and a cooker there would be no holding me back. Three days left till Christmas and I intended to be roaring on full throttle down the home straight, powered on coal and propane gas.

"There is a midnight service at the church in the village tonight; shall we go?"

John was not in any way a churchgoer, nor could I be described as a regular churchgoer but from time to time I did feel the need, the pull to immerse myself in the words and music of the familiar comforting services of my very traditional Church of England upbringing. Actually, my spiritual beliefs were very wide of the mark of the creeds, gospels and liturgy of the Christian Church and, had I lived in the village a few hundred years previously, I may have found myself in the centre of a bonfire on the village green. Yes, I respected and tried to adhere to all the principles of the Church – but then what world religion, at its roots, did not? Compassion, honesty, fairness, respect for others; few religions would argue with those concepts as a good way to live a life. It was access to the divine that troubled me when it was channelled and restricted in differing ways by differing religions through this prophet or that messiah, through rulings on how to live your life or rituals about even the smallest daily activity which, if ignored or broken, could imperil your soul. I took my spiritual inspiration from the world around me, from the people I met along life's journey, from the astonishment I often felt at the abundance and beauty and tenacity of creation, even in the face of the greed and cruelty of humankind. No, faith was not an issue for me; it was trying to fit my particular type of faith with an established path that was the problem and, while I sporadically sought for a better fit elsewhere I still continued, when I needed to, to find thinking space and peace within the walls of a traditional church, still enjoyed reciting the traditional prayers which, having been repeated by countless believers over the centuries, had acquired a beauty and spiritual worth that somehow went beyond the actual words.

And I loved a good, loud, lusty hymn.

John's response to my question over whether to go to church that night was resoundingly and surprisingly positive. Perhaps he was in the mood for some carol singing. So, well wrapped up from our heads to our toes, we banked up the fire with coal and ventured out into the still, frigid air at about a quarter to eleven. It was going to be a white Christmas, not because it had snowed but because the recent frosts had been so severe as to not entirely disappear during the days and so had built up, layer on layer, till the fields, the trees, the paths were all encrusted in a shimmering diamond white. The church of St Andrew was at the eastern edge of the village, about half a mile away and stood on a raised elevation, approached by a quite steep uphill path. There was no lighting up the path but the warm, yellow glow of candlelight spilled out from the porch at the top. We went inside, were greeted by friendly smiles and nods from a congregation of about thirty people who made little impression on the size of the church. It was a typical mid-Victorian build with fine stonework and a very high vaulted roof and, for a village the size of Westgate, it was enormous; it had enough pew space for at least two hundred people. But when the organ played out and the singing of the carols began it did not feel empty. It was filled with candlelight and warmth, the acoustics were superb, the windowsills were draped with evergreens and berries and, in the wooden crib scene, Joseph and Mary, as they always did at this point in the church year, waited trustingly by the empty manger for the arrival of the Christ child and the hope that he represented. The service was taken by a vicar who, there was no denying, looked exactly like every child of my generation's image of Jesus in their bible story books; the hair, the beard, the build, the colouring. It was somewhat disconcerting at first but he sang lustily, gave an excellent and thought provoking address and shook hands very warmly with us after the service, recognising us as strangers and welcoming us to the village. His name was Philip Greenhaulgh and he promised to come and visit us soon.

We set off on the return walk home, this time walking away from the street lights of the village into the darkness of our hillside, feeling warm and content emotionally as well as physically. Whilst we had been in church the temperature seemed to have fallen even lower, the air become even stiller. Passing alongside a stone field wall caused the sheep to stir and look towards us, their fleeces sparkling with frost crystals, their breath hanging in the freezing air but quite unconcerned by our presence;

no different I expected than the sheep with their shepherds in the Christmas story of two thousand years before. We crossed over the footbridge spanning the river at the ford, our boots making the metal deck ring. We looked over the railing at the River Wear running darkly and swiftly beneath us, fronds of frozen grass turned into icicles dangling along the bank sides. We pulled up the steep road from the ford to our crossroads, beyond which there was no street lighting and the hillside rose blackly before us, the skyline delineated only because it was ablaze with stars; myriads of pinpoints of brilliant blue-white lights hanging in front and above us.

The infinity and the glory of the universe set out before us.

And beneath the stars on its shoulder on the hill sat our house; warm lamplight spilling from a window to welcome us, the smell of coal smoke falling in the cold air, giving promise of the warmth waiting for us within. The sensation of gratitude to be there was so overpowering that I could not begin to explain it to John, so I simply squeezed his hand and said, "Happy Christmas my darling; a very, very Happy Christmas."

In the Church, the wooden Christ child now lay in his crib smiling at his mother, in the fields the sheep patiently chewed their cud, in the morning my only child would arrive back from university, in the house a small cat dreamed by the fire. God was in his heaven and all was right with the world. It was Christmas Day – and we had come home.

4

FIRES IN THE SNOW

That first winter was long, cold and hard. The hills and fields and our garden lay under snow, which then crusted over with ice. We quickly learnt the realities of life at 1,150 feet in a house with ill-fitting front and back doors that allowed a blade of perishing air to cut right through the kitchen. At first we did what we had always done, what most people in Britain at the start of the 21st century would do; switch on the central heating boiler for several hours morning and night and, at weekends, let it run all day to keep the whole house nice and warm. I had gasped when the first bill for filling the 'green submarine' which stored our propane gas had arrived but had thought, ah well, that will last all winter or more likely all year. When it ran out in six weeks we both nearly fainted; we may as well have been burning brandy! The concept of a house with all the rooms so warm all of

the time that you could go around in a tee shirt is something taken for granted by many nowadays. We needed to get back to basics, to have one really warm and comfortable room and to make sure we were dressed adequately when we ventured into the others. We bought miles of draught excluder strip and layers of thermal underwear and socks. We made sure hot water bottles went into our bed early and retired with a steaming hot drink. We ran scalding hot baths and let the steam warm the bathroom before we stripped off. In the short winter days, before darkness fell and the ground became treacherous with ice, we made sure we had enough coal and logs in for the whole evening and sticks to light the fire the next morning. Rather than regularly digging my car out of a snow drift on the drive in the morning and then careering down the icy hill, (where it behaved like a toboggan on the Cresta Run), I took to parking it down in the village. At least it was flat there, the road was snow ploughed and gritted and the walk down in the morning and up in the evening was certainly invigorating. Often, by the time I got to school there would still be a crust of snow on the car roof and I would emerge, snow booted and attired more like an arctic explorer than a teacher, into a Durham City school car park that was barely scattered with a handful of snowflakes. "It must be bad up your way?" my colleagues would say in amazement. "It's a different world," I would tell them.

We very quickly realised that the one essential to comfort in such an old, thick stone walled house was constant warmth; we awoke each morning to an unwelcome chill because the fire in the grate would not stay in overnight. Our first priority therefore was to install a multifuel stove that would stay on all the time. So, one weekend in January, John set to with a crowbar to lever out the fake Adam style fire surround and see what lay behind. Amidst clouds of dust and gasps of delight the original fireplace emerged, its hefty sandstone lintels still in place, intact and uncracked. Grooves in the uprights showed where, at one point, a cast iron range had been installed, though the original fireplace would have been open and probably dated back over two hundred years to when the house was first built. Gazing at the soot blackened hole all I could wonder about was who had once sat in front of the fire there and for how many generations. For them as well as for ourselves it was the heart of the house, the essential on which their warmth, comfort and cooking depended. We were gradually learning a little of the architectural history of the house as we peeled back layers, uncovered boxed in beams and reopened closed up openings in the walls. Although the house was a venerable age, the roof beams and trusses used when it was built clearly showed notches and grooves from having been used before in some other building, so heaven only knew what age they were. When John began to demolish a large section of wall in the living room to create doors into the entrance porch, the stone fell away cleanly on each side, which revealed a long ago whitewashed door entrance, the top of which was supported by a lintel. When removed he found that this lintel, that had once spanned the entrance, was made not of stone, nor a stout timber beam, but of an old, crudely made, wooden cart axle. It was riddled with woodworm but still had metal rims at each end for sliding the wheels into place. Recycling really isn't such a modern concept; once it was called thrift and necessity.

From our almost daily chats with Ian Dent and with others in the village, we learnt just how small and basic the living accommodation would have been a couple of centuries or more ago. The original footprint of the house was what was now the living room but only half of that would have been living space for people then; the other half would have comprised living space for their livestock. On the second floor there would have been a bedroom above the living room and store for the animals' fodder on the other side. What John had uncovered in the far wall was the long closed up entrance for the animals on the ground floor. So the family who lived there had only the one modest sized room downstairs, with its fireplace for cooking and heat, with the bedroom above accessed not by a staircase but by a ladder inserted through the ceiling beams in the corner by the fireplace. Most of the old Weardale houses were built like this, a telltale short cross beam between two of the long beams marking the spot where the ladder went through. I was told by someone else who had one that this hole for the ladder was known as a 'coffin drop', as the body of one whose soul had left for its eternal rest could not be removed from the first floor other than vertically! It was very hard for me to imagine so many people living, eating and sleeping in such a small space but then I realised that ample living space is yet another thing we take for granted; both the large size of our modern houses and our small modern families would have been an amazement then; six children in a bed 'top and tail' was not unusual then.

The work went on apace. The new stove was a glorious success, constantly heating the heart of the house and providing lashings of hot water. The new French windows in the living room allowed a lot more light to stream in from the porch and would hopefully one day provide a separate way in for bed and breakfast guests to enter the living room. That long held dream of John's was still in the forefront of our minds in all the alterations and improvements we made to the house. Our plans were endless and there was still so much to do before we could even consider taking guests; there was the kitchen to refit, a conservatory and downstairs shower room to build, the guest bedrooms to revamp, entire Artex ceilings to plaster over, the staircase to remodel in a more sympathetic way, and... and... and... We were not however in a hurry; we imagined the work would take three years or more to complete and the important thing was to get it right and do it well.
On both counts I had absolute faith in John.

Then, in February 2001, in the midst of all our busyness and self absorption something truly awful happened. It was something that did not affect us personally at all but it affected all of those making their livelihoods from the land in Weardale and the whole of the North East, indeed the whole country, and which genuinely threatened the traditional lives of our hill farmers and their flocks.
It was foot and mouth disease.
It started small and slowly with an outbreak near Newcastle but it grew and spread rapidly. The official response and solution was to kill the entire sheep, cattle and goat populations on any farm where there was an outbreak and to then burn the carcasses within huge bonfires. Watching this ghoulish site became compulsory viewing each night if you wanted to watch the news on television, accompanied by interviews with shell shocked, grieving farmers watching their entire life's work - sometimes the efforts of several generations of careful breeding and selection -

literally go up in smoke. They killed and burnt more and more animals and still it spread. They killed and burnt all animals within a certain radius of an outbreak and still it spread.

They made that radius smaller.

And still it spread.

Finally it reached lower Weardale. I was driving home from school one early evening and the ground was covered with fresh snow. I began to descend the steep Redgate Bank into Wolsingham when I saw something writhing in the air in the valley bottom below like a great black dragon, spewing out fire. Shocked, I pulled the car over to make out what was happening. Suddenly vast tongues of orange and scarlet lifted into the air and broke through the dense black smoke. In a large field an elongated pyre was well ablaze, the black smoke and the red flames made all the more grotesque by the pristine white snow that surrounded them. The fuel for the fire appeared to be railway sleepers, long square logs that could not disguise the charring bodies of the cattle laid amongst them. Blackened legs stuck obscenely upwards, horned heads protruded through the flames. It was like looking down on a vision of hell as conjured up by the most tormented of artists of the Middle Ages. I couldn't get the sight out of my head for days, for weeks and it still comes back to haunt me.

With the outbreak now only seven miles from Stanhope and the hill flocks of the upper Dale, new preventive measures were brought in. A roadblock was put in place across the road into Stanhope where you had to drive your vehicle across disinfected troughs of water and have the underside of your vehicle and wheel arches sprayed before you could continue up the Dale. I don't know whether it reassured me or terrified me more. The nights were drawing out; we were into early spring but still there was no let up. The postman was not allowed to take his van onto farms and so Hill House East became a sort of sub-post office, where those further up the hill came to collect their mail. Each day when Ian descended to collect his post he was visibly more anxious, more despairing. Even his wisecracking humour had deserted him. He shepherded three thousand sheep up Swinhope, many of them by now pregnant ewes; it was unimaginable that they could all be slaughtered. It would be the end of literally everything, of the only way of life that he and his father - now in his eighties - had ever known and it would break both their hearts. As for the flock, it may never be re-established. Hill sheep did not have nor need fences or walls on the high fells to keep them in one place. Each flock was hefted; rooted in a familiar area of territory that they had occupied over many generations. You could not simply replace a hill flock with new sheep; they would just wander off far and wide. The outbreak drew ever nearer with no sign of diminishing. It was now besieging Upper Weardale on every side – there were outbreaks in Teesdale, Allendale and lower down Weardale. One more 'jump' of the infection in any direction and we would be in a 'killing out' zone and we began to brace ourselves for the awful inevitability of this happening. Prayers were said fervently both in and out of the churches and chapels and I prayed as hard as anyone for all the farmers but especially for the flock on the fellside above us. Defra decided on a change of tactic; disposing of the carcasses by burning was too time consuming, too costly and too upsetting for the general public. It was therefore decided to bury them and a cavernous hole was dug on the moorland behind Tow Law, some twenty miles from Westgate; soon large, closed, tarpaulined wagons began to converge on it from all over the north of England. My route to school lay over that moorland road and if I found myself behind one of the lorries the stench was enough to make me gag, even with all the windows closed. I also watched as fluids dripped onto the roads from the back of those lorries, presumably escaping from their grisly cargoes, and wondered how much that might add to the spread of the disease. In the end it was said that roughly one hundred thousand carcasses were buried in those pits and the entire area stank for weeks with the sickly, sweet smell of decomposition.

But, by some miracle, the weeks stretched out into spring and the outbreaks grew no closer. The ewes' bellies swelled with the new crop of lambs and still it spread no nearer; in fact cases in our part of the world began to diminish as quickly as they had first spread. Very cautiously, for fear of tempting fate, we began to hope that perhaps we might be spared. And when the lambs were born in April that hope had grown to an almost certainty that the disease had come and knocked on our very door but had not found a way in. It was as if a protective hand had been held over us, covered us, kept us safe in the high reaches of Weardale. There were those who said our prayers had been answered but I was sure that others in different parts had prayed just as hard as us to be spared but had nevertheless been infected, so there was nothing special about our prayers. Nevertheless, that our few special square miles should be passed over was, to me, indeed nothing short of a miracle and to the Dents of Glenwhelt nothing short of salvation. Local people said, 'Thank God', 'Thank goodness' or 'Weren't we so lucky?' according to their persuasion but, amidst the relief and the gratitude, there was also an undercurrent of feeling akin to how the survivors of a horrendous plane crash must feel; why were we chosen to be spared when so many others have gone?

That the farming community up and down the country had suffered a savage blow I fully understood. But rejecting the argument that our farm animals should be vaccinated against the disease (as they are in other parts of the world) so that such a thing could not happen again?

That, I could not understand.

They were very, very dark days for Weardale and all the surrounding countryside and the year was nearly into September before the outbreak was officially deemed to be over, the disinfection stations dismantled and the postman allowed to deliver mail up Swinhope once more.

Despite the foot and mouth outbreak things still went on apace at home. The first bedroom John decided to tackle was our own. There was no cupboard space, so he began to build a fitted wardrobe across one wall. To our astonishment, when this work began, he found that what we thought was a part of the wall was in fact a row of massive, heavily tarred timbers. We later found out from 'one who knew' that they once had been the sides of an old railway truck for carrying stone or coal. It was another example of what we now call recycling from a time when the phrase used was 'mek do wi' what ye've got'. They had been used to partition off a very irregular shaped chimney breast for some reason. We thought the chimney breast very characterful and so freed it from goodness knew how many years of being immured behind those dark sentinels - which disturbingly reminded me of a prehistoric wood henge. Another discovery, when we took the pink nylon carpet up, was that the original wide, pine floorboards were still in place. Well, mostly in place. At the point when the owners had decided to turf the animals out of their half of the house and create a two up, two down dwelling they had put a staircase in the middle, between the two rooms. When in the 1970s those two rooms had been knocked into one long living room the staircase had been moved to the far end of the room. But the hole, cut out of the original pine boards to put the middle staircase in, had not been repaired with sympathetic, lovely wide pine floorboards - it had been filled in with chipboard and carpet put on top to disguise the sin. We wanted the original pitch pine floor back and so John was going to have to mend the hole. This was not as easy as it sounded because the floorboards were much thicker and much wider than modern floorboards and we had to have them specially made.

"Now are you sure you don't want me to put a temporary cover over that hole in the floor?"

"John," I reassured him, "When you walk into the bedroom, what is the first thing you see? A gaping great hole in the floor. Of course I'll not step in it; I'll see it and walk around it!"

"Well, OK. But I know what you are like; Calamity Carol. The new boards won't be here till after the weekend; you're sure you won't do anything silly?"

And indeed, all day Saturday and most of Sunday I was very careful to give the hole a wide berth whenever I went into the bedroom, whilst quite enjoying the novelty of being able to look straight down onto the living room floor. On Sunday afternoon I decided to change our bed, which was not a silly thing to do. What was silly was to take a step backwards while shaking the sheet out over the bed. My descent through the hole in the floor was so quick that I have no idea how my reflexes

43

worked fast enough to allow me to throw my arms sideways over the edge of the chasm, but mercifully they did, and I found myself clinging onto the rough edge of the planking by my elbows with the rest of my body dangling into the room below. I bellowed for John who soon dashed in and, after momentarily being stopped in his tracks by the sight of my dangling legs and torso, ran upstairs and began heaving me back up into the bedroom by my arms resulting in the more, shall we say, womanly parts of my chest being well scraped and splintered on the rough sides of the wood.

"I knew it! I knew it! I knew I shouldn't have left that bloody hole open; I knew you would fall through. Good God – if you had fallen right through you could have broken your legs, your neck, everything."

"Well I think I'm all right, apart from splinters in some very sensitive parts, though I expect I will ache all over tomorrow"

That turned out to be a grave understatement. By the next morning I was black and blue all over, could not bear to raise my arms, had one knee like a pudding and a wrist I was sure was sprained. There was no way I could go to work so I took painkillers, strapped up my wrist and hobbled around slowly all day. The throb of a quad bike announced the arrival of Ian Dent mid afternoon. It was uncanny how I only had to think about a cup of tea and switch on the kettle and he would materialise.

By now he even had his own extra capacity mug.

"Not at school? Are ye bad or summit?"

I held out my bandaged arm and hobbled over to fill the teapot.

"No, I've had a bit of an accident; you see I went right through the bedroom floor."

His face lit up and he roared with laughter.

"Bye hell! Bye hell! Did ye now? Mind that teks some doin'! Sunday afternoon an' all! And did John yell, Geronimo!?

I thought it best not to tell him about the splinters.

It took us months to realise that when John dashed into the living room and saw me dangling there all I had to do was let go and drop into his arms. It would have saved me a lot of discomfort and pulled muscles but not made such a good tale to tell!

44

It was May time, exactly a year since we had first found ourselves standing in a long neglected garden and gazing at the glorious view. Twelve months on I was back in that garden wondering where to start. Whereas John's efforts were going into restoring the inside of the house, my mission was to make something out of the garden. In the centre of the garden, choked with weeds and grass, there was a grid of vegetable and flower beds, all edged with concrete paths. This gave me encouragement that it must be possible to grow some vegetables and flowers, even at our high and windswept altitudes. When we purchased the house our boundary ran only to the actual house and its garden. But the house was surrounded on three sides by a field and just over the wall from our drive, in a small paddock that Ian called a 'gaff' there was also a very dilapidated small stone outbuilding. Ian Dent referred to it as a 'hemmel', which apparently meant locally a small outbuilding or byre for housing a few animals in. Alas, the field, the gaff and the hemmel did not come with the house and were rented out by their owner. Ever curious when Ian Dent dropped local words I did not know into the conversation, I consulted my Dictionary of North Eastern Dialect. A gaff was just a distortion of the word 'garth', meaning a small paddock or an enclosed space; this gave a whole new understanding to John's Weardale family name – the Westgarths. And hemmel had very deep roots, back to the old Norse word 'hame' meaning simply home; so a hemmel was a home for animals. And you just have to listen to a true North Easterner saying, 'Well, ah think ah'll gan heyem' to know the Vikings really did settle here!

I was applying myself vigorously to the garden fork when I heard a voice in the field behind me.

"Good morning; are you the lady that is renting the field out?"

There had been a few sheep roaming around over the winter, which belonged to some farmer or other who rented the field. When I thought about it I realised that the sheep had disappeared a couple of weeks ago and the field was now empty.

"I saw the advert in the paper shop in Stanhope and thought I would come and look."

"No, it's not our field, more's the pity. I don't actually know who it belongs to – but I could find out."

"Thanks, but I've got a contact number here; I just wanted to have a look first."

I was curious.

"What do you need the field for? Do you have some sheep or ponies? Oh, I'm Carol by the way."

"Hello; I'm Ian."

Another one!

"I want it for some llamas actually."

"Llamas?"

Had I heard right? Were we to have a touch of Peru on our doorstep?

"Yes, two actually, well to begin with. They are being retired from a circus and are in need of a home and I have always fancied having llamas. But I've got the possibility of another two – oh, and some alpacas, I like those as well."

And so it was that Eric and Ernie, circus retirees, came to live over the garden wall. They were followed shortly after by Pongo and Ginger and, in due course, were joined by four alpacas. We now had two Ians in our lives! We avoided confusion from then on by calling Ian Dent 'Denty'. Somehow the name stuck; in fact it stuck so firmly that, long after the camelids and their Ian had moved onto pastures new, Ian Dent was always referred to by three generations of our family as Denty – our unique and invaluable neighbour and friend.

The curious camelid group became quite a local attraction, drawing onlookers from the village and the neighbouring caravan sites. I was looking out of the porch window one morning when a group of Boy Scouts, camping in the village, foll-der-ree-ed up our hill and were halted by their scoutmaster.

The boys weren't too sure what to make of the strange animals that were craning their long necks over the wall in hope of tasty treats.

"Can I give him something to eat?" a small scout asked of the scoutmaster.

"Yes, I think so; they seem very friendly."

The small scout dug about in his backpack and then proffered Eric a banana.

Eric took a large bite, made a guttural noise in his throat and then ejected a large gobbet of slimy, green mucus from his mouth, straight into the small scout's face.

I quietly withdrew from the window before the irate scoutmaster and the traumatised boy could blame me for having such loutish llamas.

Slowly, the farmers and shepherds began to build their flocks and herds again, look to the future and come to terms with what had been lost. Slowly the grass regrew and covered the charred, blackened grounds where the fires had raged and consumed timber, flesh and bone. Slowly the stench from the great burial pit was cleansed by the air. Slowest of all the horror faded; but it was never quite cleansed from memory.

Woollen Friends

5

THE RAISING OF LAZARUS

The fields that surrounded Hill House East amounted to some five acres, far more land than was needed to keep four llamas and four alpacas. So, towards the end of the year they were joined by yet more unusual animals; a small flock of Hebridean sheep. Like most animal breeds that have developed to live in the tough conditions on far flung Scottish islands, Hebridean sheep are small, fast and extremely independent. They also proved to be very suspicious of, in fact downright hostile towards, humans. At half the size but twice the speed of the local Swaledale sheep and with, not one, but *two* sets of sharp horns, they looked like small, black, devilish imps as they pranced across the hillside. Trying to herd them together into one place was nigh on impossible as the group would explode off in every direction rather than clump together for safety.

"Ah tell ye what; ah'd rather try an' round up hens!" was Denty's exasperated comment after he, his quad bike and his dog had spent a fruitless half hour chasing them round the field. This combination of llamas and sheep was apparently one much favoured in South America, because the llamas acted like guard dogs for the flock, chasing off any would-be predators. Given the somewhat neurotic disposition of Pongo and his pals I personally thought these roles were reversed on our hillside!

Yet another long cherished ambition of mine had been to keep hens; not only would a daily supply of free range eggs be very desirable, especially when we got the bed and breakfast up and running, but I really liked hens. They were so full of their own importance, had very individual characters and made noises that ranged from the amusing to the very soothing. I had spent many happy hours as a small girl sitting quietly in the corner of my Uncle Albert's henhouse just listening to his hens croon to each other. We were given permission to use a corner of the rented field to put a hen house in and, in return, we could watch over and feed the menagerie when the need arose. Denty helped us to find an old hen house in need of John's clever touch and, before long, we had collected and installed our first flock; six Blackrock point-of-lay pullets. Blackrocks, we had been advised, were a large, handsome, hardy bird, well suited for our weather. They had shiny black feathers on their backs and wings that glowed with blue and green iridescence in the sun and their extremities were a warm copper colour. They were 'hard feathered' so that, instead of getting soaked through, rain just ran off them, rather like the proverbial duck's back; a distinct advantage where we lived! Our new girls soon settled in and began to lay glorious dark brown eggs with almost orange yolks, which I collected with a childlike joy, rummaging around in their warm, downy bloomers. They coexisted completely happily with the llamas, alpacas and 'Hebs' with whom they shared the field, pecking nonchalantly between their legs and taking naps on top of warm, woolly backs. The Hebridean flock had arrived complete with their own ram – or 'tup' as every farmer in the Dale would say. He was a feisty, black, devilish looking beast and very horny - in both senses of the word.

I called him 'Satan'.

In the autumn he very quickly got through his allotted supply of ladies in the field and got frustrated. Nimble as a mountain goat he escaped over the stone walls a couple of times but was recaptured, no doubt having spread his devilish spawn around locally. After one final great escape he was sent off to another farm in Northumberland to be used there. He was locked up securely overnight in a farm building but the next morning there was only a splintered window frame left to show he had ever been there and he disappeared into legend.

We spent our second Christmas at Hill House East warm, snug, well fed and extremely happy. Only the need to go out into the real world and travel daily to school in early January spoilt the rhythm of the short winter days for me. Despite his brief time with us, Satan had obviously fulfilled his prime function and, as the year progressed into spring, the Hebridean ewes became visibly rounder. They were, we were informed, very independent lambers who required no assistance to birth; they were just best left to get on with it. This was just as well as, personally, I did not think they would let anyone near them.

Around this time we acquired a new resident. Ian of the llamas was going away on holiday and he asked if Rocky could come and board with us for a fortnight. He once had a small number of hens that he kept in his garden but one night they were all massacred, not by the culprit that usually gets the blame, Mr Fox, but by a polecat. These were the scourge of poultry owners and, though small, could clean out an entire hen house in one attack, killing - it would appear - as much for pleasure as for food as they did not, and could not, take away all their victims. The only survivor of just such an attack on Ian's hen house was one small, wiry, white bantam cockerel called Rocky, who was left traumatised having witnessed the slaughter of his entire harem. He lived on, a lonely widower of seven years old wandering around the village and up the middle of the road, getting in the way of the local bus from Stanhope. Ian explained he did not like leaving the old chap alone for two weeks, even with ample food and water. We pointed out a snag; we did not have and did not want a cockerel. They made too much noise and I had heard horror stories of how dominating and brutal they could be to their terrified wives. Our hens were all models of maidenly virtue; how would they react if we suddenly introduced a male of the species? There was no problem, Ian assured us; Rocky would come with his own small hen house and run where he could stay for the entire fortnight. I agreed that he could come, provided he was kept in his bachelor quarters. However, within three days of arriving Rocky had created a trench inside the run through pacing up and down throughout the daylight hours, gazing longingly at our nubile girls strutting their stuff on the other side of the wire. Eventually I became worried he would die of exhaustion. It was decided – experimentally – to allow an introduction but I was emphatic that if he harmed a feather on one head of my girls he would be back in solitary. His door was opened and Galina, our chief Blackrock hen, strode in and took a quick peck at his bowl of food. She received a quick peck back on her head for her cheek. What followed can only be described as a scene from Andy Capp; the one where he comes home the worse for drink and his wife sets about him with a rolling pin. A ball of feathers, fury and squawks comprising Rocky and Galina locked in combat rolled across the field. When the ball came to a halt, Galina – three times Rocky's size and a third of his age - dusted herself down and strode off with an expression that clearly said, "Hmphh" and, when he finally staggered to his feet, Rocky wobbled back to his run, minus several feathers and with blood trickling down his face from a serrated wattle. After that I decided the girls would be quite safe, though I was not quite so sure about poor Rocky. However, things became so harmonious that, when the time came for him to leave, it was decided it was best to leave him where he was.

He had a very long, happy life, strutting around regally with a magnificent plumed tail and with an ego to match. Rocky certainly outstayed his two weeks holiday but never his welcome; we came to love him dearly, especially as he greeted each morning with his own distinctive crow of 'Cock a Doo!

Somewhere along the line Rocky had lost his 'Doodle'.

51

When the time came, the Hebridean ewes certainly lived up to their reputation and, one by one, they dropped their lambs without anyone seeing or interfering at all. They would just appear with an already dry, tiny, black demon galloping along beside them on sturdy legs and already wary of humans.

All except one.

Doing his round of the field, Ian found one mother with a seriously tiny black lamb who made no effort to flee when he approached; in fact it seemed to have trouble standing at all. Between us we managed to get mother and son into the semiderelict old Hemmel near the house; her maternal concern overcoming her suspicions of us when her lamb was carried in before her.

The building was a miserable, damp, draughty place. There were whole sections of the roof missing, the doors and windows had long since fallen in and the cold wet floor offered little comfort. We propped up the broken doors as best we could but they made a poor, draughty fit. We found some lumps of musty old straw to make some sort of a bed for mother and child. I did not know much about newborn lambs but I was sure that, by now, the little fellow should be up and sucking milk. Ian managed to catch and wrestle the ewe to the ground, tip her over and squeeze her teats, which yielded a stream of thick, creamy milk, so the supply was certainly there. He smeared the milk on the lamb's mouth and then tried to get him to 'latch on' to the teat. The lamb made a halfhearted attempt but soon gave up. "Best just leave them to it, Mother Nature knows best. We are probably just making things worse; they need to be left alone to bond properly. I'll be back in the morning."

Later that evening, I just had to creep back to see how the bonding was going. By the wavering light of my torch I saw the mother curled up on the straw in one corner and the lamb lying on the cold, wet floor at the bottom of the old door, with a chill wind blowing all around him. I picked the pathetic little creature up and, murmuring encouragingly, laid him by his mother. She promptly sprang to her feet and batted him away with her head and he staggered off, miserably, back towards the door. Her maternal instincts were telling her that this lamb was a nonstarter;

not worth wasting her care on. Mother Nature was agreeing with her, saying that out alone on a wild Hebridean island, this lamb did not stand a chance. My maternal instincts however were telling me that this little scrap of life was in desperate need of food and warmth and we were not in the Outer Hebrides. I tucked the cold little thing into my coat and took it in the house.

"It's not yours; you shouldn't interfere," John pointed out.

"I know, I know – but *look* at him; he's going to die!"

Taking a warm towel off the rail in front of the oven I put the lamb my knee and began rubbing it gently.

John sighed.

"Well you had better give Ian a ring; it's his lamb."

"No point if he doesn't make it through the night – but I want to phone Denty."

It was by now nearly nine in the evening; Denty was busy with his own lambing and had probably only had a few hours sleep in the last week.

"You can't disturb him at this time!"

"I just want some advice, that's all," I pleaded, "Just some advice."

Within ten minutes of listening to me, the quad bike throbbed down the hill, bringing both Denty and his wife Lynne, who was probably just as sleep deprived as he was.

"Now then, let' hev a look; what's up wi' little chap?"

"He won't try to suck and now the ewe doesn't want him anywhere near her."

"Not surprised; skiddly little bugger is'n he? Give us him here an' ahl tek a look".

Huge but extremely gentle hands examined the tiny lamb.

"Pass us that bag Lynne; get the iodine out."

Ian held the lamb while Lynne got hold of its damp, trailing umbilical cord and dipped it into a bottle of iodine.

"That'll stop any infection getting in." she explained.

"Jug of warm water please." – that to us.

"Mek' up a bottle of colostrum." – that to Lynne.

Once the bottle was made up and warm, Ian tucked the lamb between his legs and used a finger to ease its mouth open so he could get the teat in. The lamb, gulped, choked and spluttered and sprayed milk everywhere.

"By hell that's a tiny mouth! Ah divvent think ah'll get the tit in there!"

We had once reared an orphan kitten and for some sentimental reason I had kept the tiny kitten and puppy feeding bottle and teats. Scrambling through the contents of the cupboard under the sink I actually found them.

"How about these?"

Lynne nodded "Anything is worth a try."

With the warm milk in the small bottle with a tiny teat, Denty finally got it into the lamb's mouth and it began to suck as if its very life depended on it; which of course it did.

Then something very strange happened.

No sooner had the milk gone down its throat than about half of it reappeared through its nose, causing it to sneeze and splutter.

"Now that's queor," Denty admitted.

But by persevering with tiny quantities of milk and a good pause between gulps the flat belly began to fill a little.

"Nowt mair we can do the night; let him rest and try him again later and again afore bed. As long as they get a bit colostrum in them, it's amazin' how lambs come round."

Thus spoke the man who would know, the man who had grown up with orphaned and weakly lambs lying in boxes in front of the fire, the man who had birthed so many hundreds, if not thousands, of sheep, that one would think he wouldn't be bothered over the fate of a tiny scrap that wasn't even his. But Ian Dent was a shepherd, son and grandson of shepherds and there was no way he would not have turned out that night; it would have been unthinkable to him. After he and Lynne left, with our profuse thanks, John hunted out a cardboard box and I slipped a warm water bottle into it and then lined it with old towels, the best imitation of the lamb's mother I could come up with. I tried him twice again with a little milk in the little bottle before I went to bed but, on both occasions, almost as much milk came out of his nose as went into his mouth. But at least when I left him he was warm and dry and curled up in an exhausted sleep in his box; I went to bed in much the same state! I awoke very early and crept down anxiously to the kitchen, not knowing what to expect. To my joy the lamb stood up when I went in and began to bleat. I mixed and warmed milk, put it in a bottle and sat him on my knee to feed him. He was certainly hungry, pulling and sucking hard on the teat but, yet again a fair bit of the milk seemed to return via his nose and then he would cough and splutter till it cleared. I put him on the floor to stretch his legs; some milk must certainly be going through him as the first thing he did was to make a puddle.

I phoned Ian as early as I dared.

He was thankful, yet still concerned, when he saw the tottering black lamb. Already this one was no demon like his cousins in the field; this lamb would come straight up to a person rather than run away, this lamb was now a pet. And he was absolutely, irresistibly adorable with his tight curly black coat and his little nubs of horns. Thankfully it was a school holiday so it was decided to leave him in our care, though the responsibility was quite scary for a couple with no previous experience of sheep. Still, I had raised puppies, kittens and a daughter – so why not a lamb? As the day passed I really began to wish the responsibility was not mine. The lamb was getting weaker rather than stronger, each feed seemed less successful and yet his belly appeared distended. He seemed to be wheezing when he breathed. I also noticed that his knee joints were becoming swollen and his little hooves were curling upwards. I was completely out of my depth. There was only one thing to do; phone Denty.

"I'm so sorry to pester you but I don't know what to do. If you could spare five minutes at any point ..."

"Nee bother, ah' was comin' down anyhow soon as ah've done up here."

Denty examined the listless lamb and listened to his wheezy laboured breathing.

"Ah thowt so; its perishment."

"Perishment?"

"Aye, he was too long wet and cold and nee suck in him."

"Oh, you mean like pneumonia?"

"Aye, perishment."

"What about his tummy?" I asked, "It seems all bloated yet it can't be full of milk; most of it seems to have come out of his nose."

"Rattle belly," Denty pronounced.

"Rattle belly! What's that?"

The explanation I was given did not enlighten me greatly but I think it had something to do with insufficient irregular feeding and infection. I was getting really worried.

"And what about his legs?" I almost wailed, "His knees are all knobbly and his toes seem to be curling up!"

"Oh that's joint ail; don't fret yersel' wi' that, it'll come reet if the rest does."

I took a very deep breath and tried to get my head round the diagnosis.

"So, he's got perishment, rattle belly and joint ail?"

Denty nodded sagely, "Ah reckon."

"Is there anything we can do?"

"Oh aye!" he said cheerfully, producing a bottle of pills and a syringe, "Ah'll give him a bit antibiotic and one of these pills; grand they are – saved a few ah' thow't were gonners."

He deftly slipped the needle under the lamb's loose skin and then grasped him between his knees and opened his mouth to pop the pill in. Thank God, I thought, that will put him right.

"Mind," Denty's voice suddenly became cautionary, "Ye'll hev to give him a few more of these pills."

"I can do that."

"Aye, well Lynne thow't she could too. Treatin' my best tup lamb she was and pill slipped down wrang pipe; bang! Stone dead in seconds! It's easy done when they're that little. Ah've done it mesel'," he added by means of encouragement.

I didn't feel encouraged, I felt petrified with responsibility and I must have looked it because Denty added, "But divvent fret yersel'; poor little sod's got now't gannin for him anyway!"

He left us with instructions to feed the lamb much smaller amounts, much more often and more pills. In the early evening I could avoid it no longer; the lamb needed its pill. With trembling hands I tried to imitate what Denty had done, got it between my knees, opened its mouth and popped the pill in. At that very moment the kitchen door opened and Ian walked in, come to visit his lamb on the way home from work. The next moment the lamb spluttered once, went limp in my hands, stopped breathing and fell on the floor.

"No, no, no!"

I dropped to my knees, laid the lamb on the kitchen mat and began rubbing its lifeless form desperately.

"No! You can't do this to me!"

John and Ian watched in silence as I squeezed and rubbed the lamb and even blew air into its mouth, willing it to show some sign of life, but still it just lay, limp and still. How could it go from life to death in a single breath? How *could* it?

With nothing to lose I picked it up, held it upside down and began to shake it almost violently.

"Come on!"

"Carol, I think that... he's dead."

There was a tiny splutter and a spasm passed along the lamb's flanks. I turned him the right way up and his eyes opened.

It was I who had the joint ail now; my legs just would not hold me up and I sank to the mat cradling the lamb.

"Well, that was dramatic."

"Too dramatic for me," I agreed shakily, "I tell you what, he's your lamb; from now on you give him the pills."

"Actually, I've come to take him to the vet, I've made an evening appointment – to try and find out why he can't feed. There has to be a reason."

"Well, when you get him there they will want a name to put on his records."

"Really? But it's just a lamb."

I smiled, "No, he's not just a lamb, he's a very special lamb and, as we have just apparently witnessed the miracle of him coming back from the dead, there is only one possible name for him!"

So Lazarus went off with Ian in his car and was kept in for twenty four hours at the vet's to have intravenous fluids and more drugs. When he returned the next day he had a bandage on one foreleg and a tiny cannula still in place in case he needed more intravenous fluids. He also had an unexpected diagnosis; Lazarus had a cleft palate, which was why he couldn't feed properly and why milk kept appearing from his nose. There was nothing that could be done to correct this but the vet reasoned that as long as we were prepared to get enough milk into him he would probably make it, although he was unlikely to be the strongest or largest of lambs and may not have a great lifespan. Denty obviously thought we were all sentimental fools taking on the care of an animal that, even if it lived, would have absolutely no useful function in life. A pet lamb to him was one that had to be hand reared because its mother wouldn't or couldn't do so but once it was up it would join the flock and either be used for breeding or meat. Our pet lamb came with a need for food, care, shelter and probably a vet's bills for life!

He kept this opinion to himself, but I knew what he was thinking.

I pointed out to him that Lazarus had special needs and, seeing as I spent my working days with young people with special needs, it would be very hypocritical of me to turn my back on a little creature with the same problems.

His only response was, *"Ah'm sayin' nowt."*

The only person around all day was John, and so the lion's share of the bottle feeding fell to him. It was like having a tiny baby all over again with night feeds and nappies in the sense of a daily pile of damp towels. There were however, at three days on, no dirty towels.

"Do you realise Lazarus hasn't had a poo yet?"

John pulled a face, "Well, he hasn't had much to eat yet really, has he?"

"No, but even so, I would have thought he would have produced something by now."

It was yet another thing to worry about and yet another thing to ask Denty about. When I heard the distant throb of a quad bike on the hill I went out to catch him and ask him about it. But it wasn't Denty that pulled up; it was Avril astride her quad bike with a very dead lamb, legs in the air, across the front of the bike.

"Bloody sheep," she groused, "Born with one thing on their mind – how to die. Now't wrong wi' this one yesterday; now look at it!"

Avril was a very tough, independent, middle aged lady who lived on a small farm that lay between us and Denty at Glenwhelt. After her husband died she took on the running of the farm herself, with a minimum amount of other assistance.

"Anyway, how's your lamb doin'?"

We had quickly learned that news travelled fast and wide on invisible rural telegraph wires in the Dale.

"Well, he is just about holding his own. But I'm worried because he hasn't produced anything from his, um, back end yet."

Avril pursed her lips; "Has he got an arsehole?"

"Sorry?"

"An arsehole – has he got an arsehole? Sometimes they don't ye' know. Get some Vaseline on yer little finger and push it in. If it doesn't go in then he hasn't got an arsehole and he's buggered."

"Erm, thanks for the advice, Avril."

But she was already revving her engine and setting off up the hill, still grumbling about bloody sheep, her dead lamb's legs waving their sad goodbye. The good news was that Lazarus did have the necessary orifice and, probably as a result of the laxative effects of the Vaseline, he began producing copious amounts of what John described as 'mustard plasters' soon after. It was a case of 'be careful what you wish for'. And Lazarus did survive, and even thrive, in his own special way. On 'Lambing Sunday', a special service that the Rev Philip held in our village church of St Andrew to give prayers for the year's crop of lambs and the shepherds who tended them, Lazarus was the chosen one who toddled up to the altar with me on a collar and lead to be blessed on behalf of all the lambs in the upper Dale. He behaved impeccably and I was like a doting parent at a school prize giving!

As he grew up, he remained smaller than the usual Hebridean but with a huge personality. He never reintegrated into the flock of sheep. However, he was adopted and fostered by the llamas and alpacas, who he followed everywhere like an adoring younger brother, trotting behind them with the small sheep bell he wore tinkling gently so that we always knew where he was. He continued to have eating problems throughout his life and it was really odd to see pieces of bright green grass emerge from his nose when he had been grazing. Somehow, however, he managed to get the nourishment he needed.
He also had the worst halitosis of any animal I had ever come across; but I still loved him.

A year or two on, his owner Ian bought a new house with enough land attached to graze his strange menagerie. So they were all loaded into a trailer one day and driven away to their new home in Cumbria. Now, I had never truly warmed to the llamas and alpacas; they were too haughty and snotty. I also thought they had a really peculiar smell, akin to mouse pee. It would have been impossible to befriend the Hebrideans anyway. But Lazarus, little Lazarus, oh how I would miss Lazarus.

He was the last to load and trotted willingly and happily up the ramp, without a single look in my direction it must be said, but I would miss him sorely nevertheless. He was the first sheep I had ever known intimately; though in that sad moment I had no inkling that he would not be the last. He would not be easy to visit regularly in the future and, anyway, what would be the point? As it turned out, there was no need to visit him. A few weeks after leaving Hill House East I got a sad email telling me that Lazarus had died; quite suddenly and from no apparent cause. The vet had said at the beginning that, because of his digestive problems, he would be unlikely to have a long life. So it should have been no great surprise that his time had obviously come. And I knew there would not be a second resurrection; not into this world at least.

6

BLACK SHEEP IN THE FAMILY

All his working life, as his father and grandfather before him had done, Denty had shepherded Swaledale sheep on the fells of Swinhope. Tough, wiry, sharp sheep suited for hard conditions on the high fells. They were what he knew and where all his expertise lay. So what persuaded him one spring morning to arrive home from a sheep sale with two very black and very big ewes that were visibly pregnant, I couldn't fathom.

"They are *what* breed?"

"Zwartbles!" he repeated.

"Zoo-are-bulls? Where on earth did you get them? And why?"

"Well..."

Any lengthy explanation from Denty always began with, "Well..." and required a mug of tea.

He had, he said, seen the breed the year before for the first time and had been 'tickled'. They were a large, long legged sheep, jet black except for a white blaze down the front of their face, four white socks and a white tip to the tail, as if it had been dipped in a paint pot. They originated in Holland – where 'Zwart' meant 'black'. They were actually a dairy sheep, hence the long legs for easier milking. Having long been domesticated as dairy sheep they were very friendly and biddable, were excellent mothers and produced ample milk for two or even three lambs. Also, he'd been told, the meat was delicious and was low in fat and cholesterol making them good all-rounders. So, having been 'tickled' he'd decided to buy two ewes, in lamb with twins, at the sale. His newly unloaded purchases nuzzled our hands and took in their new surroundings.

"Well, they are very friendly and strikingly beautiful – and very large!"

The last black sheep I had had anything to do with had been the Hebrideans, who barely came up to my knee; these girls were at least three times that size.

"There's another sale next week wi'some in; a'hm thinking of gannin' for another couple o' yows," Denty confided.

That was exactly what he did but he did not come back with two sheep, he came back with three.

"Good God!" I gasped, "What's *that?*"

'That' was the largest sheep I had ever seen. It was huge, not just height-wise but also width-wise; I had seen ponies with narrower legs and smaller feet in my time. The beast reached up to my waist.

"That," he said proudly, "is a Zwartbles tup. He's got a few years on him but apparently he produces grand lambs. The owners had to sell him because their flock would get inbred if they used him anymore, so I beat them down to fifty quid and I got him! He's not related to the yows I got last week, nor is he father to the lambs in these new 'uns. So, there'll be a good few crops of lambs out of the fower yows before 'ees spent."

Tups – or rams to the uninitiated – have a dubious reputation: they are not to be trusted. They can be sweetness and light one minute and charging you at a hundred miles an hour the next. When their hormones are raging, so are the tups; most of Denty's missing front teeth were as a result of coming off worse in an encounter with a tup.

Beware of tups!

So I looked at this giant with a mixture of awe and fear. He looked back at me and stuck his lower jaw and pearly front white teeth out at me in what looked for all the world like a winsome grin. Then he manoeuvred his head under my hand and gave me a beseeching 'scratch me' look which, tentatively and nervously, I did.

He gave me an even bigger grin.

"He seems friendly," I admitted.

"Oh, they say he's a right softy, aren't ye lad?"

The tup gazed at Denty with eyes that were amber and chocolate then nudged me for another scratch.

"What are you going to call him?"

"Call him? Why ye daft, soft thing; ah'll call him the Zwartbles tup!"

"Oh, he has to have a name; he's magnificent! He's proud and tall and strong. And jet black. I think you should call him Zulu."

"Zulu! Give ower ye daft woman!"

"Zulu," I said emphatically.

Since the departure of 'the menagerie' from the field, we had taken over the rental of it. Of course, having nothing to graze on it, we offered the grazing straight to Denty for his own small flock of Swaledales. Fields need grazing or they cease to be fields; they revert to scrub land and then forest – a contentious point with those who would wish to see our uplands rewilded.

"Look, if you want him to graze in the field here, then I need to know what to call him!"

Denty conceded defeat. "All right, all right; but you're ganna hev to put yer thinkin' cap back on for another name. See them two new yows? Both carryin' twins by the way. Well, one of them is yours: tek yer pick – one or t'other."

"*Mine?* Well, ours? Surely not!"

"Surely yes; you an' John hev' been grand neighbours since ye came here. Now ye hev the field I think it only right ye should hev at least one o' yer own sheep on't. So, gan on – pick one!"

I was for once speechless. Our own sheep? And in lamb with twins, so soon three sheep? Of our own?

"No, no you can't; that's too generous. I am really very touched but... well; I know nothing about keeping sheep or lambs!"

"Now that's not quite true; ye did pretty well with that last skiddly little black lamb. And ye've had yer midwife lessons from Lynne, remember?"

Remember? How could I ever forget?

The previous year when they were full on with lambing up at Glenwhelt I had popped up with a bit of something tasty for them to eat. Mealtimes were often erratic or nonexistent at that time of year; it was more a case of grabbing something when you needed it and when you had a spare minute. The same actually went for sleep. Lynne would take her annual leave from work at this time so that they could be there for the sheep both day and night. I found her in the maternity ward where all the ewes expecting twins were kept; they were more likely to need a bit of a hand.

"How's it going?"

"No sign of it slowing down yet! But, so far so good; no real problems or losses. This one's been bothering on a bit too long without getting anywhere though. The trouble with twins is that, if the first one doesn't get born quickly enough, the one behind it can get a bit challenged with all the pushing and going nowhere – they can even get fluid on their lungs, maybe die. So, I am just going to get this lamb out now."

She had the ewe on her side and was using her knee to keep her there while she inserted her hand into the rear end. The mother-to-be was not impressed with this and blared loudly. Lynne completely ignored these protests and had a good feel around.

"Good lass; nothing in the wrong place, it's a big lamb though. A bit of a pull and we'll soon have it out! Have you ever pulled a lamb?" she added so casually that I didn't quite believe what I was hearing.

"Me? Deliver a lamb? Good heavens no!"

"Time you learnt then and no better time than now; this lamb is in exactly the right position – both legs stretched out in front of its head, jut ready to dive into the world. As long as you don't mind getting mucky that is!"

However romantic a notion it is, and however great a privilege to be there, birth is a messy business; there is going to be blood, amniotic fluid and a lot worse besides. With a hill sheep, her long tail encrusted with poo ranging from dry to very liquid and lying on soiled straw bedding on a concrete floor, it doesn't get much worse. But none of that mattered to me at all; I am not squeamish and had spent many years mucking out horses on a daily basis, so getting my old jeans and jumper and hands filthy was not even a consideration. What was bothering me was the responsibility for bringing this little creature into the world; what if I did something wrong?

"Are you sure? I'd be, well, 'honoured' is the only word I can think of. But I don't know what to do!"

"Don't worry, I'm here. Just don't over think it and don't rush it; take your time. Just slide your hand in – there's plenty room, honestly – and just feel around. It's not your eyes that see inside the sheep, it is your fingers, let *them* see for you; see what you're touching. In a normal presentation you should feel the tips of two front hooves, lying more or less side by side. Back a bit further behind them and you'll feel the ankle joints. Slip your fingers between and around the legs and grip tight; when she has the next contraction give a good steady pull. And I mean a good pull; it takes more strength than you imagine."

My hand slid into the sheep, into an interior world that was silky wet, warm and a strangely safe feeling place, far removed from the cold, dirty, prickly world where she lay labouring. I indeed did feel two tiny cleft hooves and, sliding my fingers a little further, the bulge of the ankle bone behind. I grasped the legs with fingers between and around as the sheep suddenly had a strong muscular spasm that gripped my hand very firmly.

"Okay! Pull now! A long steady pull; that's it, *pull!*"

And seconds later a long, thin, creature covered in yellow mucus slid out in a gush of warm water, membranes and slime. Lynne immediately wiped its face and cleared the mouth and nose from any obstructions before rubbing its flanks with some dry straw. The little chest lifted into life and the mouth opened to emit a warbling bleat, which caused its mother to immediately turn to it, sniff it and then begin to lick it so vigorously that it fell over every time it tried to get up on its very wobbly legs. A few minutes later the mother 'cleansed', expelling a placenta that resembled a red jelly fish. Then her flanks began heaving again and, with little effort and no help from us, her second lamb dived head first into the world. It was one of those intense and memorable moments that I felt truly privileged to have experienced.

"Perfect!" Lynne smiled.

"Yes; it *was*."

Over the next week or so, I helped with more births. In that time, I learnt about situations that were not quite as perfect; lambs lying with a 'leg back', lambs coming chin, rather than nose first, lambs that were 'arse first'. With a breech birth, Lynne explained, the fear was that, because the lamb was facing backwards, the contractions could push fluid *into* its lungs rather than squeezing it out so that it might drown, literally before it was born. For all these reasons, and sometimes for none at all, the small wet creature that slid into the world was not going to live in it. Stillborn, it would lie motionless in the straw; sometimes the mother would try to lick and revive it, sometimes she would know there was no point and just turn away. The list of things that could go wrong seemed endless; sometimes it was the mother that died and not the lamb and then there was the choice of bottle rearing or trying to foster it onto a mother who had lost a lamb. Savage though it may sound, the best course of action to make a foster lamb 'tek' was to skin the little body of the dead lamb and to fit this skin, like a coat, over the live lamb. A ewe identifies her lamb by one thing only – its smell. By tricking her in this way both mother and infant have a much happier and more natural outcome. Then there are ewes, with plenty of milk, that will drive off their healthy lambs and not allow them anywhere near to suck. Denty's solution to this was something called 'purgatory.' The unwilling ewe would have her head placed through two narrow bars, where she could access food and water, but with her head held tied in place by her very useful horns. Unable to turn around and butt the lamb away she would usually have no choice but to let it get under her and suck. Once it was sucking regularly the mother would then usually accept it. Not *always* though – one day I went into the barn to hear a long and loud string of expletives.

"Yer bitch! Yer useless au'd baggage! Get ower – get ower there!"

Denty emerged from the pen with a pretty, though tiny, lamb under his arm, still cursing.

"Cunning au'd bitch! See that – Ah've got her head tied up in purgatory so she has to gi'e her lamb a bit suck and what's she dee? Sits on the poor little bugger and near flattens him! Aye, well that's yer last chance;

ye did this last year and this year but ye'll not do it next – it's the mart for you this autumn my lass, that'll fettle ye!"

The rescued infant blared loudly and indignantly.

"Hadd yer whisht, hadd yer whisht! Ah've got yer bottle ready here."

He handed me the rejected lamb and a bottle of milk.

"Here; see how much o' that ye can get down him"

There is a knack to feeding lambs, especially tiny ones not used to the bottle, but I had successfully done it for puppies and soon got the knack.

"Well, ah reckon ye've earned yer first midwife stripe this year! It's where women have the advantage o'er men at lambing; the hands."

"Hands?"

"Aye, small hands; men have the strength but women have small hands, long fingers, more sensitive touch. Sometimes that's what's needed at lambin'."

I looked at his hand, which was somewhat like a small shovel with five fat pork sausage digits attached and took his meaning.

So fast forward to my current dilemma - "Hawway woman! Pick yer yow!"

There was so very little to choose between them. They were both beautiful, placid and happy to gaze at me with their liquid golden eyes. But one held my gaze just that little bit longer before demurely lowering her long, black eyelashes.

"That one!"

"Grand choice; ye've got a good eye. Let's get them all in the field. So, what fancy name are ye givin' her then? Something beginning with 'Z' to go with the tup? Something dark an' African?"

Panicking, I stupidly thought of the plastic novelty a friend had given me recently: battery powered, it was in the shape of a sheep which – when switched on – was a small handheld vacuum to suck up crumbs from the table. It was called a 'Crumb-Pet.'

68

"Crumpet!" I announced, "I'll call her Crumpet!" whilst all the time thinking, "How stupid is that?"

"How stupid is that?" Denty said and shook his head in disbelief, "But it is your sheep!"

The two new ewes were put in the field with the first two; Zulu went up the hill to Glenwhelt to spend the early spring where Denty could keep an eye on him until the lambs were safely here. When we went to bed that night it took a long time to get to sleep.

"We have a sheep; our very own sheep. She's Dutch and huge and pregnant. And I've called her 'Crumpet'. Why? A Dutch dairy sheep; wouldn't 'Edam' or 'Gouda' have been better? She is having twins; what on earth do we do then? Then we'll have three sheep...three sheep..."

Counting sheep did not help me get to sleep that night!

7

LAMBING STORMS

We were technically in the last month of winter but, although the days were getting longer there was nothing you could truly call spring-like in Weardale that February. Gales blew so strongly that I feared for the elderly fir trees around our garden as they bent and tossed. The wind was accompanied by rain that came in solid sheets rather than droplets. Going out, to put the hens to bed in the evening, was like walking into a pressure washer. The whole Dale was awash; every stream and gully overflowing with racing water, all desperate to find a route down to the river. We awoke one morning to find the cowl from the chimney blown into the field and, rather alarmingly, a section of stone garden wall tumbled down. The cause of this could only be that the rocking of the fir tree in front of it had been so violent that the roots had been lifting in the earth and had caused the wall to collapse.

Denty phoned, "We're scanning on Sunday so gatherin' tomorrow – are ye busy?"

John prepared himself, best he could, for a 'trip on't fell'; a prospect he was not relishing given the weather outside.

"Damn modern wellies!" he said in exasperation as his second bicycle puncture repair patch failed to stick across the hole in the heel, "These must be made of plastic, not rubber. It simply won't stick!"

He was not looking forward to yomping over the sodden fellside in a pair of leaky wellies in search of sheep. So, muttering, he went off to search his garage for some suitable adhesive. Not to be thwarted by modern technology, and determined to avoid wet feet, he reappeared triumphant with a new strategy; a plastic bag put over his sock, held firmly in place by an elastic band round his ankle, before inserting his foot in the welly.

However, he was about to find, before the morning was out, that it was going to take more than a plastic bag and an elastic band to protect him from the elements. At an elevation of eleven hundred and fifty feet, Hill House East woke to what would be called a wet and blustery morning. Up at Glenwhelt, at fifteen hundred feet, there was a howling wind, accompanied by lashing rain. Once they got up onto the top of the fell to gather the sheep – at nearly two thousand feet – the weather was appalling "Not fit for man noo'r beast" Ray Dent, Ian's father, had muttered to them as they left, even though he had gone out in such weather onto the fell countless times in his long shepherding life. The bitter wind drove the heavy, cold rain through every chink in their clothing and they were soon wet through, chilled and exhausted. John said there were times when they simply couldn't see into the wind nor barely stand up. The dogs were working out of sight and out of earshot. The sheep huddled, sodden and cold, wherever there was a bit of a gully or stone wall to gain shelter and were less than inclined to move, even if the dogs could find them. The men made it back with only about half the sheep they had set out to gather.

"We'll have to try for the rest the 'morra," Denty had finally conceded, "and hope to God the weather improves by then."

Although the wind and rain were somewhat abated the next day, the trip up the fell was harrowing and sorrowful. The streams and gullies were pouring in full spate and overnight, when the waters had risen, some of the sheep who were sheltering in the sides of the gullies had been engulfed and drowned. Denty and John found their sodden, thick fleeced bodies at the foot of the fell. Almost worse, when they did start to round up the surviving pregnant ewes, they found that some of them appeared panicked, disorientated and unable to keep with the main flock. Their eyes, scalded by the driving wind and rain for days on end, had been blinded. Others were showing clear signs of pneumonia or, as Denty

71

and Ray far more graphically described it, perishment. Both these conditions could be resolved hopefully by rest, good feeding and, in the worst cases, antibiotics. This, however, meant turning the Glenwhelt fold yard into an infirmary with more work for the already overstretched Dents and worrying cost implications. Normally, even at this time of year, sheep on the fell could find some of their own sustenance, which was supplemented with daily hay and sheep nuts. But once inside, or in the fold, they needed all their feed and bedding providing, plus medication where needed. The previous summer had been a dreadful one and the hay crop poor. Hay prices had soared as a result. In addition, the global harvest had been poor, which had meant the cost of animal feeds had also risen sharply. The only thing that had not gone up was the prices at market. Farmers all over the country were reeling from rising costs and lower profits and now this prophesied to be a long, cold, wet spring with gloomy forecasts for the summer to come. For some, it was just too much; the Craig family, who reared the only remaining milk herd in Weardale, decided enough was enough. After generations of their prized red and white cows lumbering heavy uddered from the meadows into the farmyard twice a day there was to be no more milk from Weardale. It simply wasn't worth producing any more, given the low prices it sold at. Words like 'shameful' appeared in the headlines of the Weardale Gazette.

And it was.

But beyond the Dale no one noticed or cared; it was just another dairy farmer out of business.

At Glenwhelt, and many other hill farms in the Dale, the most keenly felt and daily rising cost was to be a very bitter one.

The knacker man.

Every animal, no matter how small, had to be disposed of officially and correctly in the post mad cow disease world. Every sheep cost fifteen pounds to take away and even the smallest newborn lamb cost five. Given that some sheep after one to two years of rearing, feeding, worming, drenching, dipping and clipping brought only around twenty pounds at mart, the books were hard to balance. The ewes brought little enough profit if they lived; any that died soon ate away at that profit. And die they did.

Every day we saw the grey, unmarked wagon of the knacker man climb the hill beside our house and, every day in those bad weeks, we knew that six, eight, ten dead sheep were being picked up from Glenwhelt. Some succumbed to the pneumonia, some aborted their lambs, or gave birth to them so prematurely they could not live. Some, simply ground down by the conditions on the fell, just seemed to lose the will to live. For the first time in the seven years I had known him, I sensed that Denty too, was being ground down by it all. He was working very long, very hard hours, often in awful weather, every day of the week and, despite his best efforts, there was nothing that he could do to really improve things. Only the return of some decent weather and grass could do that. He was now approaching sixty and I knew how that felt for me; less energy, less strength, more aches and pains. I considered that when Ray, his father, had reached this stage, Denty would have been in his thirties - in his prime. Before that, when his grandfather George (who was the first Dent to shepherd at Glenwhelt) began to feel the toll of his years, Ray would then have been in his prime. But Denty had no son to take on a major share of the heavy work. The only help that he could call on was from John. John was always happy and willing to help out if needed at the farm and he and Denty were firm friends; comfortable in each other's company, appreciative of each other's talents. However, John had never imagined he would find himself spending a significant proportion of his time and energy on sheep. He had soon discovered that shepherding a flock of Swaledales on a wild, high fellside had little to do with the fluffy white creatures of popular imagination. These sheep were stubborn, suspicious and uncooperative. Their long shaggy coats were more grey and matted than white and curly and they were generally malodorous and prone to a variety of revolting conditions such as worms, foot rot and maggots. Affectionately, and only half in jest, Denty began to refer to John as his 'undershepherd' and in the years since we had arrived, John had become swept up into the annual cycle of lambing, shearing, dipping, horn branding, tagging, drenching and winter feeding. It was a mutually beneficial arrangement in that Denty got the help he so obviously needed, John got a lot of fresh air and exercise, and they both got to enjoy each other's company. John also got to know a great deal about Swaledale sheep, a topic that, even after three generations of discussion, Denty never tired of waxing lyrical about. We, however, still struggled with the terminology at times; we obviously understood the difference between a tup – a ram – and a ewe - a female (always pronounced as yow, as in cow, in Weardale) but we struggled with gimmers, hogs, wedders and shearlings and sometimes just nodded in agreement, having no idea what Denty actually meant when talking about his 'gimmer shearlin' yows'.

But that awful spring, I did worry about John at times. He would sometimes return home so exhausted and aching from being out on the fell that I feared he might also succumb to the 'perishment'. Three thousand acres, three thousand sheep, one shepherd with a quad bike and a couple of dogs, a wife who worked long hours in her own full time job, the only additional help from a father in his eighties and John who was coming up to sixty; how on earth could Denty run Glenwhelt virtually on his own? It seemed like madness and yet somehow he managed, as he had done all his life. His devotion and determination were all the more incredible when you remembered that the Dent family were merely the shepherds there. Employees. When Denty reached retirement, that employment would cease. And Glenwhelt, with its surrounding fields and fells, where he had been born, raised and learned his shepherding from father and grandfather, where he had always lived and worked, would be his home no more. Glenwhelt, I found out, meant 'wild valley'. When he ceased work it would not just be wild, it could be lost. It would need someone very special, who knew it and understood it as much as the Dent family, to take over its custodianship. But those days lay in the future and the problems were of the present. There was simply nothing anyone could do except what they always had; do the best they could and wait for spring to finally come.

It was something best not to even begin to hope for before April in Upper Weardale.

Even then, it could be biting cold with the hills covered in the sudden vicious snow falls known and dreaded as lambing storms.

After one such event, two of Dent's ewes dropped twins on our hillside prematurely and one set were dead by the time he got to them. The others were taken to the farm for intensive care; the mothers, having no milk, had just left them.

When our part of the world finally tilted into April and the days really lengthened, the time drew near for the Zwartbles lambs to be born. Denty took his ewes, who were due first, up to Glenwhelt to lamb and John carried out some basic repairs to the doors, window and roof in the Hemmel to make it a reasonably comfortable and weatherproof place for Crumpet. We had no idea of a date that she would be due but with each passing day she seemed to get bigger until we thought, 'surely today or she will explode?' And each day Denty would feel her udder and say, "Aye, not long – but not yet!" I truly hoped that she would give birth while I was at home and not at work but, as this limited it to evenings and weekends, the odds were against me. Of course, I was safe in the knowledge that when her time came, the Dents would be around to hold John's hand through it all if I were not there. She was checked throughout the day, then when I got home from school, again early evening and twice again before bed.

"I think something might be happening" John reported late one night, just as I was really feeling the call of my bed.

"Really? What?"

"Well, she is restless."

"Define restless."

"Well, she looks sort of anxious to me."

I abandoned all thoughts of the warm security of bed.

"Is she getting up and down all the time? Wandering round in circles? Making funny noises? Pressing herself against the walls?"

"No," John admitted, "But she just seems, well, different. I'd feel much happier if you'd come and look."

It was hard to put on damp, cold wellies and go out into the chilly night. Just exactly whose idea had it been to give us a sheep? Pregnant with twins at that! John switched the light on in the building and Crumpet looked at us very much as she had done two hours before.

"Restless?" I asked, a little scathingly.

"Well, she was, honestly."

"Don't you think that it might be you that is a little anxious and not the sheep?"

John looked very crestfallen.

"I tell you what; we are both out here now, so why don't we give it an hour? If anything is happening there should be some sign by then. You go and get us a nice big mug of hot tea and a slice of fruitcake and I'll go and get some warmer outdoor gear on. We may as well make ourselves comfortable."

Sat side by side on a bale of hay, gratefully sipping hot tea and hoping it would bring back circulation to my toes, we two very amateur shepherds watched our flock – of one – by night. Just as I was losing the fight with my eyelids and the call of my warm, soft bed, Crumpet suddenly lay down, got up, panted a bit, then lay down again. Adrenalin is amazing stuff; within seconds all thoughts of bed and sleep had vanished again.

"Something's happening!" I said, digging an equally dozy John in the ribs. Something certainly was happening, and happening quite quickly.

Within minutes Crumpet was lying down to have quite visible contractions then getting up, walking round and lying down again.

"Shouldn't we be timing her contractions or something?" John asked anxiously.

"I've no idea how often a sheep has contractions, so that wouldn't help!"

"Shall I phone Denty?"

"At this time of the night? Sorry - morning! And why? If his Zwartbles were anything to go by, these lambs just seem to fall out! He said he saw a foot sticking out of one and the lamb was born before he got the main lights put on in the barn!"

76

As if on cue, after a loud grunt, a small black bulge appeared at Crumpet's back end.

"Oh, look! Look!" I gasped, grabbing John's arm.

But this lamb was not going to just fall out. Crumpet bleated, panted and pushed. She got up, she lay down, and she leant against the wall. The black bulge got a bit bigger but, whenever she stopped pushing, it seemed to disappear again, although there was one wet, stringy bit that always dangled outside and I took this to be the foetal membrane. After half an hour, she was becoming visibly – and audibly - tired and distressed and so were we.

I remembered my midwifery lessons with Lynne. I also remembered her saying that if a sheep 'bothered on' for too long it could be a bad outcome for the lamb. I have never liked feeling helpless and 'grasp the nettle' had always been my personal motto. I went into the pen and made what I hoped were comforting noises.

"What are you doing?"

"I've no idea; just having a look at the moment. I'm sure there shouldn't be just one leg sticking out. And why is it dangling?'

I pushed Crumpet into a corner against the side of the wall and felt around her nether regions.

"Oh, God!"

"What's the matter?" John enquired frantically.

"It's not a foot dangling out. It's a tail - this is a breech birth; go and get Denty – *now!*"

John shot out of the Hemmel and in a couple of minutes I heard the car roaring up the hill towards Glenwhelt. I cursed myself; why hadn't I sent John to get him as soon as we knew she was in labour? How stupid to assume that just because all the other Zwartbles had lambed without effort that this one would? How arrogant of me to assume we would not need help? Crumpet continued pacing, getting up and down, heaving and bleating. It seemed to me that the black bulge, when it did appear was getting bigger but then it would all disappear again, apart from the pathetic little black tail, tipped with white in true Zwartbles fashion. After only a few minutes I heard the car rushing back down the hill, it stopped, the door slammed and John ran into the stable. Denty was not with him.

"Is he following you down?" I asked urgently.

"He's not there."

"What!" My heart sank to the depths of my wellies.

"I banged on the door, shone headlights in the bedroom window and the dog is barking her head off. His vehicle isn't there though Lynne's is. But I've just remembered him saying something about them having a night away, just before the Swales start lambing."

"Right; well we'll just have to do the best we can," I said, trying to fool myself into feeling positive and calm. Nothing in my brief sheep midwifery course from Lynne nor my Girl Guide 'Emergency Helper' badge had prepared me in the least to deal with this situation. I began to try and think logically; what exactly was preventing this lamb from coming out? A feel around the bulging opening beneath Crumpet's tail revealed two hard, angular bulges just inside her body.

Of course!

They must be the hock joints of the lamb's back legs and perhaps they were preventing the lamb from slipping up and out. Lynne would flip the Swale ewes expertly to the ground and deliver them lying down. With Crumpet being the size of a small Shetland pony there was no hope of me doing this. I nudged her over to the wall and pressed her there with my thighs.

"Get in here John; hold her head and press her front end to the wall!"

The next time she gave an almighty heave I slipped my hand into the wet warmth of her body, found her pelvis and hooked fingers under the bony hock joints of the lamb and tried to lift them up. My eyes were tight shut as I probed and felt around and I realised that I was indeed seeing with my fingers. Crumpet did not enjoy the experience in the least and bellowed her discomfort at me. The extra pressure she exerted by bellowing was just what was needed however, and as soon as the hocks were free of her body, a large slimy lamb slid out onto the floor of the Hemmel. Almost as soon as it hit the deck it was wriggling, moving and, within seconds of birth, was bleating and actually trying to stand. There was no sack of waters surrounding it; they must have burst a while back, and so I could see it all quite plainly as soon as it was born. It was a fine healthy lamb with all the required Zwartbles markings in all the right places – jet black with four white socks, a white tip on its tail and a white blaze. However, just above the nose, in the middle of the white blaze, it had a single, perfect, small black circle. While Crumpet anxiously licked and nudged her new offspring making low, encouraging and very loving noises to it, I took a quick look between its hind legs; it was a gimmer lamb.

"Dot!" I pronounced to John, "We shall call her Dot!"

Crumpet had a daughter.

Minutes after birth, a determined little Dot was staggering around on her four white socked legs, and clamping her little mouth around a large, pink teat. Crumpet, only minutes from an exhausting and traumatic birth, was cleaning up her lamb and encouraging her to suck like a veteran whilst simultaneously dispelling the placenta that had nourished it.

She then began to birth her second lamb; not many humans could do that!

The second lamb, it must be said, began to appear almost automatically, with none of the effort or problems that had gone with the first one. This lamb appeared within an intact foetal sack, which grew and grew in size until gravity took over and it plopped, wetly onto the straw and burst.

Inside a small black shape lay, unmoving, inert.

"Oh no, no, no!"

This lamb had arrived so effortlessly I had imagined all would be well. It was small; very much smaller than Dot and was making no effort at all to breathe or to move.

Crumpet gave it a quizzical look and turned away to continue licking Dot. "Come on!" I urged it, wiping away the glutinous membranes that seemed to encase it, smother it and giving its bony little rib cage a vigorous patting, "Breathe!"

I had heard that shepherds did things like swing lambs around by their hind legs to get them breathing but I did not know how to do that, besides which this little thing looked too fragile to be swung anywhere.

"Is it ..." John asked anxiously.

"I don't know, I really don't know!"

"Kiss of life?" he suggested in desperation.

"Why not!"

There was simply nothing else I could think to do. I wiped away as much of the wet, clinging slime as I could from its mouth with an old towel, squeezed the little mouth open and began blowing short, strong puffs of air down its throat. The mess of amniotic fluids, blood and slime I was kneeling in mattered not one bit; all that mattered was the small, cold, slippery head between my hands. I had no idea whether what I was doing was right or wrong but I simply had to do something, so I just kept on blowing, rubbing and squeezing and finally the little rib cage convulsed, the head shook, the chest heaved once more and the lamb was breathing. I cried with relief while the lamb, after a literal pause for breath, pushed herself up onto tottering legs, fell over, tried again, bleated pitifully and then headed towards the enormous bulk that was her mother. Hearing the bleat, Crumpet turned with renewed maternal instinct, sniffed her second daughter and began licking her vigorously to warm, dry and stimulate her. Two gimmer lambs – Denty would be green with jealousy; his Zwartbles had produced mostly tup lambs!

As the new lamb tottered to join her sister in search of a swollen pink teat we allowed ourselves to breathe more normally again; the last half hour or so had been terrifying and amazing in equal part. The first time mother's instincts had kicked in when required but what instincts had enabled me to guide one lamb that was hopelessly stuck safely into the world and then breathe life into another? Then I remembered Lynne's advice, 'Don't over think it; don't rush it. Your eyes can't see inside a sheep: let your fingers be your eyes, trust your instincts."

So; instinct? Beginner's luck? Mother Nature? All of the aforementioned - who knew? But I knew that I had feared we would lose them all. When both lambs were properly 'latched on' and 'footed' and clean bedding, food and water provided for the new mother and we were 'done up' for the night, we could finally get a few hours sleep. I seemed to be latching on to the old shepherding terms as naturally as a lamb to its mother's teat. I was both awed, and I admit proud, of what had taken place in the old Hemmel that night. I was also exhausted and getting up and getting to school would be a struggle in the morning. Then I felt embarrassed. How dare I even begin to think of myself as a shepherd! At the present time Denty, and all the shepherds in the Dale – indeed the whole country – would be facing six weeks or more of relentless life or death crises, very little sleep and very long days and nights.

I had just lambed one sheep; they would be tending to hundreds.

"And this one is to be called...?"
I took John's arm as we headed back to the comfort of the house and our bed.
"Well," – I was even beginning to sound like Denty! "These lambs are the bringers of spring aren't they? Sometimes a little late and hard in coming, just like a Weardale April, but although it can be tough, this can be the most beautiful month of all, so we should name her for it: we shall call her April."

8

ZULU UPRISING

A goal, which we had worked towards slowly, and at times despairingly, for eight years, was reached two days after my sixtieth birthday in December 2009. On the significant day of the winter solstice or festival of Yule in the Celtic calendar; we finally completed the purchase of the Hemmel building and the fields around the house. What had once been joined, and then separated for many years, was once again whole. It felt joyful and somehow right; and, as Denty said, "God's not mekkin' any more land any time soon!"

There was deep snow on that twenty first of December and very early in that morning there was to be a lunar eclipse. So in the freezing dark, we got up, dressed warmly and brushed away the snow to get into the summerhouse, which had a view of the moon to the west. Drinking mugs of coffee well laced with whisky we watched a perfect celestial performance, which was awesome – in the true sense of that word. Even though we knew all the science behind it, this solstice eclipse felt as if it was happening especially for us; to celebrate my significant birthday, the ending of the first decade of the twenty first century, and our purchase of the land. We now owned the land - or rather we were entrusted with it; for a while it was ours to use, to care for and to keep as natural as we could. The pheasant and curlew that nested in the rushes at the top edge of the field would not be disturbed; nor would the little covey of partridge that flittered nervously through the grass every year. Then there was the Tree – a single, enormous sycamore tree that grew against our boundary wall in the top south west corner. From its girth it had to be about a couple of hundred years old. How this single tree had thrived on land that had been grazed for centuries, when no other large tree had survived anywhere near on that hillside, was a mystery and a marvel to us. It would have seen so much unfold and change around it down the years. King George III, or maybe even George II, would have been on the throne when it was a sapling and the slave trade still flourished in Britain. A dreadful catalogue of wars, in which the young men of this land were sent to fight, had raged and ended. All the while the Tree had driven its roots deeper into the Weardale hillside, through the battles of Trafalgar and Waterloo, the Charge of the Light Brigade, the Zulu Wars, the Boer War, the Crimean War, the First World War and then the Second World War. By that time, it would have been a tall, mature tree.

It would have stood a silent witness to the stricken RAF Wellington bomber, on a night time training flight in low cloud, coming down too low and too fast and which would have crashed onto St John's Chapel village had the crew of seven not remained on board and manoeuvred the plane just that little further and higher so that it crashed and buried itself into the soft hillside of Green Laws above the village, less than a mile away from Hill House East. Six of the airmen were Royal Air Force and one was Royal Canadian Air Force.

All seven crew were killed and their names have a special place on the village war memorial at St John's Chapel:

IN

GRATEFUL REMEMBRANCE

OF THE SEVEN AIRMEN

WHO LOST THEIR LIVES

AT GREEN LAWS

ON THE 7th MAY 1943

The Tree – now our tree – would have seen the lead mines in the Dale in their heyday and in their decline, watching the tired miners pass by on their way to work in the mine at the top of Swinhope. Once, horses would have worked the land and carried people and goods on that hillside. Now cars, motorbikes and enormous tractors have taken their place. It saw the iron rails and the steam engines forge their way to the very top of the Dale in the Victorian era and watched the last train leave from Westgate Station over half a century ago. Most importantly, that tree had presided over all the families that had lived in Hill House East during its life - a mute witness to their hard work, their joys and sorrows, the births and deaths that had taken place under its roof. How I wish I could somehow access its memories; if I walked past it on a breezy day, I often stopped to listen to the leaves chattering and murmuring but, unlike the whispering grass of Greek legend, the tree has never shared what it knows with me. But we were not owners. We were merely custodians, hoping there will be a few more rings in its girth before we too become a memory. It stands out as a landmark we can see from up, down and across the Dale, a landmark that meant 'home'.

For a while at least, it had now become ours to care for and to revere.

The following spring after the lambs were born and 'up', Zulu returned to the field with the Zwartbles flock. Early summer came and the adults' wool was now inches deep and a hot encumbrance. Shearing took place up at Glenwhelt and, when it was Zulu's turn, it took a wrestling match between him, Denty and John to get him onto his back to be clipped. The next task in the shepherd's year was dipping the sheep; immersing them in a deep trough of water and sheep dip, which would kill off any parasites and prevent skin conditions developing. The splutter of an engine being switched off announced Denty's arrival. He swung his leg over the quad bike and stood to straighten his back.

"You heard the kettle being put on didn't you!"

"No, not today thanks; we're on dippin' today and ah have te' get back. A'm wonderin' if John'll be free this afternoon te gather up the Zwartbles and we'll get them done an' all?"

"No problem," I assured him, "I'm sure he's free and I'll give you a hand as well."

"Champion!"

Denty grinned and climbed back on his bike; I was just thinking how unusual it was for him to visit without tea or gossip ensuing when he paused and said, "Bye, I had a near miss this morning!"

I rose to the bait.

"Mmm?"

"I set fire to a sheep!"

"You... set fire? To a sheep?"

"Aye! I found it in a dyke back when I was gatherin' and it looked very poor. Ah reckoned it were maggoted, so I didn't want to put it in front of me on the bike – well, ah didn't want me wellies full of maggots did I?"

"No, of course not."

"So, I pushed it down in the footwell in front of me and away we went. Well, halfway back to the Glenwhelt, there was an awful smell of somethin' singeing and then I noticed the smoke comin' up in front of me. Poor bugger were too near ti' exhaust weren't it? Smoulderin' away it was, so I tipped it off and rolled it about in the grass a bit to put it out."

"And is it alright?" I asked anxiously.

"Oh aye! Mind you," he added, "Ye'll soon tell which one it was; just look for the orange stripes on its wool!'

So, that afternoon the three of us, sticks in hand, whistled up the Zwartbles – who came at a gallop as soon as they heard a feed sack being rattled – and with Denty in the lead on the quad bike we walked them up the hill to Glenwhelt for their annual MOT which involved a pedicure, a drench for worms and immersion in the sheep dip bath. It was a joyful thing to do on a fine early autumn day; sunny but with a brisk breeze that sent clouds frolicking down the Dale like so many airborne ewes and lambs. I felt very proud of our little flock as they trotted along with Zulu, quite rightly in the lead of the flock and following at a steady determined trot beside the quad bike. It made me so happy to see him looking in such fine form, his short coal black curly coat shining with health, his back broad and well muscled. He had lost a lot of condition over the last winter which left him rather emaciated and weak, his wool falling off in great patches which made him look embarrassingly like a large French poodle. We feared he might have been heading for the end of the road; there is not much future for an old tup and Zulu had been not been young when he first arrived. The problem was we were so ridiculously fond of him; he was gentle and kind, adored nothing better than a slice of wholemeal toast or a back scratch and had fathered many fine lambs. Thankfully he had picked up and put on so much condition over the summer that Denty had declared him up the task of fathering another crop of lambs.

"It's all that bloody toast yer feed 'im!"

I thought it best not to mention the sacks of carrots he had got through in the spring.

So this was an enormous relief to us and I am sure, had he known how near he had been to going into 'the last pen', also an enormous relief to Zulu. We were able to veer our minds away from the 'what happens when...' question for at least another year. We turned the Zwartbles into Glenwhelt yard and I left them to it, imploring John and Ian not to fall into the sheep dip.

A couple of hours later I had just started peeling some potatoes for supper when John roared to a halt underneath the kitchen window on the quad bike.

"They're on their way back down! Stand in the road so I can turn them into the gaff!"

I dropped my peeler into the sink and dashed out. Sure enough, within the minute I could hear Denty's gentle encouragement floating down the hill.

"Ye big bellied, skinny necked waste of space! Get out of there! Get on wi' ye!! Git on! Git on wi' ye!"

And round the bend they came, damper and less happy than when they went up. I flapped my arms and gave a mandatory but unnecessary 'Ssshhh, sshhh' call but they had no intention of passing the gate; they just wanted to get back into their field to eat grass. They streamed through the gaff and into through the gate into the top field and John pushed it shut.

"By hell" said Denty, "We only just got Zulu through that trough, what! By he's a big bugger and he wasn't keen on gannin, but he went – mind, ah nearly went wi'im! As for them imps,"- by this he meant the lambs he had crossbred between Zulu and some of his Swaledale ewes- "By, they are evil little black beggars! Fast – wicked – what! You've not seen anything like it; it was more like them motorbikes on the wall of death than a sheep dip. They were all ower the place! Ah'll breed nee mair of them! Ah'd sell the lot to the butcher but, ye'd be lucky if ye could eat them."

"How do you mean?"

"Well, if they're as fast as that on a plate, ye'll nivvor get your fork into them!"

The issue of the lamb on our plates was something friends would ask about.

"You don't actually *eat* any of those lovely black sheep of yours do you?"

"Well, actually yes, we do."

"How *could* you!"

Then I had to patiently explain that we were not vegetarians; we did eat meat but I was very fussy about what meat we ate and how well sourced it was. I avoided cheap, processed meat at all costs. Our butcher in Stanhope even knew from which farm a joint had originated. So, when you get lambs you will get girls and boys. The girls you can either keep to breed from or sell to someone else to breed from. The boys are less straightforward; the majority of them will be castrated while very young, as you cannot have a field full of rams bashing seven bells out of each other. The flesh of a mature ram is not that good to eat either, as it has a very strong flavour. So, while one or two male lambs that seem exceptional may be kept for breeding, the majority of male lambs are fattened for the meat market. It seemed to me pure madness to send our castrated male lambs to the mart to sell, so that someone else could buy them and sell them on to the butcher and I would then go to the butcher when I wanted to buy lamb. Not only was it much cheaper to have one or two of our fat 'wedder lambs' sent to the local abattoir and then put in the freezer to see us through the year, I also knew that the animal had had the best of care and conditions through its life and had never eaten grass tainted with fertiliser or pesticides. We felt grateful and even honoured to be able to eat such wonderful home produced meat.

"But you know them!" friends would wail.

"Not personally," I would reply.

Once we had around five ewes of our own lambing each year, that was around ten lambs. With them would be an even greater number of lambs from Denty's larger number of ewes. Other than the ewe lambs we kept for breeding, which would be named and stay with us for the whole of their natural life, the fields were full of anonymous black lambs. If a ewe lambed without difficulty and mothered on without help it was possible we would have had no real contact with her offspring till the time came for them to leave.

Of course, there were exceptions. These came in the shape of male pet lambs who had to be reared by hand for one reason or another and anything that got a name had a place with us for life. Lazarus had been my first experience of this but it was not too long till I had my next. Having produced two fine gimmer lambs in her first lambing, Crumpet went one better the next year when Zulu impregnated her with three. Triplets were not usually good news at lambing time because producing enough milk to rear three can be a problem – although we were assured that our dairy Zwartbles would have an abundance of milk. And maybe that was true – but not when the ewe drops her lambs early outside in appalling weather after a hard winter. And, catching us completely unawares, this is exactly what Crumpet did. It was well before her due date, she was not 'bagged up' with milk and I was away visiting the family. So I received the news on the phone.

The flock had been out grazing on the hill all day in cold, rainy miserable March weather. Late afternoon, John had gone up to check all was well and to call them down to the sheep shed for the night. They had all come running to him – except Crumpet. In the failing light he had searched the field and eventually found her against the top wall, taking what shelter she could for herself and two tiny, newborn black lambs from the trunk of the huge sycamore tree. John looked carefully for a third lamb without success so either it hadn't been born yet or the scan had been wrong. Or, the third lamb could have been reabsorbed or even expelled at some point in the pregnancy, which can happen. Crumpet responded to his voice and, tempting her with a handful of sheep nuts, he got her to her feet and she stumbled down the steep incline, her two newborns tottering after her on jelly legs. Halfway down the hill John just stopped himself from stepping into what he thought was a wet, black pile of sheep poo. But then it moved.

And then it emitted a thin, plaintive bleat.

He had found the third lamb.

Had it been born first or last? No way to tell. But obviously the lamb had been abandoned by Crumpet, who was desperately trying to protect and nurture her other two stronger offspring and was at that very moment leading them down the hill to safety and warmth, completely ignoring the cries of the pathetic, tiny scrap as she passed it. John had picked up the soaking and almost stone cold lamb and shoved it into the protection of his coat till he got to the sheep shed. Having shut the door on Crumpet and the two stronger lambs, he dashed to the house do the obvious thing: phone Denty.

Of the three rather premature lambs Crumpet had produced, the two gimmer lambs were not actually doing badly. They were small but quite strong on their legs and could 'latch on' to their mother's ample udder perfectly well. With umbilicals dipped in iodine and a dose of colostrum in them, they were bedded up in straw out of wind and rain and Denty announced there was 'now't te worry about'. Their brother, for so he was, was weak and pathetically skinny. His premature ears flopped down on each side of his face and his premature little hooves were soft and bent up at the ends, like Dutch clogs. So for him it was intensive care - and not much hope. Out came the tiny feeding bottle, the hot water bottle, the old towel and a large box for a bed.

"Nappies and fireguards again; I'm too old for this!" John had grumbled, without a great deal of conviction, when he spoke to me on the phone, "But he is seriously cute."

By the time I got home a couple of days later, it was thankfully clear that the little chap was making progress.

And that he had bonded firmly with his 'mother' – not Crumpet, but John.

He followed him endlessly around the kitchen when he was out of his box and, when he wasn't fast asleep with a full tummy, blared constantly when he was in it. No problems of feeding or cleft palates or doubts over 'an arsehole' with this one; he could drain a bottle of milk with incredible speed and all that food passed effortlessly and regularly out of the other end.

"What are we going to call him?"

"You choose!" John replied, which was his usual get out clause disguised as a compliment.

"Well, I think it should be something beginning with 'Z'; after all he is the first son of Zulu that we have kept."

"Fine! So what?"

Z? Z? Z? – not a great deal of choice. There were biblical 'Zebadiahs' and 'Zachariahs' of course, but he did not look much like an Old Testament prophet. Then there was 'Zeus' – but he certainly didn't look like a Greek god. Then, from heaven knows where, came the memory of a stupid, grinning metal alien that used to advertise a famous brand of instant mashed potato long ago - and he was called… 'Zeeb'.

"Zeeb!"

"Zeeb! Why?"

"It's short , it's a 'Z' name – and I think some day, when he grows up, he is going to have a wide grin, just like his Dad. "

And grow he certainly did, in fact he eventually actually outgrew his magnificent father. Possibly because, at a tender age, a little rubber ring was slid in place which ensured he would be a 'wedder' and not a rampant tup. There was no need for another tup in the flock and anyway, he was too closely related to be of use to our ladies. His sisters -Crumble and Custard, named with a 'C' for their mother, and keeping the 'food' theme - also grew and thrived. When they were fully weaned I gave Crumble to Denty as a thank you for all his help with our sheep and so that, after a lamb crop of too many males, he would have another breeding ewe. The tight knit family group grazed contentedly on the hillside all summer; Crumpet with her triplets Crumble, Custard and Zeeb and their older stepsisters Dot and April with their own families. Presiding over his wives and offspring of course was Zulu, their lord and master.

Then, one morning, in late August, we detected the indescribable change of something in the air and light that announced summer was packing up to leave and that autumn was heading our way. Zulu also began to notice something in the air and began sniffing round the ladies.

"Its ower soon for tuppin' yet; he's ganna hev to go in t'other field for a month or so."

But Zulu was not at all keen on the idea of being on his own. Next day, as Denty and John enjoyed their morning tea, putting the world to rights leaning over the fence, a cry went up, 'Ye au'd bugger!! Hawway John!' and they raced for the quad bike and were roaring up the hill. By the time I got outside to see what the commotion was they were in the top field, waving their arms at Zulu and trying to corner him away from the ladies. Denty made a valiant grab for him and managed to hang on for quite a while, despite being dragged across the field flat on his belly. Eventually, when they were all running out of puff, they managed to get a rope around his neck, though it took all of their combined strength to bring Zulu to a halt.

"It were like tryin' to stop a bungalow!" was how Denty described it later.

"Did he jump over the wall to get out?" I wanted to know.

"What wall!" he pointed to a wide hole, "The bugger doesn't hev' to jump walls – he just walks through them!"

So it was into chokey for Zulu, locked in a barn up at Glenwhelt, till the time came for the high point of his year and he would 'gan te work.' This would mean him fathering lambs on the four original ewes and also on their daughters who were now 'shearlings' and old enough to breed. This was what he had been bought for after all. What I found strange to contemplate was that Crumpet would be having lambs sired by Zulu but so would her daughters Dot and April. Nothing incestuous though, as those lambs had not been fathered by him, they had arrived as yet unborn inside their pregnant mothers. Nevertheless, I still found it strange that my sweet Dot and April had their lambs sired by their 'stepfather'!

After a few weeks 'in chokey' Zulu was getting increasingly frustrated and not even interested in the wholemeal toast we took him when we went up to visit. It was not that he had become violent or even bad tempered, it was simply that his hormones had reached a point where he was ready to burst with frustration when every waft of breeze brought him more tantalizing whiffs of ladies who were ready and more than willing to succumb to his muscular, masculine charms, whilst he was penned up behind high metal bars. It was no surprise that he was bashing seven bells out of them at times. He even tried his most toothy of winsome grins on me when I went in, as if to charm me into opening the gates but I could only scratch his very musky head and tell him I was sorry, there was nothing I could do but that I didn't think he would have to wait much longer. He would give me a look in return as much as to say, 'I've heard that one before – and I am still shut in here!'

October half term came round; always one of my favourite holidays. It always fell around our wedding anniversary so we celebrated by travelling down to spend four lovely days with the family, who were by this time living in Wales. The morning after we got back Denty was down bright and early to check on us.

"Had a good trip?"

"Great thanks!"

"And Zulu? Has he finally started work, as it were?"

"Oh aye! By, ah've had a hell of a job wi' 'im! Ah've nee skin left on my knuckles!"

"Mug of tea, Denty? Then you can tell us the tale."

I smiled inwardly; Denty always left a few seconds gap between the ritual of me offering tea and him accepting – even though the final outcome was a foregone conclusion.

".......Aye! Gan on then!"

He had wanted to move all the Zwartbles into a field higher up at Swinhope, so he set the ewes away up the road first and kept Zulu back in a pen in the yard.

"Ah knew he would follow them and ah was ganna gi'e them a good head start. But bugger lugs had other ideas; he smelt them and went berserk! He battered and rammed at the gate on the pen till he just took it with him; ah managed te grab it as he went past me and pull it off him – and most of me skin! – then he was off like a rocket up that hill!"

"So he did follow the ewes to the field?"

"Follow them? He caught up in about five seconds and 'e'ed tupped two before they even reached the field! What a lad eh!"

9

FACING WEST

S ome things in life creep up on you so sneakily that you don't notice
them until you have a problem.

Like age.

Sixty hadn't hurt, but now I was heading for my mid sixties and that did!
One morning, I got out of bed, took a step and felt as if I had stood on
a drawing pin and it was stuck in the bottom of my foot. In the end I
looked it up on my computer and found I had Plantar Fasciitis, which
did not sound so grand when referred to as heel spur or worse,
'Policeman's Foot'. There were all sorts of weird and wonderful
suggestions and appliances to help this condition, which was apparently
very common but notoriously hard to get rid of. The final solution when
all else failed, was to have a steroid injection into the heel; a procedure
so painful that grown men, yes even policemen, had been known to faint.
Alarmed, I made an appointment with a foot clinic. By the time I went
for this appointment something else was happening; I had developed a
painful ache in my right hip and, watching my shadow when I was
walking home from school, backlit by low sun one day, I could see the
black shape of a person walking in front of me on the road and, at every
step, down dipped the right shoulder. I was limping; if I were a horse I
would be 'nodding' or, quite simply, lame.

Thirty years before I had been involved in a fairly horrific riding accident
when a young horse I was riding had reared, thrown me, then

94

overbalanced and fallen on me. I had fractured my pelvis in four places and dislocated my right hip. I was also very lucky; another few inches up and I could have broken my back. I had two operations and spent nearly a year on crutches and in a wheelchair and I had been told that sooner or later, possibly as young as fifty, I could need a hip replacement. When you are just past thirty, the age of fifty is unimaginably far off and I had managed to get my mobility pretty well back to normal. I could walk, swim, dance, ride - do most things really. True, I got aches and pains in my hip from time to time and I could not lie on my right side in bed but, on the whole, the accident did not really slow me up and I passed my fiftieth birthday with a rather cocky 'Ha!' in the direction of the doom mongers. Of course, now I was well passed my sixtieth birthday.

It was recommended that I wore a special brace in bed to help with the foot pain. I collected it from the foot clinic and I couldn't believe my eyes. The contraption looked like something Frankenstein's monster might have worn when he was being assembled. It was rigid plastic from below the knee to the heel and then right angled to go under my foot, it was covered in a black, cushioned velvety material and had three huge Velcro straps, one below the knee, one around my ankle and one around my foot.

"And I have to sleep with that on? In bed?"

"You'll get used to it. Honestly."

John did manage to make me smile though when he got into bed with me that night.

"Woo-hoo! That thing is a bit racy isn't it? I mean, black velvet, straps and buckles? It's a real turn on that is!"

I resorted to the 'final solution:' the steroid injection in the bottom of my heel. Then, I believed what I had been told about it making policemen pass out! Despite all this treatment, which did seem to slowly improve things with my foot, my hip got more and more painful and so I went to the doctor. She examined me and said I had arthritis in the hip, undoubtedly initiated by the trauma of my accident so long ago and brought to its current crisis by the heel problem. I asked her how I could have gone from being reasonably fit and very active to a hobbling, pained wreck so quickly and she said things about camels' backs and straws, time catching up, and how good hip replacements were these days. It did not do a lot to cheer me, in fact I felt utterly down and depressed.

We went to visit the family in Wales that weekend, the first time we had seen them in nearly two months and the long awaited treat was marred by the pain in my hip. Trying to keep up with everyone as we walked around I felt I simply couldn't walk any further. I slunk into a shop and purchased a very funky looking walking stick.

But it was still a walking stick.

Between the stick, leaning heavily on John's arm and everyone else slowing sympathetically for me, I made it home with memories of my mother with first one stick, then two sticks, then a Zimmer frame and finally a wheelchair, uppermost in my mind.

I confided this to Megan.

"For heaven's sake mother; don't be so melodramatic! If you need a new hip you need a new hip; apparently they are fantastic these days!"

Thus spoke a Job's comforter with youth on her side.

When we got back home I sat up in bed, after a poor night's sleep, and burst into tears for the first time in more years than I could remember.

"Whatever is the matter?"

"I just feel so... old, so...useless. If I were a horse you'd be sending for someone to shoot me now."

"I think not," said John gently.

"Perhaps," I sniffed, "But I mean, look at me! Trussed up in Frankenstein's boot at night, walking with a stick, having to sit down when I am teaching, not able to go for walks. And putting on weight. I mean I've finally done it; reached the golden age, semi-retired, a secure pension. All those years investing everything - labour, love, money - into Hill House East so that we can have a decade or so of just enjoying it, just living here. And what happens? I'm beginning to drop to bits! Good God, what's next? Bath hoists? Stair lifts?"

"I think not," said John for a second time, "Not yet awhile anyway."

"I have never, ever thought about my age before but I cannot get away from it; I am getting old!"

"So am I - and there is nothing we can do about it," he reminded me, "Nobody can."

He was absolutely right of course and I needed to realise that I was not the only one getting older. Denty had come down in an uncharacteristically serious mood and, without preamble – which was also uncharacteristic – had come straight to the point.

"Ah'm sending all the Imps to a sale at Darlington mart."

The Imps were the lambs he had bred by putting Zulu to some of his Swale ewes; I suggested the resulting cross could be a new breed called 'Zwartdales' but he had several other choice descriptions for them. For some reason, rather than the docile Zwartbles side being inherited, these horned black devils were wild – almost as bad as the Hebrideans – and did not take kindly to any sort of human interference.

"Ah've no intention of breeding from them – if the next generation is as wick as they are then, we'll nivvor get near them! So, old Zulu will not be running wi' my Swaledale ewes this year. Now, ah knaa he's covered your ewes already. So, the thing is…"

Another uncharacteristic pause…

"Ah think Zulu should go to the sale as well."

We were all silent, then he continued, "He's just ga'n te brekk out of every field we put him in on the place till the spring wi' nay mair yows to cover here; an' he'll be searching for mair, as ye knaa. Auld bugger just walked through a wall last year and helped himself to some of me neighbour's Swales. Ah' nearly had a paternity suit on me hands!"

Denty had decided that his Zwartbles were taking up too much of his time and effort and so had sold them in the spring, as well as a fair share of his own Swaledales; an ominous sign that, he too, felt the clock ticking towards the end of his shepherding days. As he had bluntly put it, we were all beginning to 'face west and head into the sunset.'

"So the only thing te dee is to bar him up inside aall winter – and ye know he doesn't tek well te that"

"Define 'sale'" I asked carefully.

"Well – ah mean a breedin' sale; he's well fit enough to do more work this back end – it's just we haven't the yows for 'im!"

"Not for meat then?"

"Well," Denty replied equally cautiously, "Ah would hope he would sell for breedin'. He's still in good fettle – for an auld tup – an' ah reckon he's got another couple of years work in him. But if he didn't sell, well...'"

The question was left at that point.

"But summit has te be done; ah canna spend the winter chasin' him all ower the Dale."

I took a deep breath, "Well, he is your sheep; I have to leave it to you."

Over the next few days I did try very hard to weigh up all the options. Just why I felt so strongly about this enormous black male sheep was impossible to define. A tup was not something into which one usually invested emotion. I once read in a book a description of the time honoured fate of the elderly tup: 'After a life of sex and violence they find themselves in a wagon and on the first step of their journey towards becoming pet food'. Everything inside me protested about Zulu having such an ignominious end; his life had certainly been filled with plenty of sex but I had never witnessed him being violent. In fact, for an animal of such enormous strength and power he was a gentleman, in the true sense of the word. He was the father of most of the Zwartbles that now roamed our hillside. It was pure sentimentality, I knew that, but... this was Zulu, who liked nothing better than a slice of wholemeal toast and having his back scratched, who knew his name and who came when called. But... he was also an old tup, past his prime in fact when Denty had bought him a few years before; he would not have many more years left in his natural span anyway before his teeth and possibly everything else went. But... I had always known that this day would come and John and I had discussed it at length.

I knew Zulu would be in 'the last pen' one day and have to go down the road and would probably end up as pet food, but surely it must be possible for him to live out his natural lifespan, even after Denty no longer wanted him for breeding?

"That would be a bit difficult; I imagine that breeding would still be on Zulu's brain as he drew his last breath!"

A classic male response I thought but actually probably true.

"What if we buy him from Denty and have him castrated?"

John winced visibly.

"What?"

"Have him castrated; it's the time honoured way of getting round the problem of aggression and, um, urges in male animals and making them more docile and biddable. They castrate horses and cattle – why not a sheep?"

John was still crossing his legs protectively.

"Well, I know they castrate male lambs when they are very young – but a mature tup? Can it be done?"

I raised the issue tentatively with Denty, who of course, thought I was completely deranged and I think I went down several points in his estimation of me as a sensible country woman. Why would anyone want to spend money to keep a smelly old tup, who'd had a good life, going for another couple of years as a ...pet? Crackers! Zulu, he was sure, given the choice between having the chance of another couple of years of fathering lambs or 'losing his tackle' would go for the first option.

"Ah'm bloody sure ah would!" he had emphatically declared, "Ah kna' yer fond of the auld lad but the wagon is coming for him and some others at the weekend. It's the best way, believe me."

The problem kept going round and round in my head. What if someone did buy him for breeding? They may just use him for one more year because he was old and then it would be on that wagon again and away - and we would never know how, when or where, his end came. There were horrific tales of sheep ending up on lengthy journeys in wagons to faraway places. One of the reassuring things about all the lambs from Glenwhelt that ended up in our freezer was that their journey was only half a mile to the small, well run abattoir in the village. And what would happen if he did not sell for breeding? Denty had made it clear he wanted nothing bringing back from that sale. So Zulu would just be penned up with all the other leftovers and unwanted has-beens and sent with them for the scrap market and no doubt end up in a pet food tin.

That thought pained me most deeply of all.

All week the arguments of common sense versus sentiment warred in my head until, in the end, I simply said to John, "Denty must decide what is the best thing to do. I am sorry; I simply cannot bear to think about this anymore."

I washed my hands of the whole issue, just like Pontius Pilate.

The decision was taken; Zulu would be going to the sale on the wagon, with the Imps, at 8.30 am on Sunday, the next day.

Sunday morning breakfast was a sombre affair. John made toast and boiled eggs and we sat at the table by the kitchen window as usual. Our conversation was a bit strained and very trivial and both of us were obviously avoiding the one thing that was really on our minds. In the end I could bear it no longer.

"This is the right thing for him isn't it? There's nothing else we can do is there?

"Well, yes, yes it is for the best; I mean I am sure he'll be sold to someone that really wants him. Best thing isn't it when he still has a breeding year or two left? Surely?"

"What if," I asked in a small voice, "What if he isn't? What then?"

"Well... I..."

A grinding of gears and a labouring engine cut through John's sentence. The cattle wagon was heading past our window, up the hill to Glenwhelt. We both pretended to ignore it and I tried to continue with my breakfast, but every mouthful was getting harder to swallow. Finally, in an eleventh hour blinding burst of conscience, I knew what I had to do.

"Sorry," I said to John as I left my egg, the table and him, "I have to go up to Glenwhelt – I just have to."

I grabbed my coat and car keys and set my little old car at the hill. At least I knew the wagon could not get past me on the way down, the road was too narrow. The journey was only a few hundred yards and I could soon see the large wagon backed up to the sheep pens. The ramp was up and dark shapes were milling around inside. The driver's door was still open though and Denty was chatting to him. They saw me make an abrupt halt and get quickly out of the car. Had I been able to lip read I could have bet he was saying, "Aye, now what? Ah' bet it's trouble!"

So I spat it out.

"Denty, I know this is pure, foolish sentimentality and actually none of my business,"

"Probably!"

"Well, if Zulu does not sell for breeding, then we will buy him and then will you please have him brought home?"

Stupid, warm, fat tears had begun to trickle down my cheeks.

"I'll pay for him to come back –and I'll get straight onto the vet and see what can be done. And if it's not possible to castrate him then I'll pay for him to be put down; here. Then the knacker man can have him, but I just cannot let him disappear without knowing what has happened to him. It feels wrong – it's just wrong."

Denty and the driver looked at each other, both lost for words for a while.

"Oh, but he'll sell alright – he's a grand sheep! He'll go for breeding, sure thing," the driver finally assured me from the window of his cab.

"Then that will be alright. But if he doesn't, you will bring him back won't you? Please promise me that?"

Both men were looking a bit stunned and not a little embarrassed by such emotion being poured out over an old tup but reassurances were given and I thanked them, apologised for my softness and went back down the hill.

My tea and eggs were cold by the time I got sat down at the table again. The big wagon rolled downhill past the window as I buttered some leathery toast.

Zulu was on his way.

"I do feel better; I am glad I went up," I told John.

"Good."

"But..."

"But what?"

"But... nothing really. Something still doesn't feel right. I just wish to goodness I had thought this all through more clearly, been more decisive before he was put on that wagon. I suppose I have been waiting for some sort of sign."

"I'll make a fresh pot of tea," sighed my long suffering John.

In Westgate that morning the weather was bitter cold, dark grey overcast and spitting with rain. I was going to the Quaker Meeting in Alston; an hour of quiet reflection was something I was much in need of. When I drove past Cowshill and began to climb up the hill to the Cumbrian border there was an abrupt change in the weather. It was snowing rather than raining and already, a slushy wet layer lay across the road. Barely another half mile and the snow was falling more purposefully, lying more deeply and already beginning to form into small V shaped drifts across the road. The car wheels spun and slid as I negotiated a curve that took me to the top of the hill. From there it was downhill all the way and I knew I would get down safely - but what if the snow kept up for another hour or more? Would I be able to get back up it again? It was too risky, so I did a cautious ten point turn in the middle of the road and headed slowly back for home.

"What happened?"

John bustled out of his workshop as soon as he heard the car on the drive.

"Don't worry, nothing wrong with me or the car, just too much snow lying on the tops above Cowshill to risk it."

"Very wise; better safe than sorry. I expect we could get snow here too before the day is out."

I followed him into his workshop, which was comfortably warm after the rawness outside with a wood burning stove glowing cheerfully in the corner. I went over to enjoy its heat when I heard a quad bike pull up outside.

"I'm sure Denty can see the smoke from my chimney from up at Glenwhelt whenever I light this stove," John chuckled, "He'll have come down for a warm no doubt."

On cue the sliding door opened and a cold, damp shepherd came in. He gave me a very strange look and said, "Hev' ye been to church?"

"Well, I *was* going to the Meeting at Alston but I turned back because of the snow."

"Well, ha' ye been praying to Saint Francis or someone?"

"Sorry?" I was completely baffled.

He turned to John, "Git your coat on quick; we've got to gan and get a Zwartbles tup."

Ah well, I thought bitterly, there speaks a working shepherd; Zulu's barely left and he's looking for a replacement.

"Where from; where are you getting one from so soon?" I asked, knowing that they were not something to be readily found.

"Westgate."

"Westgate?" I knew there were no other Zwartbles tups in Westgate. I was completely baffled.

"But Zulu is the only Zwartbles tup in Westgate!"

"Aye."

He paused for effect.

"An' that's who we're gannin' to get – yer bloody Zulu! The auld bugger jumped out o' the wagon when they put the ramp down to load some cattle in't village. Only a gap of about eighteen inches but he got through; driver says he's only ever seen one other sheep do that in all his years. They've managed to catch him and bar him in a buildin', so we'd better go and get him. The au'd sod!!! What!"

I really did not know whether to laugh or cry and so did both. I had asked for a sign concerning Zulu's fate and this, most surely, was it.

"Denty, I am sorry but I am so, so happy!"

"Ay, well; ye wanted him? Well he's yours. Tell yer what – here!" and he threw the quad bike keys to me, "If he's your sheep ye gan' and fetch him!"

Of course, he did not mean it, and John and he left with bike and trailer a few minutes later. I went into the house to make the best pint mug of tea for Denty that I could. I was so happy; I felt lighter and brighter than I had done in a week. The tea was brewing nicely in the teapot when the bike rumbled past the kitchen window, back up the hill, and in the trailer behind, head held high, very regal and visibly smirking, was a big black tup.

Zulu had come home.

I had to wait till the next day to phone the vet. Would it be possible, I asked, to castrate a large elderly tup? There was a pause, as if she was not quite sure she had heard right.

"Well - yes, it certainly can be done but why on earth would you want to?"

I explained as concisely as I could.

"It's his only hope I'm afraid."

"Well, he should be fine even at his age if we give him an epidural and local anaesthetic rather than a general. Have you somewhere suitable for him to have the operation? We would need a fairly clean building with good light. Oh, and hot water available nearby."

Hot water? Epidural? It sounded more as if he was going to have a baby!

"And he'll be a bit sore for about ten days and you'll have to watch out for signs of infection; you'll have to keep him inside."

"No problem!" I assured her.

We would convert the Hemmel into a private ward for him.

"Great; we can book him in for next Tuesday morning. That's all I think – oh! Except, we could do with two fairly strong men to help out?"

"Don't worry," I chuckled, "I know just the right two – but bring your smelling salts; there is one who just might pass out!"

I wondered how I could thank Denty for humouring my softness? What would he enjoy more than anything in the world? Three words immediately sprang to mind – lemon drizzle cake. So on a day that was not fit for a dog to be out, rain lashing against the windows and great dark clouds scudding across a late autumn sky, I set to baking in the warm sanctuary of my kitchen; softening the butter, beating that day's eggs from the hens and grating lemons in simple contentment to the calm accompaniment of the tick of the kitchen clock. A delicious smell of baking cake filled the kitchen and, when it came out of the oven, I poured caster sugar and fresh lemon juice over the cake while it was still piping hot, just as instructed in the hand written recipe of my mother's that I was using. Then I made myself a pot of fresh tea and was just about to pour it when there was a knock on the door. I knew it would be Denty; he could hear a kettle boil from the top of the fell. He stood on the step drenched through and thoroughly chilled, his wellies muddied nearly up to the knees. How he worked the way he did, out in all weathers, I really did not know; it was a hard, hard way to make a living. No wonder he did not have that much time for sentimentality.

"Come in, come in," I urged, "You're soaked through; have some hot tea."

He declined; which was a very rare event.

"No, no; if ah tek this lot off ah'll not get goin' again. Ah just called to see if there was news – from the vet like."

"Yes! She's booked us in for next Tuesday morning. I'll be at work so it'll be down to you and John to help – I've said we'll have the Hemmel here ready for him. Poor John; he really would have preferred it to be on a day when I am not at work and, actually, I would rather be here to. But it can't be helped."

"Nowt's the bother!" said Denty cheerily, turning to go.

"Wait! Just a sec!" I shouted, as I dashed back into the kitchen, scooped up the still warm cake, covered it with a clean tea towel and handed it to him, "That's for you. Just to say thank you."

He looked very touched.

"From you?"

"No, from Zulu actually – he knows it is your favourite!"

"He's not wrang there."

Denty gave a wide grin. He only had one front tooth left, but it was very sweet.

Snow began to fall with a vengeance over the weekend. Before long, the whole of the north east of England had the worst snowfall for the time of year for a long time. If this was what the third week in November was going to throw at us, what was the rest of the winter going to be like? Very quickly all normality ground to a halt; public transport was struggling, the airport was closed, the post could not be delivered and all the Dale's schools closed. Now, my school in Durham had a maxim of 'we never close' but there had been one or two occasions over the previous years when it had been absolutely impossible for me to get out of Weardale because of the snow. Whenever I rang the school to tell them I would not make it, I could always detect just the slightest note of disbelief in the secretary's voice:

"Oh? That's strange; there's just a light covering here."

"Of course there is," I always had to tell them, "You're not 1,150 feet up in the North Pennines!"

By Sunday evening I began to think that I wouldn't get into school the next morning. I also worried that the vet wouldn't be able to make it on the Tuesday either and we'd have to call the whole thing off. That would have been a great shame because we were all psyched up for it now - well, all except Zulu, who was in blissful ignorance. John had cleaned the whole building out, made a big airy pen and put down a deep, clean bed of straw. It was a really nice little building was the Hemmel, well built with - unusually for the Dale - a green Cumberland slate roof, windows that had once been quite delicate and pretty with four narrow panes in them and good, sound roof timbers. Many years of neglect had left it in a sorry state though; holes in the roof, slates missing, glass missing, window frames rotted, gutters hanging off. John had had to replace the stable door; it had just about disintegrated and would not keep anything in or out, not even the draughts. He had however been reluctant to spend any more time or money on the building than was absolutely necessary, as we did not own it. Actually, the top item on our wish list for life was to one day purchase the Hemmel and the fields adjacent to the house; to own them rather than to rent them. But, although we had started negotiations it was proving to be a long and very complicated procedure. If and when we did own it would become John's next big project.

"When I do do it up," he would say, "Then I want to do it properly."

And I knew, of course, that he would.

But the immediate need was to have somewhere weatherproof and comfortable for Zulu to spend the next couple of weeks, so he rigged up electric light by cable from his workshop, pushed pieces of roofing felt under the slates to block the largest holes and keep the snow out and stapled thick, clear polythene over the window frames to keep the draughts out but to let light in.

My teaching assistant from school phoned that evening;

"Good news for you! School is closed to pupils and staff tomorrow because of the snow - and probably will be till Wednesday, so you don't need to try and struggle in!"

"Thank you, thank you God!" I said with sincere gratitude.

"Thank him from me also," muttered John, deeply relieved that I was going to be with him for 'the op'.

I was up bright and early on the Tuesday morning and, by the time the vet arrived at 11.30, I had made six dozen fairy cakes (well, it kept my mind off things) for my classes' Christmas coffee afternoon at the end of the week.

The vet had only just managed to crawl up the hill despite her impressive 4x4 vehicle. As she had requested, I had a big kettle full of hot water ready on John's woodstove in his workshop and a pile of clean old towels. Despite my bravado about 'Oh, I've seen horses castrated before – nothing to it really' I was beginning to actually feel just a little squeamish now the time had arrived. When the vet said she had decided against an epidural and was just going to give Zulu a local anaesthetic, I felt decidedly wobbly; an unconscious horse is one thing but a fully conscious, large and very strong ram was another!

"I'll give him this painkiller shot first and a dose of antibiotic," she announced, spreading out her surgical kit on a bale of straw in the building.

She got the first needle into him without him noticing, but he was not at all happy about the second one. So, when she said brightly, "Right then! If you could just sit him on his backside in that corner please!" Zulu shot off to the far side of the pen. Denty finally cornered him. It was like watching two Sumo wrestlers locked in an impasse but, slowly, and grunting with the effort, Denty got him off balance and flipped him expertly onto his back.

"Bye hell!" he gasped, "Ah reckon he's heavier than me!"

"My, he is a big boy!"

"D'ye mean me or tup?" Denty asked the vet.

The vet grinned; she was used to Weardale farmer humour.

Denty braced himself in the corner, his massive arms locked around Zulu's equally massive girth, just below his front legs. John braced himself against Zulu's far side to keep him pushed in the corner – making sure that he was in a position where he could see nothing of the procedure. The vet reached for her clippers and began to shave off Zulu's short and curlies. Even pinned by both men, there was nothing to stop Zulu from kicking around with his back legs.

"Don't suppose you could come in too and sit on his back legs for me?" she asked.

Well, there was no backing out now, no sitting on a bale in the corner offering moral support from the side lines; I was going to be face on, within inches of the whole operation. I really do not like blood – certainly not if there is lots of it and if it squirts; how I would have to eat my words if I was the one that passed out! In the event, neither of these things happened and the whole procedure was so neat and skilfully done that I actually found it fascinating to watch. The vet injected large amounts of local anaesthetic, made two little slits in the scrotum, slid out his testicles, clamped the arteries, removed them, put in sutures, sprayed on some antiseptic – and it was all over in under half an hour from start to finish, with very little blood at all and just the odd stoic grunt from Zulu.

"You can all let go now."

Zulu rolled onto his side, got up, had a good shake and went to his hay rack and started to munch as if nothing had happened.

"That's a good sign!" The vet was clearly very pleased with how things had gone, "Though he will be rather sore for a few days when the anaesthetic wears off. You will have to watch out for any bleeding or undue swelling – give me a ring at once if that happens. Oh, I'll leave you some iodine; if you could wash the scrotum with a weak, warm antiseptic solution every day it would help a lot. I'll also leave a syringe with another antibiotic shot to give on Friday."

"Aa'll see to that" volunteered Denty.

Away she went down the hill and it was all over.

"Bye," said Denty, eyeing the bucket that contained what had till so recently been Zulu's manhood.

"Hev' you ever had them sliced and fried? Delicious they are; mind that's young lambs' am talkin' about – ah think them'll be a bit strong and gamey!"

Poor Zulu, I felt a sudden pang of guilt, what had we done to him? Given him the chance to live to a ripe and cared for old age I reminded myself. It was, however, a consolation to look at our ewes pulling on the hay feeder in the nearby field and realise that safe, deep within them, another crop of lambs, in a final fathering, would be slowly growing through the cold winter months and that Zulu would still be with us to see them.

He made a quick and full recovery and was a very patient patient. In fact, I think he quite liked his cosy pen with full room service and lots of tasty treats. He wasn't so keen on having his undercarriage sprayed with antiseptic daily, but as long as he had his head in a bucket of food he put up with it. When the time came to release him out with our ewes we were curious to know what would happen, even though the ewes were all safely into early pregnancy by then. He sauntered out as if he had never been away, began grazing and later in the day, lay contentedly chewing his cud with his adoring wives close by, just as if nothing had happened. That which we had so dearly wanted for him came to pass; he had three whole years of contented retirement. Laid back and utterly idle he would indulge the new lambs every spring - even though they had not been fathered by him - by allowing them to use his back as a climbing frame or to huddle up to him, like a large windbreak, against the chill spring winds. He and his first love, Crumpet, became like two old sweethearts, grazing, sleeping together and nuzzling each other whenever they could. His dearest friend and companion however was John; every time he saw him he would bellow loudly and trot over to be petted and scratched.

When John worked or walked in the fields, wherever he went, Zulu would follow like some enormous black Newfoundland dog. If John sat down on the grass he would lie beside him. If he was out of sight and John called his name he would appear almost instantly. Each morning when John tweaked open the curtain on the landing there he was, lying on the slight rise in the field we called Zulu's Hill, gazing longingly at the window apparently waiting for John to appear.

Their love affair was mutual; they quite simply adored each other.

It was over a period of time that we realised Zulu was not carrying quite as much flesh as he had. Then I began finding little wads of half chewed grass around the hay feeder. I reported this to Denty.

"Aye lass, he's cuddin; he's not able to chew his grass up properly so it's comin' out of his mouth half chewed. It's his age and his teeth; they wear out in sheep ye knaa an' then they cannat get enough food digested properly. And afore ye ask – no, ye cannat get dentures for 'im! This time there's now't ye can do."

That wasn't strictly true; I'd had a pony once with a tooth problem and I kept him going on buckets of well soaked, calorie-rich sugar beet. Supplementing his diet with this, Zulu seemed to gain some weight but I knew – and dreaded – the day that would be coming. He was, after all, now over eleven years old and that was a ripe old age for a tup.

I went to sing in a choir in Newcastle every week and, rather than driving over the moors back home in the dark, I would stay overnight with my old school friend, Maria. It was there that John phoned me quite early one morning.

"What's wrong John?"

By the tone of his voice something was wrong.

"It's Zulu; he's dead."

"Dead! But... how? He was fine yesterday; he ate all his food."

"Well, he has gone – in his sleep I think. In fact, I thought he was asleep. I opened the sheep shed door and they all came out except him. He was just lying on the straw in the corner. I even...I even poked him with my foot and said, "Come on you lazy thing!" But, he was gone."

"Oh, John, I am so sorry."

And I was deeply saddened and knew there would be an irreplaceable hole in our lives.
But part of me rejoiced; all I had ever wanted was for Zulu to live out his natural life span happily and well and the wise old thing had known it was time to go.

No marts to be taken to and sold off as scrap.
No journey to an abattoir.
No knacker man with a humane killer.
He had simply gone to sleep. At home.

I hope and pray that when my time comes I have as gentle an end.

Feathered Friends

10

A REQUIEM FOR ROCKY

When I was a girl, my great aunt Meg once came to stay, bringing with her a cage containing a green budgie called Robin. She and the budgie came for a fortnight. My aunt went home but the budgie stayed with us for four years, until it finally fell off its perch. Rocky, a little white bantam rooster, had come to stay with us for a fortnight but in the end stayed for six years. He was seven years old when he came on holiday and thirteen when his long vacation ended abruptly and not well.

Rocky had so quickly settled in with our much bigger, though virginal, hens that it seemed an unkindness to send him back to live out his days in solitary. Whether he became espoused to our girls in the full sense of the word, I don't know, but certainly there were no offspring from the various unions. He developed a particularly affectionate relationship with Galina, our senior Blackrock hen, who was also getting on a bit and they toddled around together, shared their food and snuggled up at night; an odd couple indeed, as she was at least three times larger than him. Rocky's ego was up to the task however and he would strut around his erstwhile harem regally, showing off his best feature – a tail of long white plumes that were fit for the headgear of a British colonial governor. The hens would raise their eyebrows as if to say, 'Oh God, here we go again!' Batch after batch of nubile pullets came, laid many eggs and passed away but Rocky soldiered on. However, ego alone cannot defy the ravages of time and, in his thirteenth year, he became very creaky in the mornings – as do we all – and eventually his strutting turned into a rather bad limp. There was nothing else for it; he was put into a cat basket and taken to the vet. The old chap was highly indignant about this and thoroughly embarrassed by the examination.

"How old did you say he was?"

"Getting on for thirteen we think."

"That's a pretty good innings you know. I'm afraid he has got quite bad arthritis in both hips; there's not a great deal I can do really. If you like I can just put him…"

"No! Not unless you think he is really suffering."

I knew that hip replacements weren't available on the NHS for chickens but I ventured, "Is there anything at all you could do?"

"Well… I could give him an anti inflammatory injection; that should make him more comfortable."

So the jab was given to Rocky, who gave the vet a good pecking in return.

"Now, you do realise that this bird is now inedible."

"Sorry?" I could hardly believe my ears.

"Because of the injection; he can't be used for food purposes."

On the way home in the car I was as indignant as Rocky.

"Eat him!" I spluttered to John, "Eat him? Why would anyone want to eat a scrawny, little old rooster? He would be as tough as old boots! And, had we wanted to, I would have just wrung his neck – not taken him to see the vet and pay twenty five pounds for a jab! That's more than I pay for the Christmas bird!"

His decline continued slowly at first. Like an old retired colonel he only came out to take the air when the elements were clement and took to increasingly early nights, preferably snuggled up to his old love, Galina. Eventually the Horlick's hour became too early for her; at less than half his age she still had the urge to party in the field well into the long summer evenings. On good days, Rocky would still attempt an alluring fan dance for his harem when he came out in the morning but they would just stampede over him in the rush for breakfast, clearly thinking 'silly old fool!' Then a curious metamorphosis took place in his feet; it seemed to me he was gradually losing his toenails and then his feet seemed to become shorter and shorter. I worried that one day he would be tottering around on legs like stilts; mercifully, the atrophy stopped before we reached this point. Next he began losing, one by one, that glory of his manhood; his plumed tail and then all the feathers on his neck, which made him look quite ridiculous. Nevertheless, he still seemed to be enjoying life – eating, drinking, socialising – and not suffering in any way, even though he was a very shabby old bird. Then one day, he just did not want to leave the hen house nor accept any breakfast, even in bed. He had obviously decided his time had come and we just decided to let him fade away quietly with as much dignity as possible. Normally when one of the hens went like that they are 'gone' within thirty six hours.

"Aye," declared Denty, "Once they decide they are gannin', nothin'll stop them: that's the way wi' animals."

Not Rocky.

Nearly a week later he was still with us. As it was a lovely sunny morning we decided to lift him out of the hen house onto a favourite sunny spot in the grass; he could still move around if he wanted to but not very well. Then we went out for Sunday lunch with friends, during which it began to pour with rain just as we were starting our sticky toffee pudding. I rushed home guilt ridden, imagining him suffering from hypothermia and a bad dose of perishment. We could not find him anywhere; he wasn't in the hen house and he wasn't in the garden. We extended the area to the field and, in a police-type fingertip search operation, he was discovered hidden in the long soaking grass at the bottom of a stone wall. He was a pitiful sight, soaked through and stone cold.

He had pushed and battled his way right down the field through all the tussocks of grass and forests of nettles. Somewhere on his journey he had bashed his head and the few straggly feathers he still possessed were sticking up, punk fashion, plastered with blood.

Surely he would not recover from this?

"Is he alive?"

"Just, I think."

Up at the house, in an effort to make him more comfortable, I rubbed him down with a towel and then gently dried his feathers with warm air from the hair dryer. He actually seemed to enjoy this and, warm, dry and fluffed up again, seemed very much happier; he was even, in an endearing fashion, trying to make himself more presentable by having a little preen. It was during this treatment that I discovered Rocky was completely blind. He had no idea what direction he was facing and would just walk till he bumped into something; this could have been why he was having trouble getting to his food.

"Enough," John pronounced, "He is ancient, blind, bald, can barely walk; time for a one way journey to the vet."

"Just let me see if I can coax him to eat," I pleaded.

Rocky, the indestructible, wolfed down Weetabix and warm milk when it was put right under his beak. The next morning he happily polished off his porridge. That evening I decided he needed more protein and he really enjoyed his scrambled egg – but not as much as the smoked salmon and new potatoes the next night. He spent his days in his basket in the porch but in the evening appreciated moving into the living room with us, basket by the fire, just as Lazarus had done years before.

"Enough!" John said more firmly, "He is not a budgie; he can't go on living in the porch or the living room! We have B&B guests coming in tonight; he will have to go out in the garage. And then to the vet."

"You are right, of course," I conceded, "Just let him have this last weekend and I will take him on Monday."

As it was a sunny morning I put him in a large cardboard box in the garage and left the doors open so he could take the air and enjoy the sunlight.

When I took his lunch out later on– mashed lasagne – a frightful sight greeted me.

"Whatever is it? You look ashen!"

"It's Rocky; he won't need the vet."

John put his arm around me, "Ah well, it's the best thing; has the old boy gone?"

"Yes he has, but not in the way you are thinking. You'd better and come and see. And brace yourself!"

To begin with John could not believe what he saw, which had been my reaction when I went out. On the garage floor lay the ripped and torn body of poor old Rocky, his bright red blood a shocking contrast to his white plumage as it pooled around him. His throat had been ripped out and he was just about eviscerated.

"How… what… could have done this?"

He had gone as white as I had.

"I know exactly 'what'; I saw it run off from the body, it was at his throat when I came in. It was a large polecat or a ferret, a pale one – but it was also covered in blood."

John very rarely swears but he vented his feelings very clearly on this occasion.

"Dear God, he came here in the first place as one of those bastards massacred all his wives! And now he's gone the same way! I wouldn't care but Denty just said the other day he'd seen one slinking round his farmyard; I never thought for a minute it would get down here."

The problem was that people came rabbiting in the Dale, usually, but not always, seeking permission from the owner of the land first. They would put nets over the entrances and exits to rabbit burrows and then put a ferret down the hole to drive the rabbits out and into the nets, where they would be dispatched. The ferret would then exit the hole, get a reward and be reunited with its owner. It was a traditional way of hunting rabbits for food and actually worked well, most of the time. Sometimes however the ferret did not reappear; it could get lost in a maze of burrows, maybe come out of an un-netted exit a long way off, or it could decide it liked the taste of freedom – and that of the rabbits and other creatures it could hunt for itself. So, it would be left behind and go feral, living off the land and killing where and when it wanted; chickens were something to which they were very partial.

John was still uttering a lot of words, many beginning with 'B', when something long and furry shot out from the back of the garage and went under his work bench. Normally a gentle, pacifist, animal loving soul, a man who would pick up half frozen worms and warm them by the fire, John said quietly, yet lethally;

"Right! Get out – and close the garage door; that thing won't need the vet either!"

All I could hear was a series of thumps, bangs and clatters as John pursued his quarry, pushing things aside in the garage that were in his way.

"Gotcha, you bastard!" finally rang out in triumph.

But he exited the garage dejected.

"I hate doing things like that," he said miserably, "but it came out and looked at me, its head and neck all covered in Rocky's blood and I thought, it'll be the girls next, so I picked up this piece of wood and whacked it."

"You did the right thing; it would have been the girls next, then Jean's ducks, then Alan's hens… no end to the carnage."

I went to examine the corpse. Sure enough, when I went in a long, lean, mean body lay on the floor. I drew as close as I dared to examine it – and noticed that the ribs were still slowly rising up and down.

"It's not a corpse."

"What!"

"It's not dead; it's still breathing. Maybe you just knocked it out?"

"Oh."

"You need to finish it John."

A lot of his bravado and adrenalin seemed to have left him.

"I don't think I can!"

117

He really had to steel himself to go back in and face doing the deed, this time in cold blood, but he did. The sound of a hearty 'thwack' soon rang out. No triumph about it this time, just relief that it was over.

"I'll go in and check for you shall I?"

"Hardly think you need to – I gave it a good wallop."

"I know, but…"

So, imagine my horror and incredulity to see our murderer obviously unconscious but still breathing as it lay beside its poor, dismembered victim.

"John, you're not going to believe this but…"

"No! It can't be, it just can't! Well, I'm sorry; I just cannot do that again. Sorry. But I really can't."

"Oh, for heaven's sake John! Are you a man or a mouse?"

"Squeak," he replied, as he headed for the house.

It was my adrenalin that was running high now; seeing poor Rocky's awful fate a second time demanded that someone saw justice served for him – and it looked like it was going to be me. Icily determined I walked in and closed the garage door behind me, picked up John's wood chopping axe, took my stance over the unconscious murderer and brought it down with and almighty crash, sandwiching it between the axe and the concrete floor.

This time it did not move again.

"That's for Rocky," I snarled at it, as I replaced the axe and headed for the house and a cup of tea – or perhaps something stronger.

We laid Rocky's tattered remains to rest with ceremony against the field wall where we had buried all our hens over the years. None of our hens met a strangulated end; all passed on in their own good time and then had a respectful burial. If, in a future time, someone were to have an archaeological dig thereabouts they would probably conclude there had been some sort of cult based on the sacrifice of chickens in the area. We had a small wake and raised a tot of whisky to Rocky, who had greeted our mornings and gladdened our days.

We hoped he would greet new dawns in heaven.

Denty, naturally, had to be filled in about the whole gory story and he insisted on seeing the corpse of the executed criminal.

"No, that's not the one ah' had up at Glenwhelt; it's ower pale, the one up there was browner. An' ah think bigger!"

This meant, worryingly, that there could be another ferrety-polecat in the area who could commit mass murder on our lovely girls. We became quite obsessive about luring them to bed early and locking them in; I don't know why, when Rocky had been slaughtered in broad daylight. Whilst in this state of red alert John looked out of our bedroom window when he got up one morning and said with alarm, "Come and look at this! What is it? It couldn't be an otter could it!"

Well, no it couldn't; it was far too small and too far away from the river. It appeared to be going round in erratic circles, pausing now and then to lick or even bite at a back leg, which seemed to be damaged.

"It's another bloody polecat – maybe the *other* polecat! It's a big brown one!"

I was down the stairs before he had time to reply, put my tracksuit on over my pyjamas and pulled on my cold wellies over bare feet - which is never a pleasant experience. I had no positive feelings about polecats at all after what had happened to Rocky and I went out armed with a heavy walking stick. But the sight that met me did strike a chord of compassion, even for a polecat, for that is what the creature was. I do not like to see any sort of living thing suffer. This creature had obviously had its back leg trapped in some sort of snare or trap – probably set for rabbits. It had somehow got free but the leg was mangled, swollen and possibly broken. It was also most probably infected and obviously driving the creature mad with pain. It ran in ragged circles, stopping when the pain got too great to bear and it began to gnaw at it, as if it wished to bite off the offending limb and be rid of it.

"Oh God."

I knew there was only one thing to do and that was to put it out of its agony and misery as I had done several times for rabbits suffering from the plague of myxomatosis. So, for the second time in a week, and with a heavy heart, I braced myself, raised the heavy stick and gave it a strong blow to the head. I had forgotten two things: firstly, that polecats appear very hard to kill and secondly, that after quite a lot of recent rain, the field was soft and yielding. All that I succeeded in doing was to imprint its head into the soft ground and rendering it unconscious but still breathing.

"Not again!" I groaned inwardly, raising the stick once more and dealing a heavier and, I prayed, lethal blow. Alas, I only succeeded in pushing it deeper into the ground than I had the first time. I swore loudly and audibly this time and shot poisonous looks at John, who was watching the whole performance anxiously from the bedroom window.

There was only one thing for it.

I stomped off to the garage, grabbed the heavy axe, stomped back and – before my nerve deserted me – dealt what was, thank God, the third and final blow.

Later, yet again, the whole tale had to be related to Denty as he sipped his morning mug of tea and, yet again, he went off to examine the corpse. Surely, I thought, this had to be the creature he had seen up at Glenwhelt. But after one quick look he shook his head.

"Sorry lass, but that's not it either; this'un is too dark and too big!"

So now I had been the mad axe woman to two polecats and yet there was obviously one still at large.

Somewhere.

My mother had been very superstitious about such things; bad luck or bad events would always come in threes she would say. If two occurred then a third would surely be on its way.

And, lo and behold, a few days later Denty came down with a report of an encounter with the third polecat.

"Well," he reported dramatically, "Ah was just gannin' in for me dinner and ah tossed me wellies off in the porch."

The porch at Glenwhelt, also known as the welly room, was where outdoor clothes and footwear worn on the farmyard were discarded before going into the house proper. It would be fair to say it was all a bit of a jumble in there and items without a good purchase on their pegs ended up on the floor. As his wellies hit the floor he had spied something brown and furry move rapidly in this heap of clothes.

"Ah quickly shut the outside door and the door into kitchen. 'Right ye bugga!' ah thowt, ah've got ye trapped now and, by God, ah'll have ye!"

He had picked up a heavy rubber mallet that was by the door and begun poking around in the footwear and hats and coats that had found their way from their pegs onto the floor. For a while he simply could not find the brown furry fiend – but then he saw it! Half in and half out of a welly boot!

"Ah knew it had nowhere left to run an' I thowt, 'Noo ah've got ye!'"

He was determined to make a good job of it, knowing my problems with finishing the others off.

"Ah brow't that mallet down wi' such a force, ah knew ah would have brok' its back!"

Certainly I wouldn't like to be on the receiving end of Denty full force behind a mallet and, sure enough, the creature lay there inert and not breathing.

"And?"

I knew he liked to draw out a story but my heart was pounding with anticipation now.

"Well, ye canna be too sure wi' them beggars; ah wasn't ganna put me hand in to fetch it out of the welly, so ah got the end of a stick in..."

"And was it dead!"

"Aye, it was dead al'right"

Unable to keep his face straight any longer he exploded with laughter.

"Ah'd killed Lynne's auld brown fur hat!"

The legend of the three polecats was one repeated on many an occasion for long after, though what happened to the real polecat that had started the whole saga, we never knew. It, perhaps wisely, was never seen again. However, from then on I always found myself lowering my eyes and rushing past the tent, set up every year at our local agricultural show, for the 'Ferret Rescue Society'.

11

HENNY PENNY

As a little girl, on visits with my mother and father to a rather staid Auntie Freda and Uncle Albert, I would wander off in my bored only child way and take refuge in Uncle Albert's hen house. There it was always warm, dusty and busy with plump, matronly ladies puffing themselves up importantly and making the most wonderful range of noises; calm crooning, chatty clucking and outraged squawking. I would wait and watch, entranced, until a triumphant cry announced the arrival of an egg. Her day's work done, the proud producer of this wonder would fluff herself up and rearrange her feathers before rejoining the other ladies outside. I would slide my hands into the still warm straw and wrap them around an even warmer egg, which I would carry reverently into the house. I still vividly remember, when I was about eight, letting a precious egg drop and smash. I was so horrified that my clumsiness might lead to me being banned from collecting eggs that I scooped every scrap of shell and every slimy, sloppy bit I could and hid them in a nearby hedge. I will never know if Uncle Albert realised he was one egg down that day, but if he did, he did not tell. The production of something so delicious in such an unlikely way was – and still is really – a source of wonder to me. But it was not until I lived at Hill House East that I finally achieved my childhood dream of having my own hens.

Our first hens, six large glossy black Blackrocks, had been hardy, independent birds kept in strict pecking order by the indomitable Galina, who had condescended to allow the little white cockerel Rocky to come under her jurisdiction. They laid brilliantly for a couple of years, less well in the third and by the fourth year the Blackrocks had obviously decided they deserved a long and egg free retirement. This was all very well but the economic scales did not balance when we were pouring hen food into one end and no eggs were appearing at the other.

"Time to neck 'em," Nat from Shallowford advised me as he passed by on his long daily walk, "Nee good for nowt, au'd birds – get yersel some fresh 'uns."

He was right; a prudent country wife would have had them simmering in a pan of broth long since. But, softies that we were, neither John nor I were up to 'necking them'.

Nat's other bit of advice was to get a different breed.

"Them big black things live far ower lang; do they want a pension or summit? Get yersel' some like mine; get some 'Die-quicks'."

Of course there was no such actual breed; what Nat meant was the very common, hybrid, ginger-red hens developed for egg farms. They started to lay eggs at twenty weeks, basically never stopped for over two years and then, in the third year, went 'a bit peaky' one day and keeled over the next.

"Just the ticket!" pronounced Nat.

Having been reduced to actually buying eggs something had to be done. The breakthrough came through when someone in the village offered a home to our elderly Blackrocks as all they wanted were pets, not eggs. So five of them went off to their new home - but not Galina as she was, well, a character. Next we sourced a breeder of Die-quicks over the hill in Teesdale; a lovely elderly gentleman called Mr Stubbs, who reared hundreds of chicks to point–of–lay hens for the egg industry. This was no prison camp of a hen factory though. His birds were all reared in large, light airy barns with thick, clean straw underfoot and they were healthy and friendly and would run up to him when he went in among them crooning 'Chook! Chook!' and holding a wire coat hanger.

"Now, d'ye see a bird ye fancy? That's a bonny 'un!"

And flash would go the wire coat hanger and the bird would be hooked by the neck and into our travel crate before it knew what had happened. The new hens quickly settled in and were soon under Galina's benign but iron discipline. She reminded me of a plump, spinster Girl Guide leader I had once had, who would clap her hands and say, 'Girls! Girls!' if we put a foot out of line. Galina obviously thrived in her role as matron in charge. She lived for ten years before we buried her beside her beloved Rocky, under the tree where they used to sunbathe together. But imagine how long we would have had to wait for an egg if we had kept all six Blackrocks!

The new hens were more docile and less adventurous birds than the Blackrocks but they could certainly lay eggs. One problem was that they all looked almost identical so it was hard to tell them apart and even harder to give them names – they just became 'the Girls'. There was no way we could bring ourselves to call them the Die-quicks'.

"There's a hen in the garden!" John yelled.

I muttered bad words, imagining my newly planted pea seedlings being ploughed up by sharp, scaly toes.

"Not the back garden – the front garden; in the gaff!"

Sure enough a ginger hen was strolling around, having a little peck here and another there, quite relaxed and at ease. She put up no fight at all when I stooped to pick her up; in fact she really seemed to like being carried around. How had she got out? They had all had their wings clipped the previous week to stop them lifting off and clearing the fence. The hen crooned with pleasure at having her head scratched.

"Hang on."

I extended the bird's left wing but, instead of a row of stumpy quills, all her feathers were intact.

"I'm sure I didn't miss one when I clipped them," I said, more to myself than to John, as we walked round to the hen field to put her back out.

I could see John counting.

" ...four, five, six. You didn't; all ours are here. She's not our hen!"

Now, the only other hens that lived anywhere nearby belonged to a couple in the village who owned a tiny corner of a field a little way up the steep hill to Glenwhelt. Like us, Jeff and Lesley had a long felt urge to keep hens but had no ground on which to do it, so buying the little patch of ground was their solution. It entailed either a long and steep walk every day or a trip in the car to see to them; but we are all willing to make some sacrifices in pursuit of our dreams. Jeff built a stout, roomy hen house on the plot and a little stream ran through so, as long as food was provided, his hens had everything they needed. Unlike us – because it would have meant having to unfailingly make the trip twice a day – he did not shut his hens in at night, so they could pop in and out of the hen house at will.

"I think we have one of your hens here Jeff," I said into the phone.
"Really? I thought I had them really well fenced in. Sorry about that."
"There's no problem," I reassured him, "She is quite happy; I just didn't want you worrying that you had lost one when you go up to feed them."
"Well I am coming up soon actually, so I'll pick her up then."
When Jeff pulled up in the car I had the hen in my arms, still extremely calm and content.
"Shall I get a box to put her in?"
"No! It's only a few hundred yards. Just pop her on the front seat." I opened the passenger door, popped her on the seat and for one ludicrous moment thought of putting a seat belt around her. The little hen just sat there very calm and very regal; as if Jeff's car was a taxi service she had sent for to take her home after a long day's shopping, and off they went up the hill.

That proved to be quite a prophetic thought because, over the next days and weeks, more often or not we would just be looking out of the kitchen window waiting for the kettle to boil for our morning cuppa when she would appear, striding purposefully down the hill, one scaly little leg after the other, heading straight for our front garden. She would spend the day there, pecking around, drinking from the stream but never doing anything destructive or damaging to the plants. Jeff became more and more frustrated over just how she was escaping. He erected more fences

and filled in more holes in the walls till his hen run became a hen Colditz but still she managed to get out. She got so used to her taxi rides home that all I had to do was pop her on the ground when I heard Jeff's car coming and he would lean over, open the door and she would hop in. After a while I suggested to Jeff that we should just adopt his hen and buy him a new one if she was so determined to spend her time with us.

"Never mind a new hen – just keep her!" he quickly agreed, with a great sigh of relief.

But that was not at all what the hen had in mind and so, once her taxi rides stopped, every evening when the light was just beginning to fade she would set off for home, her short legs pushing her stout body resolutely up the steep hill, her broad, feathery backside swaying from side to side. It was a long, hard pull for a little hen but this was the most determined hen I had ever come across. She reminded me of the hens in children's story books, full of self importance – like the 'Little Red Hen' or a Beatrix Potter character.

We named her Henny Penny.

Because I was away teaching during the weekdays I did not see much of Henny Penny except at weekends, although John assured me that her daily visits continued and, if he left the door open, she had discovered the wood burning stove in his workshop. So, if it was a cold or wet day and he had the stove on, she would now wander in and settle herself down in front of it for a nice warm through. I often referred to John's workshop as the Tup Club, a place where the local males of the species could wander in and out for a chat, a moan or a warm by the fire over a mug of tea whenever they saw smoke curling out of his stove chimney. The most regular members of the Tup Club were, of course, John and Denty and I would often find a cold and soaked through shepherd, clutching a large mug of tea and a cigarette, steaming gently in front of the stove on a clashy day. He even had his own chair placed strategically in front of the stove; a stubby, shabbily upholstered item that had long ago been John's nursing chair At least it was Denty's special chair till Henny Penny got her bright, beady eye on it and took possession, fluffing herself up contentedly on the cushion.

"Bloody hen! By, it's got some neck – in fact ah'll brek its bloody neck if it doesn't get off my chair!"

There was no love lost between Denty and Henny Penny, but she did have the sense not to argue with him and would strut off, clucking crossly when forced to vacate her place by the fire.

At weekends, Henny Penny became part of my life too. Because we were often down later in the mornings she would have already made her journey down the hill. I found, that as soon as I opened the front door, she would instantly appear, fussing round my legs for titbits to eat, a habit we had to plead guilty to encouraging.

There is something deeply pleasing about listening to a hen going 'puk puk puk' with delight over a tasty morsel.

Of course, this being Henny Penny, waiting at the front door when there was the possibility of even more treats inside the house, did not satisfy her for long. Soon, when the door opened, she would dive between my legs into the kitchen and strut around as if to say 'So, this is where you have your breakfast; what about me?'

I have never, ever heard of a hen being house trained but Henny Penny – perhaps sensing her first plop on the kitchen floor would be her last – never once disgraced herself and soon it was us that were trained to open the door, say good morning, get the glass jar of muesli out of the cupboard and sprinkle a handful for her on the floor. She liked bread, toast and cornflakes but best of all Henny Penny liked muesli. Except - she would pick out the raisins and nuts to devour with glee, but cranberries? No! They would be picked out and tossed to one side with an expression that said 'Yuk!' Having obviously carefully watched which cupboard the coveted muesli jar lived in, the final stage in Henny Penny's breakfast ritual was to strut in, go to the right cupboard, peck on it with her beak till it was opened and then choose and peck on the correct cereal jar – one of three, no matter which order we put them away in – until her breakfast was served. Had we lived in the days of variety theatre we could, no doubt, have made a tidy living out of Henny Penny.

My decision to stay on part time rather than to retire altogether from teaching at the age of sixty in 2010 had proved to be a wise one. I was thoroughly enjoying my work at school once more and having the illicit thrill of sitting up in bed with a cuppa on a Monday morning, at a time I would have previously been half way over the hills to Durham. This was especially gratifying when the rain or sleet were hammering on the windows. After only a Tuesday, Wednesday and a Thursday morning at school I would cheerily wave goodbye to my students and colleagues and begin my four and a half day weekend. It was bliss. My teaching assistants would mutter things along the lines of 'It's all right for some' but I would point out that my new found freedom came with a price tag - called age. When I was young, forty had always been the watershed age; according to some it was when life began and to others when you went over the hill. For me it was definitely the former as that was when I first met John and a whole new life had opened up before me. I was just as fit and energetic and certainly a great deal happier in my forties than I had been in my twenties or thirties. Fifty and even fifty five came and went in much the same way. When I hit fifty nine I thought of my mother who was widowed at that age and was considered an old lady, a pensioner. What were they talking about? I was still working, walking, gardening, keep-fitting and wearing denim jeans.

Admittedly I was a grandmother but thought of myself as a 'Groovy Granny' rather than a dear old thing in a rocking chair with a grey bun. I recognised that this state of affairs wouldn't and couldn't go on indefinitely; at some point the years would begin to tell. But I still took such a silly childish pleasure out of so many little things that sometimes I felt I had not ever actually grown up, let alone embarked on the process of getting old – whatever that meant.

For the moment, life was perfect. We had finally fulfilled our dream of buying the fields and the Hemmel adjacent to the house. John put heart and soul into the renovation of the old building and the Hemmel had become deserving of a capital 'H'; it provided a wonderful workshop and retreat for me where I could do all things woolly and crafty as well as being an imagination-feeding space for my grandchildren to play in when they visited. A long summer holiday was beckoning, during which they would come and spend some time on their own with us. Just the mention of 'Hill House East' and 'holiday' in the same sentence was enough to send them scampering upstairs to pack their bags. I was almost envious when I tried to imagine what it must be like to come and stay in Westgate at that age; to have fields to roam over, streams to paddle in, picnics in the garden, eggs to collect and their very own space in the Hemmel to turn into a pirate ship, a space station or a castle in the air. I could have only dreamt of such country delights at their age.

But then I remembered that at least I'd had Uncle Albert's hens.

By the time the children arrived for their holiday Henny Penny had become a local celebrity. Her brisk morning walk down the hill and her laborious ascent every evening became the start and finish posts to our day. The lambs born in the spring were long since out of the sheep shed; indeed they were now separated and weaned from their mothers, a process that involved a couple of nights of pitiful bleating for them and little sleep for us. Our own hens could not get from their field through the sheep-wired fence to go into the sheep shed but Henny Penny had no such restrictions and would sometimes potter off after her breakfast to have a scratch around in the straw and hay in there. If it was a particularly nice, sunny morning, however, she was more inclined to veer off into our porch, where the morning sunlight beat in through the glass, and jump up onto the bench seat. Rearranging the cushions to her satisfaction, she would lie on one side with her wing stretched out, much like a music hall fandancer, and have a nice snooze.

Had she been able to put up a Do Not Disturb sign I am sure she would have.

The first thing the grandchildren liked to do when they came to stay was to go and look for eggs. Rose, my granddaughter, was just past her third birthday and Fergus, her brother, now five and a half. They were really too young to be let loose to roam the hillside but they loved being outside and surely that was the whole point of coming to stay in the country? So the rule was set that they could go to the hen house for the eggs (which they tended to do ten times a day) and they could play in the Hemmel and in the safely fenced sheep yard and sheep shed, which were devoid of sheep and hosed clean at that time of year. There they could play bouncy castles on the heap of recently shorn Zwartbles fleeces or roll around in the hay till they got really itchy.

When they came dashing in one morning with an egg basket overflowing with eggs I was at a loss as to where they had come from – after all, we only had six hens! Ecstatic to find they knew something Granny didn't, I was pulled and tugged over to the sheep shed and shown a neat basin of a nest on top of a heap of hay piled up in one corner.

"It's Henny Penny's nest Granny. We saw her!"

"Henny Penny! Henny Penny!" chanted Rose.

So it appeared that all our free breakfasts were paying dividends; Henny Penny had been laying eggs for us for a week or more, judging by the amount in the egg basket.

Rose was by nature excitable, fidgety and always on the go – certainly not happy to play intently with a box of Lego bricks or a train set the way Fergus would. She was a dragonfly, flitting from one toy or game to another and always running in and out of the house whilst she chattered away or sang to herself. I was a bit anxious when one morning they dashed out to play and twenty minutes passed without Rose tumbling back into the house. I looked in on Fergus who was busy building a fortress in the Hemmel but she wasn't there, so I went round the back to the sheep shed. Maybe it was because I was feeling really anxious by now that I approached quietly and I was so glad that I had. There, sitting completely still and quiet on an upturned bucket was Rose Madeline, utterly entranced, watching Henny Penny on her nest concentrating on producing her latest egg.

Suddenly I was six again; the hen house was warm and dusty and I was waiting for the egg I would ask Auntie Freda to cook for my tea.

I crept away, hoping my granddaughter would be left with memories just as special.

Summer was over. The days were rapidly shortening, each week the sun set noticeably further down the northern hillside to the west of the house. Our view westwards provided us with a seasonal sundial. The hills almost formed a bowl around us, with only the wide cleft of the river valley cutting through them. Looking west, in the darkest days of December, the sun set far to the left of the southern fells. In spring and autumn it rolled gently to sleep in the middle of the valley, and on clear nights in June, it sank behind a copse of trees near the top of the north side fells. We had so few hours of real sunlight in mid winter that, when our friends from New England came to spend a Weardale Christmas with us, Doug sat in the porch sipping his coffee and shaking his head. "Y'know, that sun don't crawl up over that hill till two hours past breakfast time and it goes back down again in damn near the same place four hours later!"

One year, the evening of June 21st, the longest day, was so clear and still and warm that I decided to sit the night out on the deck of the summer house and see just how short it really was. It was the Summer Solstice, the Celtic festival of Litha, celebrated in these islands for thousands of years before Christianity arrived to absorb the ancient festivals and way-markers of the year into its own symbolism. Scandinavia is usually referred to as the land of the midnight sun but well after eleven o'clock there was still enough light to make out all the familiar features of the Dale and watch bats swooping in and out of our trees in search of their insect supper. After about three hours of what still could not be called real darkness, the skies behind the northern hill began to lighten and by three thirty the light was growing steadily. So much light, so much life active all around me that glorious summer's morning but, as at the festival of Yule in December, the solstice held a double meaning. The year had turned again and although there were the hot days of July and August ahead and hopefully a bright and warm autumn, in our northern latitudes we were now heading away from the light, a few minutes every day. The ancient Celts had perceived time as circular, not linear; the summer solstice a reminder to us that the light and warmth would not last indefinitely and the winter solstice that the darkness would end, that the light would return.

Modern life proceeds at such a pace and with such an artificial blurring of seasons and time with bright lights - even in the streets- and central heating and air conditioning and a 24/7 culture in most places, that the old rhythms of the year are fading. Only Christmas seems to be an immovable feature, although it increasingly has no connection whatsoever to its original meaning and function. It no longer celebrates the bringing of light into the world, be it through the sun of our planet or the son of God or both, according to one's beliefs; it is merely an excuse for an advertising and shopping spree that lasts for months beforehand.

But in Upper Weardale the seasons could not be ignored; the light in the sky, the rain for the grass, the warmth for the hay, the cattle grazing the fells in summer and the sheep buried in snow on the same fells in winter; these were all things we inescapably lived with.

Light and life.

Darkness and death.

Here, the cycle of the year turned as it always had and as it always should.

The blustery days of autumn made Henny Penny's trek more difficult. Sometimes, if she had a tail wind, she would use her wings as air brakes to stop her being blown down the hill. With the wind in her face the journey home could be struggle but, head down, she plodded determinedly on. She had discovered that if we were away a good breakfast – and lunch, tea and supper come to that – could always be had by foraging a bit further, so she would take a short cut across the field and head for the row of cottages on the lane below us. There she would go from house to house, rummaging around the bottom of all the dangling bird feeders from which morsels would descend, like manna from heaven, every time the birds landed on them. Sometimes kind people would throw her additional bits and pieces and she became a well loved visitor, usually known by her shortened name of 'Penny'.

We had spent the night away at a friend's house and had not long returned home the next morning when there was a knock at the door and I went to find Anne, from one of the nearby cottages, standing in floods of tears on the front doorstep.

"Whatever is the matter Anne!"

I had never seen her so distraught and I led her into the kitchen and John produced a chair.

"I am so sorry, so, so sorry; I never meant to do it! It was an accident!" She was inconsolable.

"Do what? What accident? What has happened?"

She took a big gulp of air.

"Penny, Penny; I've *killed* Penny."

It was our turn to feel stunned but I encouraged her to go on.

"I never saw her! I was going out and I started up the car; she must have been asleep in our bushes and when she heard the engine she must have come running out and then I reversed and then... then... Oh, I am so, *so sorry!*"

More very bitter tears were shed but all we could do was reassure Anne that it was indeed just an unfortunate accident that could have happened to any of us, though deep inside we were quite stunned to realise that the unique little hen would no longer enrich our days.

"It's not as if she was even our hen Anne – she really belonged to Jeff." Anne blew her nose and wiped her eyes.

"I knew that, though I know she comes down to us from you. That's why I tried to get in touch with Jeff; I thought he should be told. But that's when it went so horribly wrong."

"Horribly wrong?" I couldn't imagine Jeff being angry or upset about the loss of a hen that he rarely, if ever, saw anymore. "How did it go horribly wrong? Look, I am going to make us both a nice cup of tea and you can explain."

Sniffing over a steaming mug of that universal panacea, Anne told us what had happened after Henny Penny's tragic demise.

She didn't really know Jeff to speak to but she had found his number in the phone book and rung him. Alas, he was not in but she had left a message on his answer phone, which she admitted was a bit garbled and very tearful.

The main thrust of her message was that she was really, really sorry, it had been an awful accident and she hadn't meant to do it, but she had killed Penny. Too upset to explain more and even forgetting to leave her name and address she had put the phone down.

Coming home and finding a message from a woman he did not recognise and who sounded so upset and talking about an accidental killing, Jeff decided to have a word with our local police officer. So he had come and listened to the message and, also concerned and puzzled, phoned into his headquarters for advice and was told to leave it to them.

Late into the evening, just as they were thinking of bed, a very heavy fist knocked on Anne's door. Still red-eyed she went to answer it and was stunned to find police officers on the doorstep and blue lights flashing.

"I believe your name is Anne, madam?"

"Y…yes"

"We have traced a phone call made earlier this evening from this address to someone in the village, reporting the accidental killing of someone called Penny; did you make that call?"

"Y…yes, I did. B…b…but I explained; it was all a dreadful accident."

"How did this accident occur, madam?"

"Well… I didn't see her…"

"You didn't see her? *Who?* Penny?"

"Yes! I mean no! Well, you see, she's quite a little hen and I was reversing and she must…'

"Sorry madam, can I just stop you there. Did you say *hen*?"

"Yes! Penny! Well, I think her full name is Henny Penny, but I just call her Penny. She comes looking for the bird food you see and I didn't know that she was behind the car and when I reversed I hit her and…"

134

I would have loved to have been a fly on the wall at Police headquarters when they got back and had to explain what had happened; how they justified a search at national level to trace the phone call. At least they hadn't scrambled the police helicopter or sent in the 'SWAT' team but, once Henny Penny got over the shock of her nasty bump and found herself in the celestial hen house, I bet she was chuckling to find out her sudden departure had caused such a rumpus.

Life and death.
Tears and laughter.
The cycle rolls on.

12

MRS BUNION

Quite a lot of the characters who have warmed our hearts and our days seem to just wander into our lives unexpectedly – be they people or animals. The couple who had kept their small flock of hens in a paddock at the top of our hill were on the move. It was from that paddock that Henny Penny, of beloved memory, had emigrated to Hill House East. I knew through the bush telegraph that they had left the village and gone to a property near to Durham. With new occupants obviously in their house, I began to wonder why it was that, every couple of days or so, I saw their car either in the village or, very often, coming up and down our hill. Never backwards in coming forwards, the first time it came down our hill when I was in the vicinity, I waved it down.

"Hello Jeff! Correct me if I am wrong but I thought you had moved to Durham?"

"We have."

"Well, I can't help noticing that you are still going up and down this hill a lot, just like the old days when you used to go to see to your hens."

"I *am* going up and down to see the hens; we moved, the hens didn't."

"Really! Isn't that a bit inconvenient? I should know; I used to do that drive every day and it's over fifty miles!"

"*I know*," Jeff said bitterly.

It transpired that their new home had no place in which to keep even a few hens. They only had three 'old timers' left, Jeff said, but his wife

Lesley was very fond of them and she was fearful if they were rehoused with strangers somewhere they would be so upset they would fold up their wings and die. So, every couple of days either he or she made the journey to top up their feed and water and check they were alright.

"But you can't keep doing this indefinitely!"

Jeff gave me a sorrowful look, as if to say 'tell her that!'

Our own hen population at that point was quite low in numbers; in fact, I was just waiting for Mr Stobbs over the hill to have some point-of-lay pullets ready so I could replenish our stock. I gave a deep sigh; I knew it was inevitable what I was going to say next and Jeff, sensing this, perked up a bit.

"How many have you got?"

"Just three; one Maran hen – she's really old, bound to snuff it soon, she's over ten, and two Light Sussex. They still lay. Occasionally."

"Mmm... Look, Lesley knows how well we keep our hens down here; they have a lovely hen house, a big field to roam in and are spoilt rotten. Surely she wouldn't object to them coming here? After all, they are only getting contact with you every couple of days or so; that's no good!"

Jeff perked up even more.

"I'll go home and see what she says; then I'll get back to you!"

He did get back to me *very* quickly, just about as long as it takes to drive to Durham and back again.

"She's very happy with the idea of you having them!" he reported.

"Oh, good. When do you think we should move them then?"

Jeff turned round and pointed to a large box on the back seat.

"I may as well go and get them now while I'm here!"

That was the point at which I realised I hadn't even run the idea past John.

Good job he was a saint.

The three hens were all considerably larger than our resident browny-red 'Die-quicks'. Perhaps because of this, there was very little resentment or henpecking when they moved in. Contrary to belief, hens are not stupid; especially ours. Because the new residents were elderly birds and because they were heavily built, there were no squabbles over sleeping arrangements either. Our birds hopped up to perch and the pensioners slept on the floor of the hen house. As with all creatures that shared our lives, they had to have names. We were not very creative with the matronly speckled Maran hen; she simply became 'Mrs Maran'. The two Light Sussex, with their white plumage and black ermine- tipped cape of feathers around their necks, looked very similar to each other. There was one striking difference though; one of them had very lumpy, swollen protuberances on her toe joints; so she was named 'Mrs Bunion', though her companion became a very uninspired 'Mrs White'. Jeff had been right about one thing, the white hens did occasionally lay eggs; *very* occasionally. However, he was wrong about the frail mortality of Mrs Maran; she lived happily for another eighteen months before, as he had put it, 'snuffing it'. She went however as quickly and as peacefully as a candle being gently blown out when her time came. Mrs White and Mrs Bunion showed every sign of living just as long as she had, or even longer.

"Do you think old Mrs Bunion's looking a bit tatty these days?"

"Mmm, she seems to be slowing down a lot too; has a bit of difficulty getting out of the hen house in the mornings"

With the aging process in hens bearing a worrying resemblance to our own mortal decline, we did not dwell too long on it. However, over the next week or so, it was undeniable that Mrs Bunion had a real and increasing problem. She seemed to shuffle rather than walk, had problems with her balance, trailed far behind the other hens in the field and we were having to lift her in and out of the hen house morning and night, the jump down now being beyond her. John constructed a disability ramp at the front, with a textured surface, so she could get a good grip with her scaly, carbuncled feet and she appreciated that, heaving herself ponderously up and down it. The advantage of the little brown 'Die-quicks' was that they not only lived a short life and a productive one but that they did, well, 'die quick'; a bit listless one day, pale wattled and inactive the next and peacefully passed away by the next. A very considerate way to go that caused minimum physical or emotional

138

Then and now

Above - Hill House East garden – 2001

Below - the garden in 2020

Lambs

Lazarus, the Hebridean lamb

A midwifery lesson from Lynne Dent

Carol delivering a Zwartbles lamb

Sheep & Shepherds

Crumpet,
the original Zwartbles ewe

Zeeb, Crumpet's son,
born prematurely & very wobbly

Denty & Carol
at lambing time

Zulu
the gentle giant Zwartbles tup

Passing Seasons

the Hemmel in the snow

Hill House East at hay time

the walls above Westgate in autumn

Swinhope Fell

Denty & John feeding Swaledales in the snow

Summertime up Swinhope – the Hill Houses on their 'Shoulder on the Hill'

Feathered Friends

Rocky the bantam cockerel

Mrs Bunion in recovery

Henny Penny comes in for breakfast

The Grandbairns

Fergus riding a young Zeeb

Eve feeding Tussock,
son of Teasel the Teeswater

Rose with a full grown Zeeb

The Family

John the breakfast chef

Carol hugs the sycamore on the day
they finally bought the field

Megan, Bernie & Fergus, Rose &
Eve; Megan receiving her PhD

The Tail End –
Fudge the abandoned feral kitten

upset to the hen or us. These voluminous white birds were obviously of a different mettle.

It was coming up to a trip to Wales to celebrate my daughter Megan's PhD graduation. This marked the end of a gruelling six year marathon of study and determination, during which she had not only been mother to two small children but had produced a third, had to go part time after her maternity leave and then had tragically lost her PhD supervisor and mentor mid - course, due to a swift and cruel cancer. Now, however, it was time to celebrate her success, and amazing perseverance. A few days before we were due to leave John and I witnessed something extraordinary in the hen run. We had just let the hens out and were giving them some breakfast when Mrs Bunion suddenly began jerking and jumping as if she had been plugged into a mains socket. She completed two midair somersaults before landing heavily on the ground, twitching a bit, then lying motionless with one wing outstretched.
We looked at each other in bewilderment.
"What just happened? Is she…"
"No, no; she is still breathing'"
"But… What on earth…"
"I have no idea," I told John truthfully, "It was almost like a fit – or a severe epileptic attack. Whatever it was, that, I'm afraid, is the end of her. I'm just going to lay her quietly in the henhouse, shut the doors and let her pass peacefully."
We retreated into the house for a much needed cup of coffee.

When a sombre few hours had passed I returned to the hen house, in full expectation of having to send John for his spade. Semi-sitting, semi-sprawling, her wing still outstretched, Mrs Bunion's head lifted from her chest. She eyed me with a beady, golden-orange button of an eyeball and enquired, 'Phawark?'
Now what? I offered her food and water but she would have none of it. She was also unable to get to her feet or move at all. She did not appear to be in pain or distress but, surely, this could not go on?

"I've never wrung a hen's neck" I admitted, "If I knew how to do it quickly and well I would do it, but I am not going to start by practising on Mrs Bunion. I'll have to find someone else to do it."

John was blanching rapidly.

"Not you silly! You'd be worse than me. I'll try Denty first."

He too paled at the suggestion; "Ah, well, not really much of a dab hand at that really. Me father was – and me mother. But not me – not unless I really had to."

I let him off the hook. "Not to worry; I'll find someone."

But that was easier said than done; our new neighbour, the rugged young countryside ranger, declined rapidly as did someone in the village who seemed as tough as old boots and always kept a few hens in a no nonsense fashion. I did find a lady at the village coffee morning who said her husband had a great technique of bashing them on the back of the neck with a thick stick but it sounded a bit too hit and miss. No, it would have to be the vet and, as it was now Saturday afternoon it would have to be Monday morning.

It was such a lovely afternoon that I could not bear to leave Mrs Bunion cooped up alone. She eyed me with something approaching enthusiasm when I lifted her out and, having found a nice warm, grassy corner I gently arranged her as if she were sitting on a clutch of eggs. She murmured appreciatively and, to my surprise, did not fall over, but sat there like a stout queen Victoria surveying her Empire contentedly. She declined a bowl of hen food but gobbled with delight every morsel of bread bun and cheese I offered her, had a good long drink and then settled into her afternoon, holding court with the other hens that came to visit and have a chat.

What's the word I won't let the children use?

'Gobsmacked', that's it; and I was.

"John."

"Yes?"

"We are off on a trip to Wales in a few days."

"Yes."

"We can't leave Mrs Bunion in this condition."

"No."

"Vet on Monday?"

"Yes."

Sunday came, the good weather held and out she went. She was getting like an old housebound lady waiting for the minibus to come to take her to her day club. She had never liked being handled and yet, there she was, eyes all expectant and offering no resistance to her lift arriving at all. At tea time, when I went out to collect her, she had disappeared, her day out marked only by a dint in the grass. Not a fox, not a polecat surely? Not in broad daylight? Heart in mouth I went down to the little stream that runs across our field. Up by John's garage wall the garden fence creates a warm, south facing corner beside a small pool where all the hens we have ever had like to lounge, preen, sunbathe and take dust baths. We call it their Lido; on a sunny day it's the only place for a hen to be. Sure enough, there was Mrs B, propelling herself around like a penguin sledging on ice, pushing her body across the grass towards the Lido with her huge, scaly feet pushing from behind. The others were already snoozing, wattles nodding.

"John."

"Yes?"

"We can't have her destroyed; she is eating, drinking, pooing and enjoying life."

"No."

"No we can't or no, we have to?"

"No; we can't"

"But we can't leave her here and ask others to be her care assistant."

"No."

"So, she'll have to go to Wales with us."

"Yes."

Megan said the children would be ecstatic with the idea and would love a hen to come with Granny and Grandad. They lived in a Victorian terrace house with no real garden or shed. Where would she go all day I asked? Where would she sleep? What if she got worse again? What if she *died*?

Ah, said Megan, the children wouldn't like that.

"John."

"Yes?"

"We can't take the hen to Wales; it's seven hours each way in the car and she has no balance. What if she dies there? What would we do with her?"

"Ah."

"I need to find a care home for her."

"Yes."

Now, who on earth would want to look after a semi paralysed, possibly epileptic, somewhat incontinent, tatty, elderly hen? I knew just the lady; Jenny Spooner. Jenny and her family lived along the road and up the hill from us. They had a very old stone farmhouse, a big, rambling garden and a large assortment of hens and ducks. Jenny, as industrious as her chickens, was a leading light of village life, involved in all the village events and continually raising money for good causes. I explained carefully about our great need for help with a good cause.

"Well, I'll have her of course; it's a question of where to put her. Can't put her in with my lot; as a stranger who couldn't stand up for herself she probably wouldn't last five minutes. All I can offer I am afraid is my 'isolation cage' in the greenhouse; it's where I put ailing cases to keep them from the others. It's not very big and she will be bored to death, but it is the best I can do I'm afraid."

"Jenny, given that the alternative is to have her neck wrung, she should be jolly grateful! Bless you; you've solved a real problem. And if she, well, you know… while we are away…"

"Don't worry; Ed's got a spade."

The graduation was wonderful. There were tears, smiles, a lot of Prosecco and for me an overwhelming sensation of pride and admiration for my daughter; wife, mother of three, an academic doctor but always my little girl. Four days later it was all over – just like any celebration – and we were home after a round trip of five hundred miles. I really liked Wales but it was just so far away. As soon as we had opened the house and stretched weary legs, we set off to collect Mrs Bunion and take a large Barabrith to Jenny, to say thank you.

"Is she still…"

"Oh God yes! Bright as a button but well fed up of being stuck in there I would imagine!"

Mrs Bunion, resplendently wrapped in an old striped towel that looked absurdly like a bath robe, sat on my knee and thoroughly enjoyed her trip home in the car. I got the impression she was settled down for a nice drive out and quite disappointed when we got back home so quickly. We put her straight to bed, the others soon joined her and we left them nattering at each other while we too retired.

I was quietly pleased that the old girl was still with us.

Next morning John got up early and brought me a cup of tea in bed.

"Carol."

"Yes?"

"I just let the hens out."

"Yes?"

"Mrs Bunion; she *walked* down the ramp!"

"No!"

"Yes!"

"Well, more of a stagger than a walk. But she is standing on her own two feet."

"No!"

"Yes!"

"Good heavens!"

And over the next few weeks the heavens were indeed good to Mrs Bunion. She could walk, she could even run in a lurching way when food was on offer. She could preen herself again after a fashion, though still looked quite tatty. Best of all she could wade through the grass with her friends doing a beak tip search for seeds and insects and sun herself in the Lido again. She couldn't make it up to a perch or nest box in the hen house at night but lived a bungalow existence on the floor. Fitting a disability ramp for a hen was one thing – a stair lift was a step too far.

Over a cup of tea Jenny asked how Mrs Bunion was.

"She's in fine fettle; really enjoying life again."

"Good God! It must have been those four days in chokey – she obviously doesn't want to repeat that experience!"

"I tell you what; she'll outlive us if she keeps this up! She is a determined and wily old bird."

"Well, it takes one to know one. More tea?" Jenny enquired.

And dear old Mrs Bunion lived on quite contentedly throughout the summer and autumn. She wasn't fast but she got to where she wanted to be. She enjoyed her food and the company of her friends. When the flowers, the grass, the light and the very air of Weardale shifted down a gear to begin the journey into autumn she sensed that this would in turn lead to winter, with cold temperatures, driving rain, drifting snow and cruel winds. Very wisely she must have decided that she did not fancy that at all and would prefer to leave with her memories of fat grass seeds, sunbathing and lazy afternoons by the Lido pool. She settled herself in her corner of the hen house floor, dropped her head onto her ample bosom and slipped away, hopefully dreaming of summer.

Real Friends

13

THE SKI CLUB

John and Ian Dent had very quickly struck up a deep and close friendship. This was a bit odd as one might have thought that they had little in common. Denty had been born, bred and lived his whole life on the fellsides above us. His entire working life (and much of his social life) revolved around sheep and the circle of the shepherd's year. Romantic as this picture may sound to some, the reality is far from it. A shepherd's life involves a lot of backbreaking grind, often while getting soaked and frozen through; dealing daily with foot rot, maggots and a great deal of sheep manure. Battles with far from docile tups had also cost Denty most of his front teeth. Then, inevitably, there are the life and death challenges. I was the horsey, outdoor, country girl whilst John was basically a townie; he had swooned at the thought of gutting a trout a kind friend brought us for dinner and had never physically laid hands on a sheep before we moved to Westgate.

Well, all that was to change!

Trying to work three thousand acres, mostly by himself with a quad bike or tractor, was a challenging life to say the least and the daily tea breaks in our kitchen with Denty would often end with, "Ah ye busy at the minute?" or, "Can ye spare me an hour this afternoon?"

The help required from John might be as simple as standing in the road and waving his arms so that the sheep could be brought down to a new field without them running all the way to Westgate. Or it might be that, taking sheep nuts and hay up to the high fells in the winter months to keep the ewes fed, two pairs of hands were much more effective than one. Often, it was the ritual of 'gathering', where groups of sheep had to be moved up, down and across the fell, or down to the pens at the farm for a variety of reasons throughout the year; tupping, dipping, dosing, clipping and lambing to name but a few.

Once John had acquired the right footwear and foul weather gear that he needed to ascend and work at nearly a further thousand feet up the hill, he really enjoyed it. He certainly got plenty of fresh air and exercise and I found it heart warming to see the quad bike roar up the hill with John clinging onto the back. It was a sign of real acceptance; he had a real value in the local community. Sometimes he would return a little green around the gills having been assisting in tasks such as cutting tups' horns – always blood around – or recovering a dead sheep – always stinky. Most times he would return windswept and ruddy cheeked and say, "It's a different planet up there!"

Before long I began to refer to John as the under shepherd but Denty corrected me.

"Noo – wi' divvent call beginners that, wi' call 'em the daft laddy!"

And the first lesson a daft laddy learns, Denty told me one day, when he brought a particularly green John home after they had recovered a well decomposed sheep from a bog, is "Divvent howk leeside offa deed yow."

"Translation needed please?"

Sometimes Denty's vernacular was just too hard for me to understand. Sometimes, however he talked in broad 'Wardle', the sadly rapidly vanishing local speech, just to test me. He grinned his sparse-toothed grin and slapped John on the back as he was going out of the kitchen: "Do not dig a hole downwind of a dead sheep!"

The relationship was completely symbiotic; Denty gave John every bit as much help as John gave him. Anything that needed moving, fetching or digging and he would be there. Any collapsed walls or holes in fences and the right tools and expert hands would be on the job. Not only did Denty seem to know every sheep on the fell, he knew every inch of ground and just about every stone. If John was building something and needed a particular size or shape of stone Denty would say, "Aye; ah think ah knaa just the right chap," and in a short while the bike and trailer would rumble down the hill and, sure enough, just the right stones would be in the back. I happened to complain one day about the field gate swinging wildly in the wind because there was no 'stop' for it when it swung downhill.

"What it needs is a nice tall stone on the other side."

"I could hammer a wooden post in," John said helpfully.

"Mmm, I know you could; but it wouldn't look as nice as a stone."

Denty was enjoying his cigarette on the other side of the wall.

"Reckon she's right," he said, as he swung his leg over the saddle and switched on the bike.

Half an hour later he was back, with a beautiful tall, thin stone in the trailer. I felt quite guilty.

"Denty; you shouldn't have gone and done that now; you're far too busy to help us."

"Ah'm aalways too busy; but ah'm never too busy to help!"

The stone, a broken gate post, took both of them to heave out of the trailer, so how he got it in on his own I will never know. And the help was not over until a deep hole was dug, the stone dropped in place and a bag of readymix concrete poured around it. I see that stone every day; it is nothing special or significant to those who are just passing by but to me it is very special; as solid and cemented as our friendship with the Dents.

One way in which I showed my gratitude to Denty for all his help was with food. He, like all others who toil outdoors all day, had a great fondness for food and a healthy appetite. So, whenever I baked, there would always be a few scones or buns heading up the hill on the back of the quad bike plus, in the glut of autumn fruit, jars of homemade jam to spread on them. The way to Denty's heart or stomach (much the same thing) if ever there was a special job we needed help with or a special thank you to be made, was via a lemon drizzle cake; a lemon flavoured sponge cake oozing a crystallised, lemony, sugar syrup on the top. I always made it to my mother's recipe which, I found, had never been bettered.

"Sweetheart," Denty would drool as soon as he set eyes on one, "Ah would do anythin' for you for one of those; providin' John didn't mind that is!"

He was also creative in the kitchen himself. Some of his creations were of the 'necessity is the mother of invention' variety it must be said, but then he had grown up at a time and in a household when nothing, not a single scrap of food, was wasted. What couldn't be eaten fresh at once was preserved or salted, what was left over from meals would be reincarnated till it was gone and anything left at the end of that process would be fed to the hens or pigs, who would then enter the food cycle themselves at the allotted time.

'Waste not, want not' had been drummed into Denty's very bones.

Because his wife Lynne was out at work and worked shifts, he was long used to providing any or all of three meals a day for himself and nothing delighted Denty more than to tell us of some culinary delight he had recently conjured up for himself.

"D'ye kna what ah had for me lunch today?" was a regular opening comment over a mug of afternoon tea.

"I can't imagine," soon became my statutory response.

"Well, bein' Tuesday, all the meat from the Sunday dinner was gone like but I just fancied summit a bit savoury. So ah' dug around in't fridge and found a bit leftover cabbage and a drop gravy. So ah had a cabbage and gravy sandwich and it were grand!"

Or…"Well there were a few cold chips left over from't night before and they didn't look too appetisin' like, so ah heated up a bit cold broth and dropped them in; smashin!"

148

Or...

"Ye know them fruit scones ye giv us last week? Well, ah thowt they'd all gone but ah found a couple in a tin. Gone rock hard of course, but ah' heated up some custard and mashed them in; lovely!"

As well as being the most inventive leftovers chef in Britain, Denty also did real cooking. He specialised in roast dinners and rice puddings and, if I was very lucky, sometimes a tub of sweet, sticky rice pudding would make its way into my kitchen and, oh Lord, it was good. He also could have been a 'fusion chef'; one year an unexpected late glut of rhubarb resulted in one of his finest creations – curried rhubarb chutney.

One day Denty arrived at the door with very muddy wellies and an anxious look on his face.

"Is 'e in?"

This always meant John was needed and I went to get him.

"What's the problem?" John enquired when he reached the door.

In late spring, as well as the sheep, the home farm sent up two wagons of cattle to graze the fells, a practice (still known as the 'transhumance' in the far south of France) which has not changed in a thousand years or more here in the Dale. Simple shelters called sheilings or shields would be built to live in during the summer, but these were not able to withstand the rigours of winter, nor was there any grazing left for the cattle or sheep by then. So, in the late autumn, the animals were driven back down to lower pastures and the drivers returned to their own more permanent houses. The village of Daddryshield, only a mile from us, is supposedly derived from 'Doddery Sheiling' – a 'rickety summer shelter that was dropping to bits' - which is an evocative link to the past.

"Wey, ye knaa that cow ah've been lookin' for all week? Wey, ah've found her."

"That must be a relief?"

"Not really. She's deed; well deed. And the daft bugger decided to half fall into a bog when she deed. Ah've tried to pull her out wi' the bike an' a rope but she's well stuck. Ah've got the other bike up from home farm at present; so ah reckon we could do it wi' two on. Ah've got to get her down somehow afore the knacker man comes the morrow; canna' leave her there on't fell. Are ye up for it?"

John was already heading for his coat.

As he disappeared Denty shouted, 'Divvent forget yer wellies, 'cos by God ye'll need them!"

One of the skills John had acquired since he lived at Hill House East was to ride a quad bike safely. The 'safely' is the most important bit as, ridden recklessly, they can be very dangerous indeed and can easily overturn and injure or kill their rider. I was very worried at first but after endless trips up the fell, when Denty drove the tractor and John drove the bike to manoeuvre sheep around, he always returned safe and well.

I waved goodbye to them and got on with what I was doing.

Hours passed before they returned, enough time for an edge of worry to creep into my mind. But another unimaginable development since the days when Denty's father and grandfather had shepherded those fells, walking for hours out of touch with the farm and in real danger if an accident occurred, was the mobile phone; not a device I am fond of using unless there is a real problem and then it can be a godsend. Denty never went anywhere without his phone, so I knew that if there had been a problem he would have rung me. I was just thinking that I could not wait much longer without phoning him when a quad bike spluttered to a halt outside. Both men looked absolutely drained and were covered in filth, as was the bike.

"I was just getting worried; what happened?"

Denty just shook his head.

"Ah've got ti get back up and feed round, a'hm well behind wi' me day. An' if ah telt yer, ye might think it was one of me fairy tales. Best ye hear it from John."

John slid off the bike and Denty turned it round to head off back up home.

"Anyroad, he's been a hero, your husband; ah nivvor knew he was keen on snowboardin' mind. Mebbees he should join the ski club next winter!" he shouted.

And with that he was off.

"Ski club? You... what? Oh poooh... you *STINK!*"

John looked rueful.

"I bet I do; you may have to boil all these clothes – or even burn them! Look, get me an old pair of jeans and a top, bring them out to the workshop and I'll change into them there so I don't even have to bring these clothes into the house. Then I'll have a long hot shower, you can pour two large glasses of wine and I'll tell you all about it."

While he had a shower I reflected that one of the oddities of Swinhope was the fact that there really was a proper ski club at the head of the valley, where it rose to its highest point before plummeting down one side to Teesdale and, on the other, down to Weardale. Run by a group of dedicated enthusiasts, it had a proper ski lift, a club house and boasted the 'longest ski run in England', which the members devoted a lot of time in the summer to maintaining and upgrading. The only real problem in recent years had been the lack of snow; as Ray Dent, Ian's octogenarian father would mutter, 'They divvent knaa what a real winter is these days.' A further problem was a narrow definition of the 'right amount' of snow. The covering had to be deep enough to cover all the ruts, lumps and tussocks of the fellside. However, if it really blew a blizzard, the narrow road going up Swinhope past Hill House East, then Glenwhelt and then further up the valley past Swinhopehead, would be blocked with drifted snow, which could subsequently turn to ice. Nevertheless the ideal conditions did come around now and then and, when they did, the excitement was intense and determined skiers descended from all over the north east, all driven with the same desire; to make it to the slopes of the Weardale Ski Club while there was still snow to ski on. Some went to incredible lengths of endurance to achieve this. The club was over two miles up the valley on a narrow road which climbed extremely steeply for most of the way. Once the skiers reached the edge of the fell, above which the ski club sat, cars had to be parked and a trek of over a mile had to be traversed up another steep and obviously snow covered path, carrying their skis and other gear. It was beyond John why anyone would be crazy enough to submit themselves to this gruelling ordeal to just, as he said, 'slide down a hill on two planks', but then John had never had a penchant for sport of any kind. On 'skiing days' our house was the perfect viewpoint to watch the trail of would-be skiers setting off doggedly to get to the ski club, like latter day gold prospectors trying to ascend the White Horse Pass in the Klondike. Some cautious and obviously very fit souls left their cars down past our crossroads and set off to do the whole journey on foot; over three miles, mostly uphill in the snow, with their skis over their shoulders. Others would decide to attempt the road part of the journey by car. Even if the snow plough had been out up the hill, very often the severity of the first bend, just past the end of our drive, would result in them sliding embarrassingly back to where they had started. Not to be thwarted, the occupants would leap out and produce from the boot of their car a tangle of tyre chains, which they then tried to unravel and get fixed around their wheels. Fingers often got frozen and tempers heated during this process – especially as a queue of cars could be building up behind them, all itching to make their own attempt at the first bend and then on to the summit. The worst embarrassment was when, having finally got the wretched chains on, got back into the car and backed up to take a run at the bend with engine roaring and wheels sliding, the chains slid off halfway round the corner. Miserably, the car would have to pull over to allow the car behind to make its attempt. The most gung–ho and slightly smug skiers were those who arrived in enormous four wheel drive monster SUVs, skis all neatly tied on special racks on the roof, winter tyres sneering at the road conditions. They would sail past the chain-slippers and the foot-sloggers and whoosh effortlessly out of our sight up the hill. Strangely though, it was often just such vehicles that, at the highest approaches, the narrowest parts of the road and the tightest bends, slid (no doubt gracefully) off the road into one of the many deep, snow filled ditches. They would have to wait to be pulled out – slightly red faced as the foot-sloggers marched past them - by a grinning Denty with his brute of a tractor. The ski club certainly provided us with our own voyeuristic winter amusement but I knew it was something John would never want to join – so what on earth did Denty mean? When he finally appeared, a lot cleaner, sweeter smelling and looking revived, he told me the tale.

Denty had decided that the only way they would get the cow dragged back down the hill without her either getting stuck again or, frankly, disintegrating, would be to put it onto some sort of sledge.

"An' ah knaa just the thing!" he had proclaimed to John.

So the first hour or more was spent reclaiming a large, curved piece of corrugated iron, which turned out to have once been part of Denty's grandfather's Anderson shelter. I don't think heavy civilian bombing had ever been a real threat in Upper Weardale during the Second World War and Denty seemed to think it had been a postwar acquisition that had made a useful pig house. However, what remained of the shelter had also been sinking slowly into a bog for several decades so that it had to be dug out of the sucking slime before the expedition to retrieve the cow from her bog could even begin. However, eventually, with ropes, quad bikes and very muddy wellies the 'sledge' was retrieved and they set off up the fellside on the quad bikes, the iron sheet being towed by Denty. Apparently the unfortunate cow announced her presence by her smell long before they could see her. The first problem was that her head had slid completely beneath the ooze and in order to get a rope around her neck Denty was grappling up to his armpits and over his welly tops in bog. John, thankfully, was excused this part. The next stage – and I really couldn't understand how they ever did it – was to pull the cow away from the bog and, with ropes and quad bikes, get her pulled onto the corrugated iron sledge. Once this was achieved they tied either end of the sledge to the two bikes, so that it hung like a curved sling behind them, upon which the gruesome remains lay. The master plan was to keep the ropes taut and slowly manoeuvre the sledge down the fellside behind the two bikes. It was a good plan but had not taken into account the wetness of the grass, the smoothness of the iron sledge and the weight of the cow.

Oh, and of course, gravity.

Before long, instead of towing along behind them, the sledge was riding along parallel with the bikes, then, when they hit a slightly steeper bit of hill, it began to overtake them. The dead cow had no sense of fear and better acceleration than the bikes and, in a few seconds, she was in the lead. Now Denty and John were not towing the cow; she was towing them, and the bottom of the hill and a substantial stone wall were looming up fast. Desperate attempts were made to use the bikes as drag anchors before they all smashed into the wall.

Here, however, fate lent a hand.

At the end of the last ice age when the glacier retreated from Swinhope, it had deposited a large boulder that was now directly in the path of the snowboarding cow. The sledge hit the boulder, the bikes went either side, the cow rocketed into the air like a ski jumper before falling heavily and less than gracefully at the base of the stone wall. Had she managed to clear the wall and land on the road - particularly if some unsuspecting motorist had been passing - did not bear thinking about.

"Champion!" Denty had declared, "Just where aah need her; the knacker man'll get in that gate nee bother to pick her up. Couldn't be better! Cup o' tea d'ye reckon?"

What John was more in need of was a stiff whisky to stop him from shaking but they took the sledge back to the farm, had a large mug apiece and pondered on whether they had just invented a new Winter Olympic sport: 'Bovine Snowboarding'.

14

THE GOOD SHEPHERD

We had had a summer of changeable weather, though a change for the worse seemed to have happened much more often than a change for the better. In fact, it had felt as though we had had no summer at all. It wasn't just the rainy spells, which had been too frequent, it was that between them it had been mostly overcast with grey clouds, low temperatures and strong, cold winds: weather which I hated the most and had long ago christened 'the English Grey Death'. It was miserable for people, animals and plants alike. In common with friends in the area, my peas and beans had simply curled up their toes, or to be more accurate their roots, and withered away to nothing. My blackcurrant bushes had been so inhibited by the weather that I was seriously worried about how I was going to make the year's supply of 'Granny Jam' for the grandchildren. Only the rhubarb and the gooseberries flourished as always – though I suspected it would take an asteroid impact to set them back. The longest day in June was long gone and I was trying to avoid the fact that, week on week, the sun was setting lower and lower down the northern hillside of the Dale, even though I was still hoping it might shine for at least two consecutive days at some point. It was early August and gathering time when Denty would be roaming long and far across the 3,000 acres of Glenwhelt to bring some 2,000 sheep 'in-by' the farm for clipping, dipping, dosing and other annual tasks. It was after this monumental task that the lambs would be separated from their mothers, or 'spaned', to the accompaniment of much blaring objection. This word, like many others in the Weardale shepherding vocabulary, was new to me and it had to be explained that it meant weaning the lambs, separating them from their mothers; hence the blaring objections. Digging into an etymological dictionary to find out the source of all these old words was something I took a delight in, as words change and diverge from their original meaning so much over the centuries. 'Spaning', with regard to sheep, derived from the old French word *'espanir'*, which means 'to separate', possibly brought over at the time of the Norman Conquest. Certainly it was in use in an agricultural sense locally early on, as recorded in an expression of 1605: "He had a face that wad spane a calf fre' its mother!" When I told John this, he at once remembered 'espanired bolts'; bolts which separate and spring apart. Thus, the links of language throughout the centuries, although transformed, were alive and well – all because Denty said he was going to spane his lambs. Another word I had failed to understand until I looked it up was 'kytle', as in Denty on a fine day saying "By, it were that warm I had to take me kytle off!" at which point he would remove his sleeveless jacket. According to my well thumbed Dictionary of North East Dialect, kytle does indeed mean 'a light jacket' in local parlance, but digging deeper it appears to have the same root as 'kirtle', used in Middle English to mean a gown or petticoat, and 'cyrtel' in Anglo Saxon, meaning a tunic. Then there is the Icelandic 'kyrtiil', the Danish 'kiortel' and the Swedish 'kjortel'... So maybe the word has been in Weardale since the Irish Vikings settled at Ireshopeburn; whichever way you look at it, it is something people have been wearing one way or another round here for a very long time! Of course, the trendy young things call them 'gilets' these days but I hope that this ancient word is not lost.

Once spaned and the hullabaloo settled down, the lambs were fattened ready for the sales. The yearly shepherding cycle would then pause for a while with the close of summer and shepherds and sheep alike would have a little respite before it all began again, when the tups went to work in the autumn, creating the next year's crop of lambs.

Other vital cogs in the wheel of village life kept turning regardless of weather, one such being the monthly coffee morning for the church. My role in this was to produce scones to sell on the baking stand; six dozen of them, half of them cheese and half fruit every month. In truth, I loved making scones. I must have made thousands of them over the years in oddly diverse places such as Russia, New England and India. Always best eaten well buttered as soon as they had cooled from the oven, they seemed to me to be the icon of British baking: simple, delicious, less sweet and more filling than a biscuit, less rich and heavy than a cake. I was never happier than when pressing one of my well-loved scone cutters into floury, pliant dough on my kitchen table:

Hot cheese scones with butter and marmite.

A good fruit scone coated with homemade raspberry jam.

Wholemeal scones with chopped date and walnut.

A giant, thin scone used as the base for a pizza.

The Northumbrian girdle scone, or 'Singin' Hinny', cooked on the stove top.

Endless possibilities: all equally delicious.

As well as a psychic ear for the tea kettle going on, Denty had a long distance nose that could detect scones coming out of the oven from right up the hill and he would often appear, as if by magic, to partake of both.

"Bye, it was lucky aah was passin!" he would grin.

"And you have the luck of the devil," I would reply. His wife Lynne, now occupied more than full time with a seven day a week wool shop business, had little time for home baking but Denty had spent most of his formative and adult years coming back with his father after a long, gruelling and often inclement day on the fells to a house filled with the smell of fresh baking and the sure comfort of a blazing fire, dry clothes and 'summit tasty'. Perhaps his visits to Hill House East during the day, knowing there was neither a person, nor a fire, nor baking to be shared at home, provided an echo of what he had always known.

Making six dozen scones takes a little while and the first ones are baked and cooling while the last are still being shaped and cut to go in the oven. Sitting one day with a mug of tea, Denty juggled a scone that was really still too hot to eat, but too tempting not to.

"Whe'; ah've got to test them afore ye mak any more ti mak sure they're all right f' the church!" he explained.

He then enquired as to what I was going to do with all the little scraps and bits of scone mix left over from cutting out. I told him, sounding eerily like my cookery lecturer of forty years ago, that I only rolled and cut out the left over bits once after the initial rolling; after that the dough would have had a lot of the life squeezed out of it and any scones made with it could be heavy.

"So, what de ye do wi'it?"

"Well, I roll it into little lumps and bake them for the chickens; I call them 'Hen Balls' – they love them!"

He was visibly shocked.

"Gi'em to the hens! What a shockin' waste; me mother would turn in her grave!"

"What would she do with them?"

"Why, mak' 'huddlins out'."

"Huddlins out? Never heard of that; what is it?"

"The best bit – that's what! Aall the little bits of what ivver's left – pastry, scones, cake, what ivver – she'd knead it up, flatten it wi' her hand and pop in top of the hot oven till it were brown. Then out it'd come, pipin' hot, split in two and lathered wi' butter and jam.'

His eyes were misty with nostalgia, "Bye, it were gorgeous!"

"But why 'huddlins out'? What on earth does that mean?"

It was one of the very rare occasions when Denty answered frankly, "De ye knaa; aahv'e no idea! Mebbees because aall the little bits just huddle together in a lump, then get rolled and baked."

From then on the chickens were deprived of their 'Hen Balls' and instead all the bits and pieces left over after scone-cutting would be kneaded lightly together and shaped into a large, roughly round shape, patted down and put on the baking tray. The result was a 'huddlins out' that was probably the size of two normal scones; but then it would be insulting to offer Denty something puny. He took such genuine delight from seemingly insignificant things. A sign in our porch reads 'Do small things with great love'; nothing personified this better than the making of a huddlins out destined for Glenwhelt.

My memories of him will always be astride his quad bike - both equally spattered with mud - a cigarette clamped between his lips, a load of our unwanted rubble in the trailer, which was 'just what he needed to fill a tractor rut', a jar of still warm blackcurrant jam clutched in one hand and the smile of a man who was content with his world on his face.

We were going over to Teesdale one Friday lunch time. The offerings for the church and the offerings for Denty that I had spent the morning making were cooling on the bench. For once, the aroma must have failed to reach the third of a mile to Glenwhelt, as there had been no sign of him.

"Tell you what; I'll wrap these huddlins and we'll drop them in at the Whelt as we pass, then they'll still be nice and fresh at lunchtime. I'm surprised he hasn't been down."

"I think he said something about going up the fell to gather some more sheep for clipping," John informed me.

"Gathering in this weather? Surely not!"

The weather this particular Weardale summer's day was a morning that had started brilliant with sunshine and a child's depiction of a bright blue sky with small, cotton wool clouds. A couple of hours later, as if in a quick change of stage scenery, the sky filled with gangrenous-black clouds which promptly burst, discharging drenching, cold, penetrating rain like a celestial power shower. Yet, by the time we were ready to go up the hill, the sun was shining brightly again and the air warming. Only the group of bedraggled, dripping hens and the Zwartbles (shaking themselves like large dogs that had just been in a river) bore testament to the deluge. The farmyard at Glenwhelt was not a picturesque place, such as you find on a biscuit tin lid. It was a working place, where a flock of about 3,000 hill sheep, that roamed over 3,000 acres of high fell land, were brought into for all their caring needs. Once there had been three or four men and umpteen dogs to organise this work; now there was just Denty and his quad bike, with occasional help from the home farm for the large tasks. There was certainly not much time for the niceties: keeping the yard and buildings neat and tidy, mending gates and stable doors that were probably old in his grandfather's day, keeping on top of the general mess that farm machinery and animals generate. There was only time for that which was truly important; tending to the needs of the flock. It was always wise therefore, to go equipped with wellies. I picked my way through the puddles, mud and worse and hung the plastic bag

on the back door handle as I usually did. When he returned from gathering, no doubt soaked through and cold on the quad bike, the contents would provide a bit of cheer with a big mug of tea.

During the rest of the journey over the high fell top that separated Weardale from Teesdale I dwelt, not for the first time, on just what a special, unique person Ian Dent was. Without him, our life on the hill would have been very different. He and John had formed a mutual bond of respect, friendship and support which played out in many different ways. They knew they could call on each other at a moment's notice whenever life threw a problem up. Because of Denty, John had found himself performing tasks he had never even known about, yet alone experienced; holding tups while Denty sawed off ingrowing horns, manning a 'shedding gate' when the flock was being sorted, wrapping fleeces at clipping time, clinging to a quad bike on the high fell searching for lost sheep, riding a tractor in arctic conditions to take feed and hay to the 'out-by' sheep. It was through Denty that I learned how to pull a lamb when a ewe was struggling to birth, to get air into the tiny lungs of a newborn that hadn't started to breathe, clip an overgrown foot, attach an ear tag. But, as well as all these very practical things, there was something more indefinable that Denty brought to our lives. He, whose whole life and that of two generations before, had been spent up

Swinhope, made us feel from the day we arrived that we too would belong in this place, would appreciate deeply the privilege of living here amongst so much wealth of beauty and bird and animal life and that the more often than not poor, or even dire, weather conditions would not be a deterrent to this life. He also brought a wealth of language in a living but endangered dialect, told the most appalling jokes and could be very naughty without ever being offensive. He was, in short, the seasoning of our daily life; the salt – and pepper! – that gave it extra savour. A typical example was the day he arrived grumbling about being bitten by a cleg (a horse fly) on the side of his face; I could see an angry red bite, but told him that at least he knows what bit him. My problem, I told him, is knowing how something got through my shirt and the well-upholstered elastrickery of my bra to give me a nasty nip and leave me with an itchy lump that was plaguing me day and night.

His face lit up.

"Problem solved! Ah've got just the thing!" and jumping off his bike he rummaged around in the big green first aid box he always carried on the front, filled with remedies - some ancient, some modern – that he might need to deal with a problem when doing his rounds on the fells.

Triumphant, he approached me with a tub of cream.

"What's that?"

I knew Denty too well not to be suspicious.

"Why, what de ye think? It's udder cream! Question is -" he added after a slight pause, "Whe's ganna rub it in?"

He had, undoubtedly, inherited some of his wicked sense of humour from his father Ray. When we first moved in he was soon brought to meet us. Ray would have then been well into his seventies then but still went up from his cottage in the village most days to 'help out' and no doubt keep an eye on things up at the farm. He had been as broad, muscular and strong as Denty in his younger days; from photos we had seen he had been a very handsome man, well able to stride tirelessly all day over the vast area of fell that was his domain, in hobnailed bots with turned up toes with a piece of lamb's fleece in the bottom for warmth and comfort, a tweed hat, his crook and his dog. Age had robbed him of lot of his musculature and his hands were contorted painfully with arthritis. But nothing had diminished the twinkle in his eye. After introductions were made he took me to one side;

"Aall ah want te knaa is; are ye married and can ye cook? The furst'un doesn't matter really!"

We soon became familiar with the saga of how the Dent dynasty had arrived at Glenwhelt. In the 1920s an advert had been put in the local farming papers that a shepherd was wanted for Glenwhelt. Anyone considering the job had to be at the farm at a given date and time. Ray's father, George, was working over in Teesdale at that time but he had a real fancy for the job. The problem was that, on the designated day, a dreadful snowstorm blew up and covered both the Teesdale and Weardale fells. Undaunted, George got out his sturdy fell pony and headed up and over the fells, despite the driving snow. Not another soul had ventured out to make the journey to Glenwhelt that day so, when George and his pony plodded cold, stiff and white with snow into the farmyard the farmer just said, "He'll do for me; anyone prepared to do that to get the job deserves it". So Ray grew up at the 'Whelt' learning his craft and every inch of those fells from his father throughout his youth and, when George gave up the job, became the shepherd in turn. By then a small Ian Dent was in turn learning the ropes from both his father and grandfather and he worked many years jointly with his father until, in time, he became the shepherd. That is not to say that Ray ceased to be part of the life of the farm; until extreme old age and his contorted hands prevented him, we would see him most days chugging determinedly up the hill in his little old car. John, on his way up to Glenwhelt one day, passed him working on building up a section of stone wall that had come down.

"Are you alright there Ray?"

"Aye, grand. But aah don't know what's the matter; aah canna seem to lift these stones as well as aah used to."

He was into his eighties at this time.

Out in the garden one day I saw him coming along the bottom road in his car with a small group of sheep in front of it. His window was down and he was leaning out, waving his stick and shouting at the sheep, shepherding them from his driving seat. When he turned them up our hill I went and asked if there was a problem and if I could help.

"Aye well, if ye can help me get these blighters up the hill and int' the yard aah'd appreciate it; third time this week they've been out!"

So between us, Ray blaring his horn and I waving my arms and a walking stick, we got them up the hill, then I ran ahead, opened the yard gate and we turned them into a sheep pen.

Ray slammed the gate on them.

"An' they can stop there a day or two; bucket of water but nee food! D'ye knaa, they were in a good field with decent grass but no; had te jump out and look for summit better, summit mair. Well, couple of days in that pen they'll be well hung'ered and that glad to see any grass they'll stop put!"

He looked at me rather sadly before saying, "De ye knaa what's wrang wi' this country today? Nee'body's hungered enough; nee'body's hungered enough."

And in our modern lives, with an insatiable appetite for more and newer and better and a search for contentment that seems always to elude, many do seem to suffer from an obesity of materialism and an inability to be satisfied by enough; they always hunger for more.

A very wise man indeed was Ray Dent.

The beginning of the end of his daily trips to the farm probably began the day we were sitting having our lunch in the kitchen, saw something whizz past the window and then heard an awful hard bang. We rushed out to find Ray's car almost on its side, with one front wheel a good way up the gable wall of Hill House West and the other spinning over the garden gate. Fearing the worst for Ray, who was still at the wheel, we got his door open and found to our huge relief that he was conscious and not apparently badly hurt, just badly shaken. He managed to walk into the house with a little assistance and I made him tea, while John phoned for Denty to come down.

"Ah think I must hev got me foot on't wrong pedal! Ah went faster rather than slower round that bend!"

Once he arrived and it was established that Ray really was, miraculously, unhurt we helped him out to Denty's truck for a lift back home.

"Ah'll come back once aah've got him settled at home and ah'll bring the tractor and pull the car off the wall and onto the road."

Ray looked at his car, taking in its full plight for the first time, and shook his head.

"Why, I was tekkin' it for its MOT test on Monday; d'ye think it'll pass?"

The family decided the best thing to tell Ray was that the car had been written off. He was now around ninety and they had been worried about his driving for a while; the accident just confirmed their worst fears. Of course, it meant that from this point, trips up to the farm depended on him getting a lift and therefore a certain loss of independence. As he headed into his nineties he became inevitably more frail and took to sleeping downstairs. But he was very well visited and John would often accompany Denty to see Ray, or pop along on his own. These were opportunities to talk to Ray about a world and a life that had vanished. What astonishing times he had lived through and what unbelievable changes had taken place, particularly in fairly isolated rural life. On one visit he shared even older memories; those of his father George, who had been a soldier in the First World War. He had survived the horrors of that conflict and come home to the safety and quiet of the countryside, only to find that a fresh horror awaited; the influenza that swept the world in the wake of the war. So many people were stricken, or even died, that there were not enough souls to keep things going; whole families were bedridden with no one fit enough to provide care or make meals for themselves, let alone tend and feed the animals. Sheep went without hay, cows went without being milked and fires were left unlit. George Dent and the other lucky souls not stricken with the infection spent their days helping how and where they could, once they had seen to the needs of their own families and animals. Some fed animals and did the milking; George went around the houses of the ill twice a day with an enormous pail of porridge, doling out portions to each family and even spoon feeding those too weak to feed themselves. No wonder Ray thought we are not 'hung'ered enough' these days. Ray himself saw service in the Second World War, but, like so many of his generation, this was not something he ever spoke about when John visited. He had been a very well respected and notable shepherd; one of Weardale's greatest. The highlight of his entire life had been in the 1970s when he was awarded the national honour of 'Shepherd of the Year' and he and his wife Lena had to go down to London to receive the award. Ray appreciated and valued that trip and the award very much – but said he was glad when he got back to Weardale. I am afraid that my visits to him at the cottage were seriously curtailed by my asthmatic reaction to the merest whiff of cigarette smoke and, in Ray's sitting room, the air was more nicotine than oxygen as he and his son puffed away heartily and incessantly till there was more smoke than in the Craster kipper factory. I never forgot Ray though when baking, or jam or soup making and little gifts would be shuttled along to his cottage regularly. Mind you, if Denty was the bearer of the gift, I could almost see him worrying that I might be giving away his huddlins out.

15

OLD SHEPHERDS NEVER DIE...

They just move further up the hill. Well, I had finally fully retired from teaching in 2013, John had sort of retired, so why shouldn't Denty? He had hung on longer than us but, approaching seventy, he had decided that he had had enough of a month without sleep at lambing time, digging sheep out of snow drifts, heaving rocks to mend stone walls and breaking his back at dipping, clipping, foot trimming and horn burning time. Considering he had done this full time since he was fifteen and probably part time since he was five, it was a huge decision. It was the only life that he, his father and his grandfather had ever known. He had been born at Glenwhelt, which sat like a Roman fort with its square yard encircled by stone buildings; solid, defiant at 1,400 feet against the aggressive, invading weather. We had long wondered where Denty would go and how he would cope once he had to vacate Glenwhelt, which went with the job of shepherd on Swinhope fell. He was like one of the sheep there; hefted to the land and we feared unable to thrive anywhere else. But our fears were unfounded and his lifelong service to his employers ended better than we could have dreamt possible. Almost at the top of Swinhope there was another house that belonged to 'the Firm'. This one, much newer, was where Denty had lived as a child; the house where his parents lived, once married, until the time when his grandfather retired and they moved back down the hill to Glenwhelt. Since we moved to the Dale it had been occupied by one after another of, it must be said, unsuccessful tenants. It had suffered in this process but now, repaired, restored and redecorated, it was to be the home to which Denty and Lynne would retire: even a hefted sheep can cope with a move of one mile!

He and Lynne moved into this home, which was both new and old to him, in early September 2018. Of course, nothing as ordinary as a removal van was used. Up and down, up and down Swinhope valley went the tractor and sheep trailer, the quad bike and open trailer and his four wheel drive truck with the tailgate open; all with an array of household objects sticking out of the back. Very often John was found to be hanging onto, or out of, one of these vehicles. I helped Lynne at the other end, moving things into the right rooms, unpacking boxes and clearing spaces to put things in. Came the day it was time to move his family treasure, a long case grandfather clock. It was an actual grandfather clock, which had been made as a wedding gift for his grandfather. Too high for the sheep trailer, too long for the car, it had to be moved in the quad bike and open trailer – with John inside, hanging on to it for dear life. The opening credits of Antiques Roadshow used to show a motorcycle with a grandfather clock stuck in the side car. However, that clock did not have to make the journey from Glenwhelt to the top of Swinhope, a road that ascended steeply, was very curvy and had a surface that was corrugated like a switchback, from the wrinkles in the face of the earth caused by a glacier in the last ice age piling up everything in front of it. Geologically termed a glacial moraine, the Dent family referred to them as 'the Green Hills'. When the bike finally grunted to a stop near the back door, and Lynne and I peered out to see if everything had arrived in one piece, Denty turned round and grinned at a somewhat ashen John.

"Howway man! Ye look as if ye've been hangin' on tiv an angry tup in there!"

John climbed out on wobbly legs.

"I think I would have preferred that!"

Denty gazed at the road winding its way upward towards the horizon, on the other side of which lay Teesdale.

"Just think; last time this clock were moved, it came ower yon hill in a horse and cart; an' that were nigh on a century ago."

Now that was a sight I would have liked to have seen!

Finally the last trip was made, to an empty and somewhat bereft Glenwhelt, and the gate was shut. Now a new episode of life was beginning for Denty and Lynne in a house that stood alone, high up that moorland valley. The top of the fell, that was just above it, stood at almost two thousand foot above sea level and marked the division of Weardale from Teesdale. The views stretched endlessly in every direction across the thousands of acres of fell-land that three generations of Dent's had walked, shepherded and cared for.

We felt an immense relief; Denty had in no way been uprooted – he had merely been re-potted.

To our surprise, that back end, Denty sold his last remaining Swaledales, which he grazed in our fields: if the move from Glenwhelt had been the decree nisi on his shepherding life, this was surely the decree absolute. He had finished with sheep, he told us.

He wanted, he said, to try something different; he wanted to turn the land around his new home, which had long reverted to rough, overgrown, neglected fell-side, back to the garden he remembered his mother having there when he was a boy. So he was still going to shepherd after all, though now it would be land and plants instead of sheep that he would husband. That left us with the question of what to do about our fields, as we now were down to only four sheep of our own and that was not nearly enough teeth to cope with five acres of grass. If not regularly grazed down, our land would also revert to rough fell very quickly. The answer, fortunately, lay very close at hand - just across the road actually. The obvious people to ask were our new neighbours, Christopher and Karen, who were trying to build up a flock of Blue Faced Leicester and Mule sheep alongside their normal daytime jobs. They already used family farmland on the other side of the Dale and they did have a few acres attached to their new home but they could always do with more. They were delighted with the suggestion and it was the perfect solution; we got our fields well nibbled and they got extra grazing and would make sure the fields were managed and stockproof. So, as soon as enough grass grew that spring, we put our sheep up into the top field and Christopher put his two best tups – Billy and Casper – in our bottom field. He gave a strict warning not to enter the field while they were there, as Billy in particular was being very aggressive and had even charged at him; which was a bit foolhardy really, given Christopher's height, breadth and sheep sense. It must be said that the Blue Faced Leicester tups were impressive beasts; large, mean-lean, long legged, long backed, glaring at us down their Imperial Roman noses. Having watched Billy nearly knocking out poor Custard through the dividing wire fence when she had only come to introduce herself out of politeness, she – and we – gave these big bad boys a wide berth. I remembered our gentle giant Zulu, our Zwartbles tup who, though twice the bulk of these Leicesters, had impeccable manners. Nevertheless, I would like to have seen what would have happened if they had tried to butt him! But the meanest of tups, when not governed by their raging levels of testosterone, are governed by their stomachs. For a few days they watched glowering from a distance when John let the hens out and gave them their breakfast treats. But they drew daily ever nearer the rail that divided the hen pen from their field. Came the day they were stretching their noses over the fence in curiosity and John held a piece of wholemeal toast out and…Well, from then on they were milksops, batting long lashes over entreating eyes and relishing having their heads and necks rubbed. We did not, however, push our luck to the point of ever actually entering the field while they were there!

One May morning I was watching John let the hens out and giving them their treats. The tups, now familiar with the regime, converged on the hen house at great speed blaring like two battered bugles, demanding their share. The morning food distribution soon attracted other regular visitors; the ducks, who we called Mr & Mrs Mallard ,with no shame at all just limboed under the rail into the hen pen and helped themselves to the treats on offer; old toast, ends of loaves, cheese rinds and tomato tops, as well as the hens' morning food ration. Then the green wellied moorhen peered more shyly but hopefully from the edge of the stream and very soon we heard the rasping shout of the pheasant we called the Colonel strutting confidently up the lawn. He was soon joined by a pretty collared dove and a raucous jackdaw. Almost bouncing around John's feet were the pair of dunnocks who were now so tame and sociable they regularly came to see John when he was busy in his workshop. Resignedly John said, "All right!" to the feathered assembly, got a scoopful of corn out of the bin in the greenhouse and flung it across the lawn. The noise of the bin lid of course alerted the hens who, although they had just had all sorts of titbits, had an insatiable addiction to mixed corn. They now flung themselves like an angry mob of Greenham Common women protesters against their wire fence and demanded equal rights. So another scoop of corn was fetched to placate them, the last tailings of which were flung near the stream for the moorhen. I watched all this from an upstairs window with a smile that was both outward and inward. That so many varieties of birds were attracted to our fields and garden was an enormous privilege in a world from which garden and country birds were rapidly vanishing; that some of them felt secure and confident enough to be daily visitors to Hill House East was an absolute joy. So was the array of small birds that flitted in and out all day to our feeding station beneath the cherry tree.

"Bloomin' heck; I just filled all those bird feeders yesterday!" - we had six of them offering a variety of foods to hopefully satisfy every beak - "Before long it's going to cost more to feed the bird life here than the sheep," grumbled John.

But what price the joy of watching robins, several types of finch and three types of tit busy on the feeders? Not to mention a small troupe of the once abundant but now terrifyingly declined humble sparrow, which in turn attracted blackbirds, starlings, jackdaws, pheasants and a small vole to glean the seeds they spilt from the feeders, which fell like manna from heaven above to the ground beneath.

"I think that Billy is hobbling a bit on his right front foot," I was informed when John came in for his coffee.

"I'd better report it over the road then."

I knew how fastidious Christopher and Karen were about the sheep in their care and that Billy was their pride and joy. At least the sore foot meant that Billy had other things on his mind than butting people. Christopher grabbed him and expertly flipped him into a sitting position with seemingly no more effort than turning the page of a book. The cloven, horny toes were clipped and trimmed back, the cleat between well squirted with bright purple foot spray and an antibiotic injection given before Billy knew what was happening. Christopher gave him a thorough checkover for other problems while he was in this undignified and helpless position.

"Where have yer knackers gone then son?" Christopher asked him, examining his underside carefully while he had the chance.

It was a rhetorical question really, as the answer lay in the crop of large, healthy lambs grazing in the field above with their mothers.

Bemused and embarrassed, Billy was rolled back onto his feet.

"He should be OK now, but I'll check him again tomorrow."

"I must say, he seems a lot more placid then when he arrived."

"Aye, well his testosterone levels will be right down now."

"Perhaps," I conceded, "But maybe it's because his toast levels are going up!"

Christopher rolled his eyes heavenward, "Ye'll have them as soft as muck!"

"Not them, only Billy; Casper won't even try a bit of toast."

"Well, he is a picky blighter; won't eat any old hay, has to be to his liking. Same with his women, picky; passed over several yows last back end. I couldn't see anything wrong with them – but then I'm not a Leicester tup!"

With that he closed his foot care box and strode back across the road.

It had been very strange for a while not to hear the deepthroated throb of Denty's quad bike pulling up on our drive most days. John used to say that every time he lit a fire in his workshop it sent a smoke signal up the hill that seemed to attract a cold, damp shepherd to descend and drink tea and steam gently in front of the stove.

Now this happened less often.

Now he had no quad bike and he was rarely sodden and up to the top of his wellies in muck.

Now he was a gentleman of leisure, to be found neat and tidy, manning Lynne's wool shop in Stanhope a couple of days a week: how he kept the accounts right there I have no idea, though no doubt he had his own unique system. He had once confided in me that he had never been any good at figures or statistics at school; "The teacher once asked us ti' work out how many blocks there were in a pyramid! Ah telt him aah had no idea –but aah knew how many deed sheep ye could git in the knacker man's wagon!"

On other days he was beavering away on his landscaping project up on the fell. Of course, nothing was done on a dainty scale; his idea of a rockery was using the boulders the last ice age had left strewn in the valley. His idea of an edging for a flowerbed was a railway sleeper. He made a very useful planter for the front of the house out of two L shaped rocks that were so heavy he required a tractor and bucket to move them and it was a wonder the tractor did not tip over backwards. Think of gardening more along the lines of Fred Flintstone than Alan Titchmarsh. And he was loving it – digging drains, mending and moving walls, planting trees, shrubs and flowers; changing his little bit of fell from the wild side to the tame side.

He had no access or need now for sheep wormers and drenches and dips and antibiotics. His lifelong knowledge of sheep care, of course, remained and should we ever need him he would be there in a crack to help. But we would have felt it a bit much to ask him to drop in on his way home in his 'civvies' to wrestle with a muddy sheep with a toenail problem. But, yet again in our life we had been so fortunate in that now we had Christopher at hand; not a new shepherd, not a replacement shepherd, simply an additional shepherd to call on. And of course there was another shepherd residing at Glenwhelt now. This could have been a difficult one for Denty to deal with emotionally if someone he did not care for, or respect as a shepherd, had moved into Glenwhelt and taken over the care of the sheep and the fells of Swinhope. Yet again, it all worked out really well. John Bowes and his family moved into the 'Whelt' and he was someone Denty both liked and knew to be a knowledgeable shepherd. We soon learnt he was referred to locally as 'Bowsey'; it seemed there was a habit in the Dale of referring to people by a modified surname. Of course, they both had their own ways of doing things and advice was soon flowing in both directions! I once bought Denty a birthday card that showed an old farmer leaning over a fence, watching another man repairing a stone wall. The caption was, 'Of course, you know you are doing that all wrong?' Well, I will say no more! But in reality they got on very well and, whenever there was a large task on, like clipping or dipping or gathering, Denty would be called on to help with the work by 'the Firm' and it was deeply satisfying for him to still be involved. So it was not a case of 'the King is dead: long live the King', as old shepherds never retire, or even truly die; if they are wise they just pass on their skills to the next generation and so live on in the flock.

Physically of course old shepherds do pass on. It was in 2012 that Ray Dent had died aged ninety three. It affected Denty deeply. He had not just lost his father but he had also lost the man who had taught him his craft and with whom he had worked on a daily basis throughout his adult life. Ray had been a widower for many years and so his almost daily contact with the farm and his son had been vital to him. Ray was so well known and respected in Weardale and the wider shepherding fraternity that his funeral and farewell were bound to be very well attended. What suitable tribute could we give to honour a man whose life's work had made him at one with the hills, the fells and the Swaledale sheep that roamed them? I had, for a few years, been working with the wool that came from our sheep and using it for felting projects. The previous summer I had asked Denty for a Swaledale fleece, which I had then washed and experimented with different felting techniques. Being so coarse and wiry it was hard to make normal felt but it did make excellent boiled felt when felted long and hard and at high temperatures. I thought I had found something new but in fact I had only rediscovered something very old. Felt is, after all, only wool which through the use of water, warmth and friction, matts together because of the scales on the wool fibres. It has an ancient history; possibly the first fabric man ever created. When I showed Denty my thickly matted pad of Swaledale wool he said, "Aye; just like me grandfather and me father used in their work boots!" Shepherds then wore thick hobnailed boots with an iron rimmed heel and slightly turned up toes, which resulted in a rocking motion when walking. To make them warmer and more comfortable to wear Denty remembered his father cutting a piece of shearling fleece and lining his boots with it. After a few days wear it would have compressed and flattened and so he would add more, layer by layer until it reached the desired thickness, matted together firmly by moisture, heat and friction; it had become felt. For Ray's tribute I wanted to do something better with Swale fleece than a pair of felt insoles. I took the remains of the Swale fleece from Glenwhelt and lightly carded it till I had a plentiful supply of long, very thick wool strands. Then I plaited these loosely and, when long enough, sewed them into a circular wreath. With some wire, black and brown wool from my Zwartbles and white from the Swale, I made a curled Swaledale tup's horn and sewed it on the wreath. John made me a small wooden plaque, which I also attached and on it wrote

simply:

'For Ray; Safely Gathered.'

On the morning of the funeral, the hearse had driven first not to the Chapel but up Swinhope. As it passed Glenwhelt it was joined by the cars of close family and also by ourselves. The hearse wound slowly up the fell road, past the Low Byre, where Ray would have stored hay for the sheep in winter, past the low ground where the black grouse have come for generations to lek, over the small stone bridge and past Camp Lot, where John Wesley once preached in the open air. Finally, at the head of the valley, the hearse stopped and turned in. The back doors were opened and Denty gently placed our wreath of Swaledale wool on top of Ray's coffin, alongside his shepherd's crook. Then we all stood, silent, drinking in the hills, the air and the views down to Glenwhelt; allowing Ray to be one with that landscape one more time in the flesh, although I was in no doubt that his spirit would roam those fells and seek for lost lambs into eternity.

The funeral service was then held at the Methodist Chapel in Ireshopeburn which was, as expected, packed out. Afterwards we were all invited to a generous Weardale tea in a nearby hall. I was both deeply touched and honoured to be asked to do a reading at the funeral and what else could I choose to read but the text on the Good Shepherd? From the Gospel of St John it contains these wonderful words:

"The one who enters by the gate is the shepherd of the sheep. The gatekeeper opens the gate for him and the sheep listen to his voice, he calls his own sheep by name and leads them out... I am the good shepherd, the good shepherd lays down his life for the sheep...I am the good shepherd; I know my sheep and my sheep know me - just as the Father knows me and I know the Father - and I lay down my life for the sheep. I have other sheep that are not of this sheep pen; I must bring them also. They too will listen to my voice, and there shall be one flock and one shepherd."

When it was all over and we were back at home, I was reflecting on my reading. From somewhere - and maybe it was from Ray himself, who had a wicked sense of humour - what came to mind was not him but his son, flying round the fell on his quad bike, calling to his sheep in terms you would never find in the Bible.

"Ye evil bitch!! Move ower there! NO! Ye stupid lump o' mutton – not there! Ye old bag o'bones – git ower here!"

Yea, verily, the flock know their shepherd's voice; coming to it is not always so certain.

And old shepherds, certainly the special few like Ray, will never die.

As for Denty's retirement as a shepherd... After a full spring and summer and most of the autumn moving rocks, stones and soil and planting shrubs, trees, perennials and anything else that might possibly grow around his house, the gardening season was over and the sheep sale season was beginning. Deeply ingrained habits die hard and I don't suppose a year had gone by in over sixty years that Denty had not gone to one sheep mart or other.

"Just poppin' ower to this, that or the other sale t'day to have look at what's about and hev a bit crack like," he had said for over a week, adding, "Aah just want te keep me eye in; nee harm in that!"

By the time he had been to the first few sales he came to see John.

"Ah wondered if ye had an hour or so to spare this week?"

"I'm sure I will," John replied, "Have you got a problem?"

"Aye; the lights on me trailer aren't workin' that grand, ah think there is a wire loose or summit."

Having seen him arrive I was by now coming out with a mug of tea for him.

"You haven't lost the knack of hearing the kettle have you! What news from up the hill?"

"Well, ah'm just askin' if John can hev a look at me trailer lights."

"Oh, you're not moving something else up there are you?"

"Mebbies. Mebbies!" he said in a way that I knew meant that he was up to something, "Ah've been thinking; ye knaa there's a bit of a gaff up there at new house, which has a fair bit of winter grazing on it? Ah thow't ah would just tek a look at the next tup sale and see if ah could pick up a couple of young 'uns at a fair price and mebbies bring them on over the winter? Then ah could sell them on at a profit next year! Just a thowt, understand, just a thowt; nothin' definite like."

No, of course not – nothing definite; other than the need be around sheep that permeated every cell of his body.

Two young tups were duly purchased by the end of the week.

Retired or not, the shepherd in Denty was very far from being dead.

In fact, it had to be questioned whether it would be ever possible to keep this irascible man contained within a wooden box at all. He called in a day or two later just as we were, very sadly, leaving to go to the funeral of a friend. John was well scrubbed up and in a suit, shirt and tie and I

176

came into the kitchen, smartly dressed for once, while Denty was having his obligatory mug of tea.

"Bye! If ye weren't off tiv such a sad event aah'd say how grand ye look; very tasty!"

"Well thank you Denty."

"Ah tell ye what; if ye come tiv my funeral lookin' like that, ah'll be sittin' up in me box!"

Guests

16

THE MINISTRY OF HOSPITALITY

It took four years before we felt we were ready to welcome our first guests to Hill House East. During that time John worked steadily and purposefully to restore the original character of the house wherever possible while, at the same time, making it into a warm, comfortable, welcoming place for guests as well as for ourselves. In doing so he uncovered many secrets of the house long hidden and lost. We found that, probably as long as two hundred and fifty years ago or more ago, the house had been - like so many others in Weardale - shared equally between the people and their livestock. The original footprint had divided the ground floor into two; one half with a large chimney breast for the people, the other half with no chimney for the livestock.

We were puzzled, because there was no apparent separate entrance into the half we thought must have housed animals until John ripped off the pine panelling in the long porch that now leant against that wall and revealed the shape of a wide doorway, long ago walled up with stone. Removing this stone to create a direct entrance into the living room behind - intended to be used one day as a guest entrance - he found that the lintel that had once spanned that entrance was made not of stone, nor a stout timber beam, but of an old, crudely made, wooden cart axle.

It was riddled with woodworm but still had metal rims at each end for sliding the wheels in place.

Recycling really isn't a modern concept; it was once called thrift and necessity. We found other signs of this when we tore off the plywood panelling that covered the exposed ends of the roof beams which projected through the upstairs ceilings. These too had holes, notches and scars suggesting that, even before they held up the stone roof that covered Hill House East, they had seen service in another building. I would dearly love to have known how long ago those timbers were first cut.

The biggest transformation, and in many ways the one that restored the heart and the soul of the house, was discovering the original inglenook fireplace behind the modern fireplace surround. It still had its frame of sandstone uprights and lintel intact and unfractured; these framed a large hearth which funnelled into a cavernous chimney, intended originally for an open fire. Did saying we had an inglenook sound  over pretentious I wondered? I looked it up: 'ingle' in Old English in fact meant fire, while nook retains its meaning of place or small area even today so, yes, we did. Grooves and holes chiselled into the uprights showed that, at a later date, a cast iron range had been installed; an innovation at the time that must have seemed miraculous, providing as it did heat, an oven and even a ready supply of hot water. We installed a wood burning stove into the open hearth, so long the focal point of the room for the generations that had lived in it and, in doing so, provided comfort and contentment to both body and soul once more. At last, in early 2004, we felt we could say, we were ready. The whole house had been decorated, floors stripped to the wood where possible and carpeted where not, and curtains and linens bought. We had worked out the logistics of how to share what was, after all, our home with guests in a way that both parties could retain their sense of privacy and their own

179

space. The guests now had their own entrance, through the porch and into the living room whilst we could enter through the porch and into the kitchen. The kitchen had seen a huge transformation; John had put in a wooden floor and made all the kitchen units and their thick, solid wood tops by hand. The long room divided naturally into a cooking area and a place to sit and eat at my old pine table. Beyond this, John had built what was technically called a conservatory but which, in reality, was to be our bed-sitting room when we had guests. It was equipped with a very comfortable sofa bed that flipped effortlessly from one mode to another, proper heating, a television and, through a door into what had once been the woodshed, an extremely compact bathroom into which John had somehow fitted in a toilet, a hand basin and a full size shower cubicle. This space, plus the kitchen would be our 'staff accommodation' when guests were staying and we would simply lock up our own upstairs bedroom. The guests effectively got the rest of the house; the two guest bedrooms and bathroom upstairs and the whole of the living room downstairs. It would be, I mused, like renting a country house with staff; we would appear through the kitchen door when required to provide service but otherwise keep to our own quarters.

Total privacy for both parties.

Perfect.

Friends shook their heads and muttered, "You can't do that! After all, the whole house is your home; it'll never work!"

We worried that they might be right: in theory it would work but what if we didn't like it? What if the reality of having a succession of guests – for which read strangers – using the main body of the house was irksome, frustrating and too confining? Research was needed but how to conduct it? It was our wonderful Vicar Philip who came up with the solution.

"Why not offer free accommodation to people for say three months? I constantly have a string of people asking where to send friends and family attending weddings, christenings, even funerals here in the Dale. I can recommend you and they can stay for free – or perhaps for a donation to a charity? Or to the church!"

And so, throughout the spring, we entered our trial period. Not a flood of guests, thankfully, but a steady trickle of visitors visiting Weardale for a variety of reasons.

To our joy, and great relief, it worked wonderfully and we really enjoyed doing it. Weekday visitors were catered for largely by John, as I was up and off to school by 7.15 am. At weekends we worked together, though he was such a good breakfast chef my role was very much that of waitress. We had worked hard on producing a breakfast menu that was wide and varied. Guests could choose in the evening exactly what they wanted for breakfast the following morning. This allowed us to do the maximum of preparation the evening before, thus minimising panic in the mornings. We had also firmly decided not to offer evening meals; too much effort when I had been out at work all day and making no financial sense when we normally had only one or two guests staying. But I did insist that guests would always be met with a tray of tea or coffee and some good 'home baking' on their arrival; after a journey that could have been long and tiring that would be what I would most want. It was a tradition that was to become a firmly ingrained element of any stay at Hill House East; tea and cake served in front of a good log fire every afternoon.

Being confined to our quarters proved to be no problem at all. As well as the wraparound windows in the conservatory which gave the best views of the Dale in the house, John had given it a clear glass roof and so during the day the whole room was flooded with light and the cloud formations marched overhead. But it was the nights we spent in there that were so special. Once the window blinds were down and we were snugly in bed with the lights out we would be able to gaze up at the night sky in all its star filled glory. We lived in an area that was so blessedly free of light pollution that it became listed as a 'Dark Skies' area. Safe and warm in our glass bubble we could gaze in awe at the blue white dots of brilliant light to the point we were reluctant to close our eyes and go to sleep. Sometimes we were treated to other celestial sights such as shooting stars and we even learnt to recognise the regular pattern of some of the satellites that moved high above us; we even named them.

"There goes the 10.30 to Rookhope!" John would exclaim triumphantly. It was like train spotting in the sky.

And so, for the next three months, we had a steady trickle of guests stay with us, all recommended by Philip. There was the man whose estranged brother in the Dale had died suddenly and he needed a base somewhere nearby from which to sort out his affairs. There were a couple of family christenings and our very first guests were a family of four who had come for a wedding. They were delightful and we were extremely nervous. That first experience nearly caused us to abandon the whole idea when, in the middle of showering and dressing for the wedding, there were shrieks from upstairs as the heater for the electric shower simply gave up and died at a very premature age. We felt we wanted to die with it but they treated the whole thing with great humour. The guests I most remember from that period however were an elderly Church of England canon and his wife, who had come to stay because a new priest was being ordained in the Dale. At the end of their visit he paused before leaving and said, "You know my dear, there are callings to many ministries in this life, not just the ministry of the church; your calling is the ministry of hospitality." So from the very start I always kept this in mind and tried to live up to that vocation. Because, what we found out from that time, was that it doesn't matter how clean, organised, well-appointed or well-catered you are; if you are offering people a place to stay, even for just one night and you do not make them feel welcome, do not make them feel able to relax, if what you offer is without character or has no soul, then they will soon forget you.
They will not come back.
And they will not tell their friends.

Satisfied and reassured by our experience of being an experimental B&B we set aside the whole project for a few months to concentrate on the enormous excitement of Megan's marriage in the July, which was to be in the village church followed by a reception here at Hill House East. We gave ourselves a bit of a break after the wedding but, by the October of 2004, we decided the time had come to put up the signs, take out the guest insurance and do the job for real: 'Hill House East Country B&B' went live! With each booking we gained more confidence and more insight into what guests wanted from us. With each satisfied and highly complementary guest that left us we gained in certainty that we had done the right thing and, more importantly, we were doing things right.

It is of course impossible to remember all the guests who have stayed under Hill House East's old stone roof over so many years now. Some of those that do stay most vividly in the memory have been deserving of having their own stories told. However, there are many others whose memories linger and lead to 'Do you remember…?' moments. One of our very first guests was Jonathan, an elderly farmer with a rich south-west accent; we shall never forget him. A phone call from the cafe in nearby St John's Chapel enquiring if we had a vacancy for the night sent him in our direction. He arrived in a brand new and very expensive looking four wheeled drive vehicle.
"It's not mine you know! No, no, I'm just collecting it and delivering it for a friend. So I just need somewhere to get my head down for the night."
We were never actually able to clarify where he had got it from or where he was taking it to incidentally.
No guest has ever made himself quite as at home as Jonathan. He had ordered quite a late breakfast, so John and I were quietly having ours first when he strode into the kitchen in trousers and singlet, with a towel and shaving kit in one hand.
"Grand morning!"
Then he stood in front of the kitchen sink, lathered his face vigorously and began to shave whilst loudly singing 'Oh, what a beautiful morning!'
"Um, Jonathan," I ventured, when he had finished and had carefully washed his whiskery lather down the sink, "You do have your own bathroom upstairs you know."
"Oh, no point in dirtying that! This'll do me fine! That coffee smells good though."

"Well, you did say you wanted your breakfast in half an hour from now; I was just going to set up your table and start preparing it."

"Don't you go to no bother like that! No, no, this'll do me fine; more companionable like!"

And very companionable he was, quite happy to chat away while I cooked, cleared and washed up around him. Again, we never quite got a clear picture out of anything he said but elements seemed to include a one armed wife who had had an affair, squabbles over his family farm and either coming or going to Ireland to collect or deliver this vehicle for a friend.

"Right then! I'll pay my dues my dear and be on my way."

We were left stunned and somewhat bemused; we were, after all, newcomers to the accommodation game – was Jonathan typical of what we should expect?

At teatime the phone rang; it was the cafe again.

"He wants to know if he can stay another night?"

We knew exactly who 'he' was.

Completely ignoring the guest door he strode beaming into the kitchen, once more in the middle of me cooking a meal.

"Grand day! My, that smells nice; am I in time for tea then?"

I was about to point out that we did not provide evening meals for guests, we were just a bed and breakfast, but by then he had sat at the kitchen table and was smiling contentedly so I didn't have the heart. And anyway, there was plenty for three.

"I thought you were off to deliver the car today?"

"Yes, well, no; such a nice area this, seemed a shame to go. And I'm in no hurry, no"

The next morning followed the same pattern as the one before, down to the rendition of 'Oh, what a beautiful morning!' then he paid his bill and was gone.

"You don't think?" I asked.

"Surely not?" replied John.

But, on the button, just before five o'clock, which was when they closed, the cafe phoned.

"Not again?"

"Well, yes; I'm afraid so – but you could always say you were full up?" Alan, the cafe owner, suggested helpfully.

"No, I couldn't do that. Where else would he go tonight? Without getting thrown out that is!"

"He certainly is a bit if a character, that's for sure."

"That's one way of putting it; exasperating is another. Why does he always land up with you at tea time Alan? Why doesn't he come straight here and ask?"

"Oh, he doesn't arrive at tea time – he's been here since he had his lunch!"

"What! I thought he was exploring the area?"

"I don't think he has got much further than from you to St John's Chapel."

A thought struck me, "Alan? Why did he turn up at your cafe in the first place?"

It seemed to me an odd way of getting to or from Ireland.

"He said he had got lost."

"Well, where was he trying to get to?"

"He wasn't quite sure; said it didn't matter much."

"Ah."

And so a third night and third morning passed, all three of us seemingly now part of a strange routine that appeared to be going to go on indefinitely.

Jonathan paid his bill climbed into the gleaming new vehicle, waved and drove off.

Five o'clock came and went and there was no phone call; I then found myself worrying about him and phoned the cafe.

"No, no sign of him today, not even at lunch time."

So as mysteriously as he had arrived, Jonathan had gone out of our lives.

My mother would always say that when a stranger arrived at your door in need of something, be careful how you treated them; you could be entertaining an angel.

Jonathan?

I suppose it was a possibility.

One thing was for sure; he did not have the voice of an angel – Howard Keel can do 'Oh what a beautiful morning' much better.

Sometimes exasperating, but in the end delightful, guests arrived in pairs.

Such a pair were elderly spinster sisters with rich Highland voices.

How did they find Hill House East to spend their three day holiday?

Once again, only the Good Lord knows!

I shall call them Agnes and Jennie Douglas.

It was Agnes who phoned to make the booking.

"Now, firstly, is your property on a hill?"

"I think the clue might be in the name actually! Why?"

"Well, I suffer from a degree of M.S; do you have parking that is on the flat?"

"Yes," I assured her, "You can park on the flat right outside the front door. But I think I must point out we do not have any special facilities for disabled people; the bedrooms are up a flight of stairs."

That apparently was not a problem, nor was the next query.

"Now, I am a strict vegetarian, though my sister is not," Agnes said, I thought a little disapprovingly.

"We have an extensive breakfast menu with various vegetarian options," I assured her once more.

"That's all very well; but I am also allergic to eggs - very allergic. Now, you say you provide home baking, so will you make scones without eggs in them for our visit?"

"I can certainly do that, yes."

"Well then, that's good," - it sounded more like 'guut' - "So we shall be with you next month. In the meanwhile, I shall telephone if I think of anything else."

"Thank you, Miss Douglas, we shall look forward to it."

Or at least I hoped we would.

The Misses Douglas arrived promptly at the appointed time on the appointed day.

A cheery, comfortably plump person got out of the car first and smiled a cheery, comfortable smile.

"Hello dear, I am Jennie."

In her rich Scottish voice it sounded delightfully like 'Halloo'.

"And this is my sister Agnes."

She helped to heave a less plump and less cheery person out of the front seat.

"I hope your journey hasn't been too bad; come on, let's get you settled in. A cup of tea first or shall I show you to your rooms?"

"Tea," said Agnes emphatically, "I shall need a rest before tackling stairs."

I served them with tea, scones, butter and jam.

"There are no eggs in these I trust?"

"None, I assure you; I made them especially for your visit."

"Mmm."

Agnes still sounded suspicious but nevertheless the scones were polished off.

"Oh my dear! Those were delicious – and your own jam too I suspect?"

Jennie's warm and sincere praise made up for any coolness on her sister's part.

"Rooms I think, I need a rest," Agnes announced, "Bags Jennie?"

"Oh yes, of course dear!"

"Oh don't you go to get them Jennie; John will bring them up for you."

"Ah ye sure? I'm quite used to it you know!"

I suspected she was.

"Now which room would you like dear?" she asked when we got Agnes up the stairs.

Her sister inspected both rooms carefully and said, "I'll have the twin room; more room for my things."

Jennie agreed at once and took her own things into the double bedroom.

The evening passed without incident, the breakfast order was put in successfully, after each item had been carefully checked for any hint of flesh or eggs, and the Misses Douglas retired for the night.

The standard question for guests on appearing on their first morning is obviously, 'Did you sleep well? Were you comfortable?'

As soon as the words were out of my mouth Agnes responded.

"I never have a good night and I am never comfortable."

"Oh dear, I am sorry to hear that."

"It's part of my condition; I just sweat continuously. You'll have to change the sheets – they got soaked. And if you could let me have some big towels; I'll use those at night to lie on which will spare the sheets. I should have asked last night."

"Yes, of course, I can do that. Anything else you need?"

I was really only asking out of politeness, but…

"Yes! Water in my room, lots of it."

"Well, there are bottles of mineral water in each room…."

"Hah! I'd drunk those by midnight!"

"The water in the bathroom tap is just the same as the kitchen tap – it's on a rising main and…"

"Tap water? Oh, I don't drink tap water; only bottled water. I'm allergic."

So, when she went to bed that night Agnes had clean sheets, a pile of large fluffy towels and a whole twenty four bottle pack of mineral water in her room and, I hoped, nothing to grumble about.

"Did you have a better night?" I asked hopefully the next morning.

"Still far too hot; my room was stifling even with the radiator switched off. Can you make it cooler?"

"Well, did you try having your bedroom window open?"

"Open the window! Oh, you never know what might be floating about in the air at night; insects, things I am allergic to – anything!"

"Ah, well I am afraid I am stumped!"

And I was.

One good thing was that, after breakfast, they did go out to see things during the day and didn't come back till (eggless) teatime. One morning, just before they left for the day, there was a loud knock on the kitchen door. I opened it and there stood Agnes with two nighties in her hands. "Could these be washed? They have both been soaked with sweat and I didn't bring any more with me."

Along with evening meals, laundry wasn't something that was actually on offer at Hill House East.

"Um, well, yes, I suppose I could put them in with a load of our own washing I was going to do this morning."

"What do you use?"

"Sorry?"

"What do you use – to wash things with? What detergent? Can I see it?" My patience was beginning to wear thin as I trudged back with the product for her to inspect.

"Ah! Good job I checked! Can't use that; contains enzymes – I'm…"

Let me guess, I thought, 'allergic'?

"… allergic to those."

As well as eggs, water, air and detergent what else was this woman allergic to?

"Just a moment!"

I returned with a washing up bowl and a bottle of Eco friendly, free of everything liquid for washing delicates.

"There you go Agnes; there is absolutely nothing nasty in that. If you wash your things through upstairs and rinse them, I will spin and dry them for you."

The look on Agnes' face was one of pure horror.

"I don't do washing!"

Her sister was standing behind her. The look on her face was one of horror too – the horror of embarrassment.

"Here dear, just give them to me! I'll soon have them rinsed through for you."

By now I was getting well fed up; not just with the demands on us but of those on her long suffering yet clearly devoted sister. I decided no more 'Mrs Bend-Over-Backwards-to-be-Helpful'; I could be as curt and abrupt as she was if I chose. And I'm afraid I was! There was no way at all I wanted to encourage a return visit. Their last morning finally arrived, bills were settled and John was putting bags in their car.

"Carrier bag Jennie dear?"

It was the first time I had heard Agnes address her sister affectionately.

"Carrier bag? Oh, yes dear!"

Jennie bustled back to her room and reappeared with a large, pretty bag in which there was a bottle of wine, a box of chocolates and a pot plant. Agnes handed it to us.

"Just a little thank you – for all the little extras you know. I expect we're not the easiest of guests but you have looked after us well."

"Oh you certainly have my dears, nothing too much trouble!" added Jennie, with a lovely smile.

She had such beautiful skin; clear, luminous and barely lined, despite her age. Agnes' face was dull and much lined; there was no denying that the pain and frustration of her MS had taken its toll. She had the right to be grumpy and self-obsessed I realised, with more than a little guilt.

Of course, they returned the next year – for an even longer stay – and again the year after that. But I was now forewarned and forearmed and their stays with us developed into times of comfortable, humorous banter with me trying to keep just one step ahead of Agnes' demands and she trying desperately to come up with something to catch me out, while Jennie just beamed in the wings knowing it was all now in good fun.

"Hello Agnes! How lovely to see you again! Hope you have brought plenty nighties this time!"

"Yes, well, I hope you…"

"Don't worry! Huge pile of towels? Check! Crates of mineral water? Check! Hands not touched by an egg for a week? Check! Bedroom window hermetically sealed? Check!"

"But have you…"

"And Agnes, every wisp of bedding and the towels in your room have been washed in an ultra-anti-allergic-eco-friendly wash! You don't have any new allergies I don't know about do you?"

"Ah," said Agnes with a triumphantly wry smile, "You'll have to wait to find out!"

On their third and final visit they presented us with a little fruit bush on leaving. Despite sending a Christmas card that year, as we do to all our regular guests, we heard no more of the Misses Douglas, but the fruit bush gives us a sweetly-tart reminder of them each year.

Very, very rarely did we have a guest who was cold or unfriendly. Some arrived perhaps exhausted, or shy, or awkward but invariably, after tea and fruit cake or a shower and change of clothes and a warm through by the log stove (or all of these) they would thaw – literally and metaphorically – relax, and exchange a few pleasantries:

'Where have you come from today?'

'Have you had a good journey?'

'More tea or cake?' were usually good places to start.

By the end of their visit it was not unusual to have had someone's entire biography relayed to us.

Only once can I remember a visitor who was so unsociable it was as if he was encased in a block of ice. Walking the entire 247 miles of Wainwright's Pennine Journey on his own, he arrived late one afternoon carrying a very large pack. We only had him booked in with his surname and he seemed surprised and even reluctant to give us his Christian name. He accepted the usual offer of tea and cake with a brusque, "Yes. Thank you." and gave the same response when asked if he had enjoyed it. Being so used to highly complimentary comments on the wonder of John's fruit cake (and often requests for the recipe) I was a bit miffed and mentally labelled him as churlish. The same economy of words was employed for all subsequent queries:

"Is your room all right?" – "Yes. Thank you."

"Can I get you anything else?" – "No. Thank you."

"Do you need more coffee?" – "Not yet."

"Did you have a good night's sleep?" – "It was all right."

He retired to bed early, arrived down for breakfast at exactly the moment he had requested, ate everything he had ordered. Shortly after, his kit all packed and ready to go, he knocked on the kitchen door and said, "Can I settle up?"

And then he was gone.

We said goodbye, thank you, hope the weather is kind, trying not to sound as offhand as he had been, and he set off at a cracking pace down the hill, never glancing back.

We found his visit oddly discomfiting – yet, why? He had certainly not been rude or impolite in any way, though brusque and impersonal and at all times avoiding eye contact. Had we any right to have expectations of our guests' manner or mood? After all, surely the sole purpose of a bed and breakfast is in the name; a place to sleep and a stomach to fill before leaving? But Hill House East always offered and in return received so much more, without which, it would have been just another anonymous motel. Maybe that was the problem for this guest; maybe he found social interaction difficult or even excruciating. Maybe he liked anonymity and being unnoticed. He had no doubt booked with us because there we were, conveniently at the end of a section of the Pennine Journey, and had not expected to be the only guest that night, the sole focus of our desires to be welcoming and hospitable.

And thus insufferable.

So we decided to learn from the experience, to try and judge better what it was people were wanting from their stay under our roof and realising that these expectations could vary wildly. My always vivid imagination conjured up endless scenarios of why this man was so self contained; lack of friends, loss of friends, bereavement, a life of disappointment? Probably none of these. Probably it was just the way he was and he was quite comfortable with it. Yet, as he set off, checking his watch, making notes on his map, determined, committed to the many days of hard walking that lay ahead, I still sensed that he was carrying something heavier than the weight of the large rucksack on his back.

192

I had expected that the average guest visit would see them arriving no earlier than late afternoon and being tucked up in bed no later than 11.00 pm, so that we could do likewise soon after. Breakfast was something that would occur between 7.30 am and 9.00 am. Surely? Reality proved to be generally, yes. But there were always exceptions. When the house was full of guests staying to attend a local wedding, we would have been a long time in the land of nod before they fumbled with keys in the front door. And it was not so much breakfast the following morning but brunch.

"What's the latest you serve breakfast in the morning?"

"Oh, usually nine o'clock."

"Nine!" they would groan, "Could you possibly make it later please? Say ten? Ten thirty would be better! I expect we'll have a very late night!"

And softies that we were, and if we had no other guests due the next day, we would say, "Alright, we can do ten – but no later!"

Actually, come ten the next morning, some of those breakfasts were really easy to prepare comprising just endless cups of coffee and paracetamol on the house.

The opposite could also occur. We once had a pair of delightful nuns who stayed the night prior to attempting that famous half marathon, The Great North Run. Although Newcastle was some forty miles away they just hadn't been able to find accommodation any closer, so popular was the event. This meant that in order to be there at the appointed time before the race they would have to leave us before six in the morning. The issue of breakfast arose. At first the good Sisters would not hear of us getting up at such 'an unholy hour' to feed them.

"But Sister, you cannot attempt such a thing on an empty stomach!"

"Ah well, we can make tea in our room and maybe have a biscuit or two."

"We insist; we couldn't rest thinking of you doing that. No, breakfast will be served at five!"

A compromise was finally agreed that they would take porridge, tea and toast at the unholy hour, but nothing cooked.

The nuns, Sister Perpetua and Sister Mary Antony, were both teaching Sisters in a big Catholic school so they were not of the cloistered variety. Only the short veils covering their hair, their mid calf dark skirts, thick stockings and sensible cardigans distinguished them as belonging to a religious order; there were no long black robes or white wimples.

"Um, have you taken part in such an event before Sister?" I enquired before they retired to bed.

"Oh no! Never before! But we thought it would be a good way to raise funds for a project at the school."

"And, may I ask, have you been training for it? It's a long way you know, thirteen miles."

Sister Perpetua considered this before answering confidently, "Well not exactly training but we have both been walking much faster around the school these last few weeks, haven't we Sister Mary Antony?"

"Oh we have!" Sister Mary Antony agreed, "Much faster! But we don't intend running do we Sister? No, we will just put one foot in front of the other till we reach the end; the Good Lord will provide!"

Next morning on the stroke of five they came down to breakfast, both attired in black tracksuits, trainers and their short black veils. They consumed their porridge heartily, gave us thanks and blessings and drove off well before six.

"Sisters!" I called as they were pulling off the drive, "You will let us know that you get safely to the end won't you?"

I think John and I then went back to bed. Three days later though, we got a neat little note saying they had got to finish line with sore feet but in good heart; the Lord had been with them every step of the way.

Ever after we thought of them fondly as our 'Nuns on the Run.'

17

THE ADAMS FAMILY

A ll of our guests were nice people; some were extra special and went on to become regular guests and good friends. Hill House East was not the sort of place that would actually attract anyone looking for a rave up of a weekend, exciting night life or somewhere to be anonymous on a furtive tryst. It attracted people who were walking or cycling in the area, exploring the beauty of the Durham Dales, visiting friends or families or in the area on business. Sometimes, local people used us when they hadn't enough rooms to accommodate guests themselves when there was a wedding or other occasion. We had been advised that any Bed & Breakfast, however small, really did need a website if it wanted to attract visitors in the digital age and we were blessed to find a very patient, very understanding web designer called George who produced exactly what we wanted to convey a truthful picture of what Hill House East offered to guests. It must be said that we did not expect this development to ever attract attention beyond the North of England.

I was surprised therefore to receive an email enquiry in which simply said:

'Do you have rooms in August?

Linda Adams.

Oregon.'

I thought that in fact this must be a hoax or one of those 'spam' things I'd been warned about, perhaps because it was the first enquiry we had ever had from the USA. Nevertheless I wrote back:

'Dear Linda, if you could inform me when in August you need rooms and for how many people and for how long, I will be pleased to see if we could accommodate you.

Thank you, Carol Graham.'

A reply pinged back the next day:

'Dear Carol, Certainly! I need a family room for myself, my sister and my son and a double for my parents and we only need one night, August 6th. Thank you for your help – Linda.'

This posed somewhat of a problem, as I already had a Russian friend staying with us that week, but I was so intrigued that I was determined not to be beaten:

'Dear Linda, I am afraid we do not have a family room, only a double room for your parents and a twin bed room for you and your sister. I could, however, provide a cot or child's bed in your room for your son – depending on his age? Would this help? Kind regards, Carol.'

Almost at once I received -

'My dear Carol! How very helpful you are! The Lord thank you for your kindness but my son is twenty seven! However he is a real outdoor sort of guy and he says that he sees that you have fields and he would be really happy to camp out under the stars. So bless you, yes, book us in! In gratitude – Linda'

This whole exchange was now becoming somewhat surreal and beginning to remind me of the 1987 film 84, Charing Cross Road with Anthony Hopkins and Anne Bancroft, where an American author strikes up a lifelong friendship with a book seller in London, which arises out of a letter with a single enquiry:

'Do you have a book by ...? '

'Dear Linda,' I emailed back, 'You know, under the stars in August in Weardale can be wet, cold and miserable! We do however have a lovely snug summer house in the garden, which has heat and light and I can put a camp bed in there for your son if he would be happy with that? Also, though I don't want to pry as to why you and your family are passing through from Oregon for just one night, as I already have a friend staying and will be cooking for her, may I also invite you all to eat with us that night so we can get to know each other better? My friend is Russian – so it should be quite an international evening! And, oh, do you all eat lamb?

Warm regards, Carol. '

This completely opened the flood gates and resulted in an epic email which began-

'My dearest friend Carol – What can I say? I am overcome by your kindness! Let me tell you a little about us. Do we like lamb? OMG, we are a family of Macedonian Greeks!!! My father, Jim...'

It transpired that this family group, comprising Linda, sister Debra, son Travis and her quite elderly mother and father were indeed on an odyssey back to the land of their origins, as her father wanted to see the village of his birth one more time before his life's end. They could have done this the easy way by flying to Greece but no, like the labours of Hercules, they had decided to make an epic journey of it and were going to fly to Ireland, pick up a people carrier, 'see' that country in a couple of days, take the ferry to Scotland for a couple of days to assimilate what it had to offer before driving down to see the dreaming spires of Oxford. From there they would cross the channel and leapfrog across Europe in their 'family bus', dropping in on countries that they wanted to see before, finally, arriving at the family village in Macedonia. They would not retrace the journey by vehicle; it would be left in Macedonia and they would fly home.

(Did rental companies actually do that, I wondered?)

Somewhere in the grand plan someone had decided that the drive from Scotland to Oxford may require an overnight stop, a finger had hovered over the map of Great Britain roughly midway and jabbed down on Weardale. A B&B enquiry was inserted in the computer and... up popped Hill House East. The Good Lord had undoubtedly guided that finger Linda emphasised; something like that was no coincidence – it was a 'Godincidence' and she already knew in her heart that our short time together was meant to be and that we would become the dearest of friends. Her son Travis, who worked as a missionary for their church in the Dominican Republic, also felt that finding us was a true blessing and they simply could not wait to meet us in person.

And that is truly how a one line email unfolded.

The absolute truth.

It left me, in the weeks running up to the visit with a mixture of curiosity, disbelief and more than a little anxiety.

On the appointed day, my Russian friend Galina and I roasted two legs of Weardale lamb, prepared a mountain of vegetables, the biggest trifle imaginable and waited.

The phone rang mid afternoon.

"Carol! Oh my gosh, is that really you!"

"Linda? Where are you?"

"Well, we are near a town called 'New Castle'; say, do you know where there is a laundrette in that place – we've been on the road a week now and, sheesh, do we have laundry to do!"

"I'm sorry, I wouldn't know where to begin to direct you to a laundrette in Newcastle Linda; it is just too big!"

"That's OK – guess we can use the one in your 'Wear Dale'!"

Oh God, oh God, oh God!

"Well now Linda, I'm afraid Weardale is too small to have one!"

"Oh dear."

"But, just get yourselves here, with your washing, and we can do it here tonight."

"Are you sure? There are five of us you know!"

"Just get here; and phone again if you can't find us!"

A little over an hour later the phone rang again.

"We have made it to Westgate! The satnav says go straight on – but we seem to have come to a river?"

"Well, actually it is a ford, so yes, just drive straight over and head up the hill, over the crossroad and you will be here!"

She sounded somewhat doubtful; "You want us to drive through the river?"

"The ford; yes, it'll be okay, honest!"

A male voice in the vehicle shouted "Okay, I'm on it; here we go!"

The phone was apparently left on because the next thing I heard was a medley of screams; male, female, young and old, ranging from excited to terrified.

"Oh God!"

An awful thought had just hit me, which I shared with Galina.

"You know that really heavy rain we had last night? Well, the river could be well up, the ford could be flooded; they could be swept away!"

Galina replied in something dark and Russian and we both shot out of the house to run down to the river to see whether our guests were now bobbing down the River Wear towards Durham.

What stopped us before we got halfway down the hill was a large people carrier with water streaming off its bonnet and doors, wipers swishing frantically.

Doors opened and people started climbing out, right in the middle of the road.

First to reach me with arms wide open was a cuddly brown haired lady with a smile as broad and warm as midsummer.

"Carol!"

I was squeezed so tight and with such genuine affection that I could hardly breathe, on both counts.

"We've found you! Thank God! I feel I know you already!! Oh – here's my son Travis – and this is my sister Debra – my mom Anne and my dad Jim!"

"I am so sorry about the ford! You know, I've just been so excited about you coming I forgot about the heavy rain last night!"

"Hey!" smiled Travis, a tall, dark haired, well-put-together and extremely good looking young man, "Know what – that's the most fun we've had since we left home!"

I am not sure that his elderly grandparents shared his view but they were polite and gracious in the extreme.

"OK! Grab your luggage everyone; I'll sort the laundry as we go in! I got them all to put it in separate bags from their clean stuff last night," Linda confided to me.

An organiser! Who thought ahead! About the important things in life – like laundry; we were going to get along just fine.

The Adams family began to stream into the house like a file of leaf cutter ants, all bearing their burden of bags.

Linda stood at the back door directing operations.

"Our room Debra. Laundry, laundry. Mom; that's laundry, Dad take that bag to your room. Your bag Travis; laundry. Laundry; my room…"

It was like watching Denty shedding sheep after they had been gathered for clipping.

Eventually, all the laundry made its way to our little utility room and Linda stared with disbelief when I pointed to the washing machine and suggested she started loading.

"Yes, I know, it looks tiny! My American friend Judy once told me they had a larger one in their camper van! But don't worry; we'll get through it all in time."

Though used to the enormous top loading machines that everyone has in the USA, Linda smiled gratefully and began loading up. Every hour of the afternoon, evening and up to bed time required a check on the laundry, a transfer to the drier – "*Jeesh!* That's dinky too!" - and a reload. The process began again very early the next morning almost to the point they were due to leave. Whilst the laundry marathon was in progress our houseful of guests relaxed, drank a socially lubricating quantity of wine, chatted, laughed and generally got to know one another. Nose twitching, salivary gland teasing smells of roast lamb and garlic wafted through from the kitchen and tummies rumbled. Debra, Linda's sister, was having a photo frenzy, dashing everywhere and snapping her camera at everything – even the lambs' legs roasting in the oven. The house and its contents were described as, 'Amazing! Gorgeous! So quaint!', the garden and our views, 'Wow! Awesome! So beautiful!' The summer house, which was to be Travis' roost for the night was inspected with gasps of delight and renamed 'the Adorable Cottage!'

Five Americans, one Russian and two Northern Englanders shared a memorably huge and convivial meal, well washed down with yet more wine. Oh that those nations could always share such friendship and warmth; perhaps more roast lamb and trifle is the key to world peace? We all found out interesting and amazing things about one another; that Linda, Galina and I were all teachers, that Linda and I were both teachers of students with special needs, that Travis had the biggest appetite of anyone I had ever met. I was stunned that such a lean, fit young man could pack away so much food, but helping after helping disappeared with relish.

"Can you help me with this Travis dear; I have too much meat!"

"No problem Grandma!"

Linda patted his arm with maternal indulgence.

"You know, when he is living and working at his Mission he has to live so frugally. So, we like him to get stoked up when he gets the chance."

Travis beamed and took another helping of trifle.

After dinner, taking advantage of our long, northern summer's evening, Travis set off for a yomp up our hill to see the fells at the top, striding effortlessly as though the steep gradient simply was not there. Debra took off in a flatter direction with her camera, Anne had a rest, Jim couldn't resist the lure of John's workshop and Linda and I... well, we discovered something rare and precious. I have few truly close friends; those I have are much treasured and tend to have been in my life for a very long time. To discover someone with whom I shared exactly the right chemistry, with whom I felt I could confide with complete confidence, with whom I could share a good laugh, or a cry on such short acquaintance surely couldn't be possible? But that we were drawn to one another, across so many miles and by such unlikely circumstance, was undeniable. That a fully committed member of a very Bible based evangelical church, complete with electric guitars and drum kits in their services, could find anything spiritual in common with a very non doctrinal Quaker, used to sitting in silent Meetings for worship, just did not make sense. Yet, we talked and talked until we just had to give in to the call of our beds.

Before they retire for the night, all our guests are given a form that lists all of the items that are available for breakfast the next day. They are of course free to put a tick against as many items as they would like. But, before the Adams family visit, no one had ever ticked everything on that menu. We viewed the line of ticks marching down Travis' form the next morning and wondered if he had understood it. Then we remembered his prodigious appetite from the night before and decided that he may well have done. And, after all, the customer is always right. After he had tucked away the preliminaries of fruit juice, fruit and cereals we began to serve the cooked breakfasts. I found I had a logistics problem; with two large sausages, two bacon rashers, two fried eggs, mushrooms, tomatoes and baked beans on his plate I simply had nowhere to put the three egg cheese omelette he had also ordered.

I stuck my head round the door.

"Travis, did you want your omelette before, during or after the rest of your cooked breakfast? I am having trouble getting it all on one plate!"

"Oh, just stick it on top; that'll do fine thank you."

And it did do him just fine and dandy and every mouthful went. I was about to clear the cooked breakfast plates away when he got his eye on a lonely sausage sitting on his Grandma's plate.

"Can you not manage that Granma?"

"No dear! Too much for me!"

As the speared sausage headed towards his plate, I looked at the empty toast racks; all three of them.

"Could you do with some more toast with that Travis?"

"Oh, thanks, that would be great; there are all these lovely preserves of yours to try!"

His digestive marathon has been known ever since as the Travis Challenge and no one else has attempted it.

Inevitably, after breakfast, bags began to make the return journey to the 'bus' and then came the time for the people to go with them. There were many hugs, kisses and back pattings as they piled in. Linda and I held each other's eyes because the words were hard to find.

"Oh, I wish you…"
"I know."
"Maybe someday…?"
"I shall hope and pray so."
"Keep in touch!"
"I will."

Then their vehicle was heading down the hill, turning away from the ford this time, and they were gone; continuing their odyssey heading across Europe and on to Greece, their less than one day stay with us having been decreed by the fates and the stab of a finger.

They left behind a ridiculously large amount of cash for having done their laundry and a warm and vivid place in our memory.

"Such nice people," Galina declared.

I hugged her arm; she had become a dear friend through another chance meeting, when I went to Russia on a teachers' exchange.

"They were a very special family; I would have loved to have spent more time with them."

Galina shrugged her shoulders in the universal expression of 'who knows?'

"Perhaps you will," she pronounced solemnly in her grave Russian way.

And indeed, since that one night stand with the Adams family we have been reunited twice in Oregon and once here, when Linda came to us for a wonderfully unhurried two week visit. Future visits are planned to visit in both directions for as long as we are blessed with health and indeed life; after all, we are both getting on a bit! But, having found this precious friendship quite late in life, we fully intend to share it as much as we can.

'Do you have rooms in August?' Who could imagine what that simple question led to? As Linda is prone to say, "Put your trust in God; he does all things for a purpose".

18

WALTZING MATILDA

Occasionally, though not often, we were blessed with visitors from the New World at Hill House East. Although sharing the mother tongue of English with these guests, sometimes it wasn't quite as we knew it. This was not a problem of vocabulary or dialect, rather one of tone, inflection and social niceties. This led us, at the time, to think that some of our New World visitors were a bit curt, outspoken or maybe even slightly discourteous – all right, rude – but we began to realise the problem probably lay with us – all right, me - in that I had been drilled in the good old English school of manners, manners, more manners. Say please and thank you in every sentence and, of course, do not discuss things of a personal nature with someone unless you had known them just about from birth.

The railway line that once took passengers from Wearhead at the top of the Dale to the metropolis that was Bishop Auckland, thence to Darlington and thence... well... to the world, had been closed since Doctor Beeching swung his axe. There was enormous excitement in Weardale when it was announced that the line was to reopen; admittedly not exactly to the world, but along a six mile stretch between Stanhope and Wolsingham. This wide gauge line would boast vintage carriages and diesel engines, as well as that holy grail of train spotters - a real steam engine! It would encourage a host of visitors to the Dale and lead to a huge expansion in the tourist economy. The project was hoping to receive a lot of funding from America, where there were apparently quite a lot of wealthy people who still had an abiding passion for old railways and trains.

With a huge fanfare in the local press, a weekend of events was planned when the hoped for American investors and their entourage would visit to take a look at Weardale and its railway line. It was a large party; most of whom were to stay at a nearby country house hotel guaranteed to tickle the fancy of transatlantic visitors, but overflow was needed. Could we accommodate two of the party?

I assured the owner that we would be delighted to.

I was actually earthing up potatoes in the garden when a long, low, shiny black car purred to a halt. The driver swiftly opened the back doors for his two passengers. One was tall, hawk eyed and somewhat unnerving when he cast his penetrating gaze over the house and then me but did not say a word. The second man was smaller, moustached and seemed rather on edge. Cases were removed from the boot by the driver and placed in the house. I wiped my hands vigorously on my gardening trousers, uttered the usual pleasantries- 'Hello!', 'Have you had a good journey?', 'Welcome to Hill House East', 'Let me show you to your rooms!'

None of these statements seemed to elicit a response, as the moustached man was in conversation with the driver and the tall man was still scanning everything with a penetrating gaze. Finally, in an almost resigned way, he simply stated, "OK; where do we go?"

The accent was broad American; not western, not eastern but somewhere in the middle I guessed.

"Just follow me!"

I led them upstairs, where their accommodation was viewed wordlessly.

"I'll leave it to you to decide who has which bedroom; your bathroom is the door between them. Can I offer you a cup of something once you have settled in? Tea? Or coffee?"

"Coffee?" the word was spat out with a derisory snort, "Haven't had a decent cup of coffee since I left home. But I sure as hell can't drink tea, so I guess I'll have to risk it."

Man number two nodded in meek agreement.

"So, home? Where would that be – or should I say which part of the US?"

"Chicago."

Nothing else was forthcoming so I risked an, "Oh! That's a long way! My name is Carol by the way, my husband is John; you'll meet him later. As you can see I was gardening – the weather is so nice; would you like your coffee out in the garden?"

"Mmm." said Mr Terse.

"That would be great," said Mr Timid, "And I'm Mike by the way and this is Mr... this is Don." "Well, it's nice to meet you; I'll go and get the coffee. And perhaps a piece of John's famous fruit cake? To keep you going till you go to eat with the others tonight? I'll leave you to settle in." I had just made it back down the stairs when Mike appeared close behind me.

He looked anxious.

"Could you explain the bathroom protocol?"

I'd never been asked that one before.

"Well, there is no protocol really; it's your bathroom for you both to use during your stay."

"Just the *one* bathroom?"

"Just the one I'm afraid; this old house won't expand to create ensuites."

"OK. So what's the towel protocol?"

I was puzzled: "Is there a problem?"

"Well, there are just those tiny towels by the washbasin; do we share those too?"

Mike was flustered and embarrassed.

"Good heavens, no! Those are just hand towels if you need them when you've washed your hands. You'll find you each have a supply of large, fluffy towels in your rooms; you may be sharing the same bathroom, but you certainly don't have to share towels!"

"Oh God!" I was thinking all the time I made coffee and laid out a tray, "Oh God, God, God! This is going to be it; our first awkward customers! I don't think they even understand what a 'B&B' is; they look more like five star hotel types."

John appeared in the kitchen door; "I take it our guests have arrived?"

"And then some! They are going to take a lot of pleasing I'm afraid. They have already pronounced English coffee undrinkable and telling them they have to share a bathroom was like telling them they are spending the night in a doss house! Please come with me while I take this tray to them in the garden?"

Our guests were sitting on a garden bench with faces that betrayed nothing.

"Here we are! I've made you a big cafetiere, and there is plenty of cake." Glances fell suspiciously on the creamy white sticks propped up beside the wedges of cake.

"Oh! And that's Wensleydale cheese – a mild, creamy cheese from the Yorkshire Dales. It's customary to eat cheese with fruit cake in these parts; the sharpness really offsets the sweetness of the cake."

Their faces plainly read, "We are in Outer Mongolia and we are being offered rancid yak butter."

I poured the coffee.

"This is my husband, John: John Graham."

At last Don's face registered interest. He replaced the cup he had been sipping from.

"Graham? Did you say *Graham*?"

"Why yes; that's us - Carol and John Graham."

A broad grin split Don's face.

"Hell no! I've had my people checking out my ancestry and, guess what! I come from Graham roots in Scot- Land! That's right Mike isn't it?"

Mike nodded vigorously.

I decided it would not be politic to disclose that John's roots were probably not descended from the Scottish clan, but from the Border Reiver Grahams; the most wicked, devious terrorists of those violent times. Better to let him think they were distant cousins from the

Highlands I instantly decided. Or even better, *close* cousins. While Don expounded on his family history with enthusiasm Mike was tucking into John's fruit cake. In a moment of abandoned recklessness, he picked up a stick of Wensleydale and inserted it into his mouth, along with a bite of cake. A look of sheer astonishment crossed his face, swiftly followed by one of pure delight.

"Good, isn't it?"

Wordless, he just closed his eyes and nodded his head slowly.

"So," I ventured, as cracks did seem to be appearing in the ice, "I take it you are here because you are connected with this new Weardale Railway venture?"

Don took a long draught of coffee and something approaching amusement crossed his face.

"Sure; I like trains. I'm involved with a few railways over in the States."

"But, dare I ask, why are you staying here? Why are you not staying somewhere with fourposter beds, room service and all the trimmings?"

"Ah hell, I didn't want to stay along with that circus; told them to find me somewhere on my own. Well, apart from Mike here; he sort of sees to things for me – that right Mike?"

An enthusiastic, "Yes sir, sure thing!" finally clarified their relationship.

"So why don't you go find out what time we have to go 'eat and greet' at this place tonight Mike?"

"Yes sir!" and Mike was off, as Denty would say, like a sheepdog in pursuit of a lost yow.

Don took a last drink from his cup, pursed his lips and nodded slowly. "Good coffee."

We took it as a great compliment.

By the next day I found I could even tease Don a little and that he relished it. So, on the morning they were leaving and the driver was loading their luggage into the boot of the big shiny car, I was brave enough to say, "So, back home to Chicago eh Don? Mmm, I hope there is a violin in that long case he is putting in the boot and not a sub machine gun?"

He smiled enigmatically and tilted his head as if to say, "You'll never know!"

The railway project proved to be a troubled one that did not, in the end, result in hordes of tourists chuffing up and down the Dale in steam trains; though there are still some enthusiasts who live in hope.

One blazingly hot June day, a great rarity in these parts, I was wilting languidly under the canvas canopy in the front garden awaiting the arrival of two walkers, when I heard a bell tinkling very faintly. I thought at first it was my overheated brain, but no, slowly and steadily the sound grew nearer. Then, around the corner walked a short, grizzle bearded man with a barrel of a chest, an even larger belly and calf muscles like prize vegetable marrows. He had a heavy looking pack on his back and the heavenly tinkles, I realised, came from a small brass bell on one of the straps. Dressed in serious looking walking boots, heavy drill shorts and a bush hat, he was a man that looked hot and tired; sweat was pouring down his face. I had no idea *who* we were expecting as guests because this booking had been made by a travel company that specialised in long distance walks; all I had was names and dates. This single walker most likely was one of them I decided, and got up to greet him.

He dropped his pack on the ground and before I could get a word said "Hill Haa-ses?"

I nodded opened my mouth again but was cut off with a loud, heartfelt, "Streuth! That's a baa-ger of a moor to get over ain't it?"

I got in this time, "Certainly is; especially in this heat! What can I get you? Water? Tea? Coffee? My name's Carol by the way; and you are?"

"Beer? Dunno if that's possible, if not, tea. Lots of it and weak, really weak. And I'm Jack; Stu's on his way. Christ knows when he'll arrive; too busy stopping to look at birds and flowers. Tea? Lots!"

By now he had removed his boots, socks and shirt and had collapsed on a seat in the shade. Taking the 'tea' as an imperative, I excused myself to go and make it. Although his appearance was uncannily like a cross between Father Christmas and Crocodile Dundee, it was his accent and the iconic expletive that marked him as an Aussie; perhaps he *was* the

Australian Father Christmas, taking some downtime out of season? All he needed was some corks round his hat brim to complete the image of a swagman in dire need of a billabong.

By the time I took out a tray laden with tea, fruit scones and homemade blackcurrant jam, his walking companion had arrived and was wriggling his bare feet in the grass. Stu was as tall and thin as Jack was short and wide, his beard as neat as Jack's was unruly. He was dressed much the same as Jack apart from, incongruously in the heat, a woolly pompom hat.

"This is Stu; Christ, that tea's brown! Waa-dar – bring *cold* waa-dar; big jug!"

By now I was beginning to feel like pouring a jug of water over him; the man had not said a pleasant word since he arrived and Stu hadn't had a chance to say anything at all. I returned with the water just in time to see the last of what had been two large scones, well laden with butter and jam, disappear down his throat. He filled his teacup - which was about an eighth full of tea - with cold water, knocked it back, refilled it, swallowed that and sat back with a contented smile.

"Y'know, on the rigs, I made my own tea with a litre of hot water and three dips of a tea bag; me mates said it looked more like cat's piss than tea!"

"Well I like weak tea too; my mother used to call mine Maiden's Water." He roared.

"Well, a bit more ladylike than me I guess!"

"Just a bit."

The ice was broken.

"Say, it's a beautiful place you've got here, and those scones – or is it sc'ow'ns? – bloody gorgeous; life savers."

"Mmm," mumbled Stu, his mouth still stuffed and his beard full of crumbs.

"Well you're eating at the local pub tonight; you'll get well fed there. And, if you like beer..." He patted his belly as if to say, 'Can a platypus swim?'- "... He brews his own; it's called 'Weard -ale'."

"Weird ale? What's weird about it?"

"Nothing! I hear it's a great beer, but you are in Weardale here – the valley the River Wear flows through – and it is just a play on words. In the same way, of course, those of us who live here are all 'Weardalians'!" He roared with laughter, even louder than before.

"I think it's time I showed you up to your rooms; you can fight over who has the double bedroom and who has the twin."

Stu was ecstatic.

"Rooms? Did you say rooms? One each? Dear God, a night without listening to him snoring!"

"Bah!" Jack said scathingly, "Too soft, that's his trouble, not used to sharing quarters. Now on the oil rigs... Well, you slept where you could, when you could and with whomever else was in that bunkroom and bloody glad of it. This bugger has been jumping ship some nights on the trip cos he 'can't get to sleep'; I've found him sleeping out on the landing a couple of times! I'll take the single; give him a treat in the double. Oh, look at that! A barth; a proper barth!"

And so the ablutions began for this unlikely pair of fellow travellers. I retreated to the sanctuary of my kitchen but it was not long before there was a tentative knock on the door. I opened it to find a worried looking Stu in his vest and underpants.'

"I can't get the shower to work!" he said anxiously.

Don't let it be broken, not today, I pleaded inwardly, but said,

"Well that's strange; it was fine this morning; all you have to do is press the large button in the middle. Do you mind if I come and look?"

He padded upstairs behind me.

"I pushed and turned everything," he confided.

"Hope you are decent; I'm coming up!" I yelled as a warning as I went up the stairs and a loud laugh came from Jack's room; normally we never go upstairs when guests are there. Stu had indeed pushed and turned everything; the temperature was so high that the thermostat had cut the shower off for safety and the pressure was turned down to its lowest. I

212

reset it for him and then noticed a soggy heap in the bottom of the shower cubicle.

"Socks?" I enquired

"Yeah, I reckon they needed a rinse through."

"Pants?"

"Yeah; well they were going in when I got in," he mumbled.

"How on earth do you expect them to be dry by morning? I'll put a laundry basket on the stairs and put anything you want washed in it. And tell him too!"

"Will they be dry by bedtime? I'll need my pyjamas."

"When's bedtime?"

"Ten o'clock sharp," Stu said, still obviously worried about having his pants (figuratively) whisked away.

"Don't worry; all will be dry by ten o'clock. And tell your friend the laundry service is free - but I charge for scrubbing backs! Oh, and air your boots on the hearth by the stove; they will be more comfy – or at least less smelly – by the morning."

I retreated once more to my kitchen feeling rather like a matron at a prep school, checking up on the personal hygiene of her small charges. Then there was a very loud rap on the door and I opened it to find a beaming Jack handing me a full basket of washing, wearing only a bath towel tied somewhat perilously round his waist – though, I use that term figuratively as well, as he didn't really have one.

"Barth salts?"

"Sorry?"

"Barth salts? Any barth salts?"

"Sorry Jack, only the bath foam on the side of the bath."

He gave a derisory snort, mumbled "A bit poncy, but it'll have to do", turned round to reveal two plump, rosy, hairy buttocks sticking out of the towel and stomped upstairs. When he came down again he was surprisingly fresh and tidy in a fresh shirt and cotton trousers.

"Stu's givin' the pub a miss; says he's too tuckered out to eat a meal or go out again."

"Oh, well he'll need something; I can always rustle up a sandwich for him."

"Naa...says he's got cheese & crackers somewhere in his backpack. Christ knows what state they'll be in but he'll be quite happy. Between you and me, he's a bit on the, shall we say, frugal side, is Stu," Jack lowered his bushy head conspiratorially, "Not used, shall we say, to the better things in life? His wife died a few years back now and I don't think he looks after himself that well."

"Is he an old friend of yours?"

"Christ no! Only met him once before this trip! I belong to the Bungawalla Bush Walking Club; gave a talk about doing a long distance walk in England a couple of years back and how I hoped to do the Pennine Journey? Well, this bloke comes up and says he'd like to do it too. That's how I met Stu."

"But you seem – if you don't mind me saying - a bit of an odd couple to be doing this together; do you think you'll last the course?"

"Well I tell you, I dunno if he will cope, but after life on the rigs I can get on with anybody when needs must. Streuth, I've got a thirst! What's happened to that lift to the pub?"

John set off down the hill with his hungry, thirsty passenger and I began to sort through a basket of clothes to wash. The evening was cooling rapidly, as happens at our altitude no matter how hot the day, so John had lit a fire in the stove and Stu settled in front of it to write his journal, refusing all offers of food though accepting a cup of tea.

"Will you have to wash all that bedding in our rooms after just one night? Or do you just steam it or something and use it again? And do you do it yourself or do you send it to a laundry? Seems an awful waste of water, energy and time to do all that when someone's only spent a few hours in the bed?" Stu seemed very concerned about the ecological ethics of running a B&B.

I assured him that yes, his bedding would be washed, as well as his towels and that I did it all myself.

"After all," I said, "You wouldn't want to sleep in sheets that had been used by someone else would you?"

Stu did not seem entirely convinced by this argument.

Just before ten o'clock I produced a basket of clean laundry, still warm from the drier, which contained amongst other things Stu's pyjamas and some of the biggest pairs of underpants I have ever seen.

"It's washed and dried," I told Stu, "And I could make a fair guess of what is who's but I'm going to leave it to you to sort it."

He took the basket gratefully and padded upstairs and was, as he had said he would be, in bed by ten. It was a lot later than that when John got the call to come and retrieve Jack from the Hare and Hounds; it seemed he had taken quite a liking to the 'Weard-ale'.

Next morning, even though John is always up very early to get things ready for guests' breakfasts, Stu was up long before him, picking his way quietly up the hedgerow and garden, camera in hand, snapping at every flower and bird he saw. Jack appeared, none the worse for wear it seemed, promptly at the appointed hour for breakfast.

"Your teapot, with maidens' water, sir and Stu's with proper tea."

"Thank you ma'am," said Jack, quite meekly.

"Did you both sleep well? Were you comfortable?" – The standard enquiry.

"Dunno; was asleep, so I must have been I guess."

"I, uh, I just slept on top of the bed," Stu added, "So you won't need to wash those sheets."

"That was unnecessary but very thoughtful." I told him.

Jack shook his head in disbelief and just as I was disappearing back into the kitchen I heard him patiently explaining, "That spoon's for your grapefruit, not your tea Stu; that's why the edge is serrated, to cut through the pieces, see?"

When I'd finally finished replenishing the toast rack for Jack, breakfast ended and it became time for goodbyes. They were both tying on their walking boots in the porch when Stu suddenly asked, "I see you've one of those bee-days in the barthroom? Is that because you have a lot of French visitors? I've heard they like those bee-days, the French."

Jack visibly winced, as if fearing what was coming next.

"Well," I replied honestly, "It's there for any guests that want to use it; but remember it's our bathroom when we have no guests and I have always been very partial to a bidet myself!"

"So what do you use it for?"

Jack shook head slowly, "Yer digging deeper Stu mate; yer gonna sink any second."

"Well... My granddaughters delight in calling it the 'botty washer' but it's actually very useful for all sorts of things - such as washing your feet or soaking your smalls!"

"Oh," said Stu, sounding only partially satisfied.

"I told you he'd led a sheltered life," said Jack sadly, then, "Right, come on Stu, let's get this bloody show on the road while it is daylight."

"Why the bell?"

"Sorry?"

"Why the bell on your rucksack? Is it to warn people you are coming?"

I said this with humorous flippancy.

Softly Jack told me, "It's for my wife, my lovely, lovely wife. She died just over six months ago but I promised her I would do this walk. The bell is her; with me every step I take."

Warm, fat tears filled his eyes and rolled down plump hairy cheeks. I hugged him, kissed his cheek on a beard that was soft as silk and smelt clean, warm and comforting.

"And I am sure she is, Jack, I am sure she is."

We watched them walk down the hill, one surefooted boot after another, rucksacks swaying, until the soft tinkle of Jack's bell became imaginary.

19
SPRING VISITORS

Spring arrived in 2019 in its usual sporadic, infuriating way that took us from summery giddiness one day, to frigid, dark wintriness the next. Mid February gave us a couple of freaky 'rip-your-vest-off' days in the mid twenties while, just into April, we plunged overnight into freezing iciness and four inches of snow. This did not amuse Teasel, our Teeswater sheep. I adored my Zwartbles but one can get tired of spinning rough, itchy wool which in turn knits into hardwearing but itchy jumpers, all of course in black. I longed for something soft and silky and white so that I could dye it whatever colour I wanted. I saw my first Teeswater at a Woolfest gathering locally and fell in love at first sight. A rare breed I was told and local – just from over our hill into Teesdale. It was a big sheep with a coat of silky ringlets which hung down each side almost to the ground and, endearingly, dangled between her ears and over her forehead like a permed fringe. I was shown samples of the carded wool from said sheep; it was a silky, lustrous white with the texture of angel's breath about it.

"Lovely nature," I was told, as the sheep batted long eyelids beneath her curly fringe, "And it just so happens, I've recently weaned her off twin gimmer lambs... and I can deliver..."

Indeed Teasel was lovely, gentle and was happy with the Zwartbles and gave me a beautiful shearling fleece the next summer. In the autumn, the week after the first frost, all the wool simply fell off her back and rump, leaving it entirely bald and weirdly shiny, rather like an undercooked pork sausage. Each spring her wool grew back but only very short and useless. Every autumn it all fell out again. The vet scratched her head, finally pronounced an undiagnosable alopecia and sent us her bill. As she grew I had to purchase a succession of personally tailored, quilted, waterproof but breathable coats at considerable expense to protect her naked back from the elements; that single fleece I got from her cost me very dear. We had removed her coat by mid March because of the clement weather and so the April shower of the thick and white variety landing on her warm and shiny back was not received well; we found her in the morning, her large, soft eyes baleful yet accusing. Of course, two days later the snow was all gone and you could just about hear the grass growing.

Easter was very late that year, right at the end of April, and the entire Bank Holiday weekend – an event which is almost guaranteed to bring bad weather – astounded the nation with three days of clear blue skies, no wind and record temperatures. Even at our altitude the air temperature reached 23º C, whilst the outdoor thermometer on a south facing windowsill reached a blistering 38º C. With everything bursting out of their pots in the greenhouse I decided to plant out my lovingly nurtured runner beans, peas and sweet peas; after all, it was nearly May, the earliest date I usually dare do this. The May Bank Holiday followed very swiftly on the heels of Easter. It brought with it rain, wind and an overnight temperature that plunged into heavy frost. We were warned about this and I expressed my concern for my tender, fledgling plants to Alan, who lived by the river and was passing our garden on one of his long, daily walks.

"Noo… divvent worry about yer beans; tough bloody things them are." Surveying the blackened, frostbitten tips the next morning, I was filled with regret and remorse and also wondered what superhero varieties Alan must plant. In a classic 'shut the stable door after the horse has bolted' act, John and I carefully protected them with bubble wrap the next night – only to find them sweating profusely next morning in glorious sunshine. You really cannot win up here, where the weather delights to be fickle, unreliable but never boring. The old adage, 'Never cast a clout till May's right out' is probably the best advice. Now I know this, but... desperation to believe we have seen the last of winter makes one impatient. Like a slow, reluctant learner I was, after twenty years on our hill, gradually internalising the fact that spring is not the end of winter here; it is a long process of often halting preparation for summer. And don't hold your breath that that will be up to much either.

Some things, however fickle the weather, do occur annually and reliably as a reassurance that we are heading out of the cold, dark months. The most obvious of these is of course the lengthening days and then there are the lambs, which emerge wet and warm into a world that is often wet and cold and yet mostly thrive and grow and scamper and blare up and down the Dale. The most joyful, the most soul uplifting sound and sight for me however is always the return of the curlews. Their long mournful call, which builds towards such a glorious climax, never fails to stop me in my tracks and look up, goosebumps rising and spine tingling, with awe and gratitude that they have made it safely back. As their numbers decline so worryingly over much of the British Isles, how blessed are we to have them on the high moorlands of County Durham. To be able to stand in our garden and watch them swoop and circle and defiantly call out on the skyline of our own field; how priceless is that? And equally welcome and an equal joy are the lapwings, the redshanks and the snipe who, at dusk, swoop and dive above us uttering their eerie, vibrating sound. Upper Weardale is one of the last sanctuaries for these spectacular species.

Another equally welcome seasonal visitor, of the very hardy variety, tended to arrive in early May. We would spot her wearily but steadily plodding up our hill, towing an equally weary – and very reluctant - heavily set horse. On the top of this large mare was a pack saddle, to which were strapped many bulging bags and a canvas pouch, out of which stuck the head and forelegs of a tiny Jack Russell terrier, obviously well happy at not having to toil up the hill.

Jane, Diamond and Dinkie had arrived at the end of the first day of their annual trek to Derbyshire and back to Northumberland.

For perhaps five years or more we have witnessed this annual trip, at first with curiosity and astonishment, and later with great admiration. Jane was a diminutive lady to whom it would have been hard to put an age - though elderly seemed somehow an insult. She wore an unusual assortment of clothes, all perfectly suited for her outdoor life on the road; heavy leather walking boots, knee length  wool stockings, trekking trousers hacked off just above the knee (with what appeared to have been a penknife), several layers of padded or waterproof apparel, that could be taken on and off to suit the weather, and a very old, battered riding hat. She also wore a pair of yellow tinted goggles, one eye of which was blacked out with a patch. We were later to learn that this was because some years earlier one of her cows had taken her eye out with its horn. As we got to know her better, we also learned that on her pack saddle was absolutely everything she needed for herself, the horse and the dog; with the exception of top-ups of water for all three and grass for the horse each night. In that compact space were her tent, flysheet, sleeping bag, spare clothes, cooking and eating equipment and supplies, first aid kit and even tools for emergency shoeing problems or saddlery repairs for the horse.

The first year we saw her go past we had nodded politely and said hello; the second year she actually stopped to speak and we patted the horse and learned that she was on a round trip to Derbyshire to visit family and would camp that night in a neighbour's field at the top of our hill. The following year we assured her she would always be welcome to camp in our field, where there was plenty of grass and water.

The year after that, she took up our offer. The neighbour up the hill had moved on and sold the property to someone who had their own horses. In no time at all, the horse was untacked and rolling with pleasure in the grass, her tent was up and her little kettle boiling. She politely but firmly turned down any offers of food or drink, saying all she needed to know was where the outside tap was. Next morning we got up early to make sure she was alright but not early enough, as she was already packed up, tacked up and ready for the off.

Her arrival the following year, was on a cold, wet and windy late afternoon; a real clashy day, as Denty would say. I decided on a firm course of action.

"My word, that was a hard first day! Is it alright to put Diamond in the field and camp for the night?"

"Of course Jane, just turn her out. But... there is no way you are sleeping in a tent in this weather."

"I'll be fine," she insisted, "I'm well used to sleeping out in this."

"I am sure you are, but there is a much better alternative."

I think she was worried I was going to say she must have a room in the house; she knew we were a B&B and therefore had guest accommodation.

"No," she said firmly, "I'll be fine."

"Just please come and look in here," I persevered and led her to the Hemmel, "See, there is a clean wooden floor to sleep on, there's a tap and sink, a gas cooker and a wood stove if you need it. There is even a sponge mattress we can put down for you. It would make us sleep easier if we knew you were in here – and you wouldn't have to pack up wet things in the morning."

Jane looked around, nodded and let down her defences.

"Well, that's very kind. I don't want to be any trouble..."

"It's no trouble at all," I assured her as Dinkie, her little dog, trotted inside and sat happily on the rug, "And look, Dinkie is quite settled already!"

Dinkie was a dear little dog who never left Jane's side. She had been born with deformed front feet which were oversized and turned outwards at right angles to her legs, so that she looked like a very small, old fashioned, cast iron bath. Jane had taken her under her wing and they had been together for eight years. Riding in the pouch on the pack saddle allowed her to accompany Jane on her epic trips, although even a Jack Russell with sound limbs would have found it hard to do the mileage Jane and the horse put in each day. Once again, Jane refused any offer of food or drink and prepared her own food. However, as she was all ready to leave the next morning, I pressed a bag into her hands.

"Just a couple of hard boiled eggs and a twist of salt, oh, and a bit of homemade bread; it's a gift from the hens, not me!"

She smiled, accepted the bag gratefully, and set off with a wave, towing a morning-stiff Diamond up the hill with Dinkie grinning at us from her pouch.

A few weeks later we received a letter from Jane. She had completed her trip successfully, was now back home and all was well. Would we like to call in some day and have a soup and bread lunch with her at her cabin? A phone number was given.

We were delighted to accept and set off, intrigued, on the appointed day. The address and directions were rather vague; a very small hamlet in Hexhamshire, which seemed to boast a pub but little else. We found the pub and enquired as to where we could find the 'cabin'.

"Oh, are you going to see Jane?" beamed the lady behind the bar. "Up the track behind the pub, you'll come to a gate, go through, up past some wooden buildings and she's at the top."

And so she was. We went up a track with buildings on either side which were showing signs of age and disuse. We learnt later that these had been the buildings from which Jane had run a riding school for many years. At the end of the track we came to a wooden hut of modest size, which stood on wooden legs with steps up to a door. Wood smoke issued from a chimney pipe at the rear.

Jane greeted us warmly, "So you found us; come in, come in."

'In' was a very compact space, yet one into which Jane had managed to organise all her living needs as efficiently as when she trekked with a pack horse. There was a small wood burning stove giving out cheery warmth to the whole cabin. There was a cold water pipe laid on to a small sink and a compact Calor gas cooker. The bare minimum of cooking pots and utensils hung above it and a very small cupboard housed her entire supply of crockery. There was one armchair by the fire, covered in rugs, and a bench seat with a lid that lifted for storage ran the length of the opposite side below a window. Lunch was delicious; mugs of a hearty vegetable and lentil soup, ladled steaming into mugs from a pan on the cooker with an equally hearty rye bread that Jane had made herself.

"I make all my own bread, can't be doing with that shop stuff."

We learned more about Jane as the afternoon wore on. Her family had owned the house and farm on the hill above where she was now. But it had had to be sold and the family had dispersed, though Jane had managed to hang onto the two large fields in front of us, some woodland and her beloved riding school. Presumably it was at this point that she began living in her cabin.

In an age when we are all guilty of over and needless consumerism; at a time when we all eat too much and exercise not enough; when we all require so much energy to power the 'must have' items that dominate our lives; then, if all the technology, cars and supermarkets were to disappear overnight, Jane is one of the few people I know who would be able to cope without noticing that much of a difference.

She cuts her own firewood for her stove and has no electricity, so has no fuel costs. She has no car, she has a horse. She keeps two cows which supply her with all the fresh milk she needs and also keeps hens for eggs. She grows a large vegetable garden each year, so has her own fresh produce. Her fields provide winter hay for the horse and cows. Most remarkably of all, we learnt that Jane was seventy seven. We left, not just a little in awe, but also somewhat ashamed at our own efforts at 'sustainable living' which are, frankly, pitiful in comparison.

The one 'mod con' Jane allows herself is a telephone and we were pleased, though a little surprised, when she phoned the next May to say she was just setting off on her travels to Derbyshire and would it be all right to stay overnight. I was surprised because she had admitted, when we visited her, that with waning strength and energy she did not know if she would be up to a trip the following year.

"You will be very welcome Jane, we would love to see you, but on condition you sleep in the Hemmel; we are having some really cold nights at present and the days are not much better. At least spare yourself getting cold and wet your first night out."

I went to tell John that she was on her way to us and his response was, "That's great, but what about the tups in the field?"

"Oh Lord! I had forgotten about them."

Christopher's tups, not being 'at work' at the time were grazing in our bottom field and this was the field that Jane would use to graze Diamond for the night. But there was no way we could let either of them in whilst the 'big bad lads' were in there. So, heavily armed like riot police with sticks, though not quite shields or tear gas, we got them safely moved back across the road for the night and the field was safe for Jane when she appeared about 6 pm, plodding wearily up the hill. To our surprise she was not leading Diamond; she was riding her with Dinkie alongside in her canvas bag. She climbed wearily down and, before she had time to argue I said, "Perfect timing Jane! I have just put a quiche, some new potatoes and salad on the table; you will join us won't you?" Unlike previous years she did not refuse but, as any true horsewoman would do, however tired, saw to the needs of her mount first. After her meal she went over to the Hemmel which was warm and welcoming. I noticed that by nine o'clock the lights were out. My parting comment to her had been, "You will join us for some scrambled eggs before you leave in the morning Jane?" having decided that saying things as a statement rather than a question was the best means of persuasion. So well fuelled with eggs, toast and marmalade and tea, she tacked up Diamond, somehow managed to secure her bags and Dinkie on top and set off, pulling a very reluctant horse up the very steep hill. She intended to make it to Cotherstone in Teesdale by teatime, where there was a field she was always welcome to camp in. Watching her determined, plodding figure disappear slowly up the hill John shook his head and said, "How does she do it? I brought those bags out of the Hemmel for her and I could barely lift them!"

225

The weather was cold and grim and by teatime, a steady miserable rain was falling.

That year Jane was seventy eight years old.
She was already planning another trek to Dumfriesshire in the autumn.

By 6.30 pm we had finished our tasks for the day and I had just retired to the sanctuary of the conservatory to read a book, have a glass of wine and look out at the awful weather just on the other side of the glass. I was warm, snug and almost smugly protected from what was going on outside. My thoughts kept straying to Jane and how far she had got and whether she was warm and dry in her tent when the phone rang. Groaning, I wrenched myself off the sofa.

"Hill House East," I said in a polite 'phone voice'.

"Oh hello, that is the B&B isn't it? We are a couple of cyclists, touring and camping, and we have just pulled into the Westgate Campsite. But to be honest, it is such an awful, cold, wet night we can't face sleeping in the tent. Would you by any chance have a double room available?"

Now, as it happened, Sarah had just been that morning and we had changed all the beds for guests later in the week and she had given them and the bathroom a good going over.

"Well, we weren't expecting any guests tonight, but as a matter of fact we do have a room available; when do you want to come?"

"Now?" came the swift and desperate response.

By the time John had the stove lit and I had flown round seeing to towels and so on they were up the hill, stowing their bikes for the night and very soon after tucking into tea and fruit cake in front of a roaring log fire.

"It's not fit for a dog out there tonight," the lady cyclist said.

I thought of Jane under a flimsy sheet of canvas, Dinkie stuffed down her sleeping bag for warmth and Diamond with her ample posterior braced against the wind and rain.

I shook my head, smiled and said, "No, it isn't really is it?"

226

20

ANCESTRY

There had been one category of guests whom we welcomed over the years that we had never really imagined having when we first opened our doors as a B&B; the ancestor hunters coming to seek their root stock, from which many branches and seeds had sprung over the years. One such couple coming could have just been a fluke but, by the time we had had three or more couples booked in for this specific purpose, I realised there must be more to it. Most of our ancestor seeking guests seem to come from the New World; America, Canada, Australia, New Zealand. What drew them all to Weardale was that they all had ancestors who had emigrated from here. It is with shame that I admit that my knowledge of the reason for, and the scale of, those emigrations was limited. Yes, I knew that this had once been one of the largest lead producing areas in the world and the ruins and remains of that were clear to see in the Dale, although they were now softened by time into an almost romantic part of the landscape. So I tasked myself to learn more and found that there was nothing romantic at all about those ruins, or the lives that were ruined with them.

Some history is called for. The hills and valleys of Weardale have an extremely long history of mining and quarrying; it is thought that the Romans mined for lead and possibly silver in the area around two thousand years ago. From the twelfth century onward, all the Weardale mines had been granted to the Bishop of Durham who, along with the Rector of Stanhope, was to profit from them greatly for centuries to come. Lead mining was always firmly linked to farming; the earliest miners were probably farmers first and miners second because of the irregular, uncertain income that came with lead mining.

The price for lead rose sharply in Elizabethan times to supply the demand for lead shot, roofs and windows and, as a result, the mining industry in the Dale also increased. And the mining was not just confined to Weardale; lead mining was the principle industry over to the north in Allendale and over to the west in Nenthead. The land around the three lead producing counties of Durham, Northumberland and Cumbria, where they meet at a point on the fell tops not far from Westgate, was known as the Lead Triangle and it was the greatest producer of the mineral anywhere in the world at the time. The demand for lead rose sharply again in the mid nineteenth century because of domestic demand – remember all water pipes were made of lead at that time - and the Napoleonic wars. This was the height of the Weardale Lead Rush which, like the Klondike Gold Rush brought a quickly soaring population with the need for dwellings and land. Water power was harnessed to mechanise draining systems and crushing plants at the mines and the Weardale landscape was changed forever by the spoil heaps, the ditches, sluices, dams and water wheels. Whereas the local miners had been farmers first, the new wave of families moved to the Dales as miners first and they had to make their homes on increasingly higher and less productive land, sometimes almost up on the fell tops themselves, which provided a very poor living. The term should really be smallholder rather than farmer, as their small amount of land and livestock were often barely sufficient to provide for the basic needs of their families and they needed both incomes to survive; a desperately insecure way to live.

In his seminal work on the history of Weardale, its people and their lives, 'Clearing the Forest', Peter Bowes personifies the hard working, desperately underpaid and undervalued life of a Killhope miner of the time who says, wryly rather than bitterly, in a Wardle accent even thicker than Denty's : 'Duz te know onny weer else which hez see monny farms wi twee yikkers and a coo; and nowadays leed's little mair value er snow iv a dike back.'

This translates as –

'Do you know anywhere else that has so many farms with only two acres and one cow? And these days lead has little more value than snow lying at the bottom of a wall.'

In the Killhope valley, the largest centre of lead mining in the Upper Dale only 3% of the population were aged sixty or above; more than half were under twenty one. The average age of death at Killhope was twenty two and the most usual cause was lung disease, especially tuberculosis. I know that 'hope' in the place naming sense in Weardale means 'valley' and thus Stanhope, Rookhope, Swinhope and Harthope and so on. But what does Killhope mean? Whatever the true meaning, could that place ever have had a more evocative name?

The early 1870s were the economic boom time. The land and mine owners profited both ways by getting the extra miners they needed and by getting rent for land and accommodation. The valley between West Black Dene and Brotherlee in the Upper Dale had a very high population density at this time, probably ten times that of the present day, particularly around Westgate, the largest settlement in that area. The tenant holdings there were only around ten acres or less and this would have to support the family's livestock all year, including land set aside to make hay for winter feed. And it would have to support the family as well, at a time when families were large; five, six, seven or more children. A wonderful character who became my close friend when I lived in Eastgate in the 1970s was the diminutive Willy Watson, who hailed originally from 'Up Dale'. He would have been born in the 1890s I expect and came from a farming family. He was one of thirteen children, his mother having had two sets of twins within eighteen months at one point; she in fact gave one set away to a sister who was childless. He recalled hard times. The children had no shoes to wear most of the year and a long walk to school. His mother took in extra sewing to make money so that they could have wooden soled clogs to wear in the winter. The teacher at the school discriminated against those pupils who wore clogs rather than leather soled shoes, saying they were 'awful clattery things' and made the wearers leave them in the porch and sit in the coldest part of the classroom. I am sure a lot of the lead miners' children had similar hardships to face - though perhaps the boys had to have boots by the age of twelve when many went to work outdoors, in all weathers, on the ore washing floor at Killhope.

The end, when it came, was shockingly swift and very cruel. In 1882 cheap Spanish lead flooded the market, the price plummeted and rendered mining in Weardale uneconomic. It was W B Beaumont - 'the largest mine owner in the world'- who had to shoulder this drop in value but, in addition, he had the extra financial burden of rents and royalties to the Church Commissioners for his Weardale mines. He requested that they lowered his rents and put in a sliding scale of royalties so that he could afford to keep the mines open and the miners in work. The Church Commissioners, acting for the Bishop of Durham, reminded him that he had made handsome profits for himself out of the mines over the years and declined his request. Thus at one stroke of genius the Church, often accused of neglecting the welfare of the souls of their parishioners in the high reaches of the Dale, now brought about the total loss of any income on which they could support their bodily needs - and of course cut off their own income from the mines in the process. The Church Commissioners' hold on the mineral wealth of the Dale continues to this day; only recently John and I, along with all the other property owners in the area, had to sign a document affirming that the Church continued to retain its rights over any minerals which may be discovered below our property.

In 1883 Beaumont closed all his Weardale lead mines. The result was swift and chilling; with no mine work there was no money for food and essentials nor rent for the smallholdings. The attendance at the Newhouse school, near Ireshopeburn, fell from 210 to only 80 pupils in 1882. In June of that year the school log book read; 'This school will be closed tomorrow owing to depression of trade in the Dale.' Another entry for that month reads; 'Thomas Bee withdrew - going to New Zealand.' His was one of the endless lists of families who left to seek employment in the coal fields of the North East or who emigrated to work in the lead, coal, zinc or gold mines of South Africa, North America, Australia or New Zealand. Families and communities were split apart, fields and homes abandoned; many decayed and became derelict well into the 20th Century.

The terrible losses of the First World War further stripped the Dale of strong, young men; those that did return to their families then had to face the terrible Spanish Flu pandemic that swept the world in 1919. Weardale fell into an empty, haunting decline. In the latter part of the century, many of the houses were bought up and modernised and used as holiday cottages or lived in by commuters and retirees: Incomers. Many had utterly incongruously flat roofed extensions put on, often paid for by grants from the council; Hill House East is just such a house and I am just such an Incomer. Many small farms simply collapsed and gently dissolved back into the rocky land from whence they had sprung; Christine Ruskin has carefully recorded these in her sadly moving book, The Disappearing Farms of Weardale. Of all the families that were forced by necessity to leave the Dale, Peter Bowes' final comment is, 'Most never returned'.

And indeed, most never did, though some did prosper in their new lives and their families thrived and grew in a way that probably would not have been possible in the lead mines of the Dale. It was the descendants of these families that did return; seeking information and understanding about their past relatives, who risked everything to leave the only area they had known for generations and travel to very alien shores.

Killhope to California? That would be a big culture shock now - but a hundred and thirty years ago?

Mr and Mrs Johnson were the first ancestor hunters to stay with us. They arrived on a mission to find out more about family who had lived and worked in Weardale; the Byers family. Their research to date had located them to Weardale and in fact to Westgate, which is why they had chosen to stay with us. The first person I put them in touch with was Ken Heatherington at the Weardale Museum. Ken had developed an incredible data base about the families that sprang from Weardale and was always happy to help seekers with their research. When they returned from seeing Ken, the Jones' were both excited and stunned; not only had the Byers family lived in Westgate – they had actually lived in Hill House East.

This was incredible, something beyond coincidence, and we were stunned too.

Edward Byers, a many times great grandfather born in 1745, had lived a very long life for those days and had died at Hill House East in 1820. He married his wife Hannah, (maiden name Kirk) in 1766 and they were living at Burnfoot, near St John's Chapel with at least two of their four sons in 1775. By 1810 they were living at Hill House East, not as tenants but as owners of the house and land and three of their sons had already left home; presumably because of lack of space in what was, at that time, a very small house. However one son, Thomas, born in 1773, married Hannah Vickers in 1799 and they continued to live with Edward and Hannah Byers at Hill House East and they had six children. My mind reeled; four adults and six children living in what was then basically a one up and one down accommodation? Sadly, though not uncommonly for those days, one of Thomas' six children, a daughter called Hannah like her mother and grandmother, died in 1803 aged two. Then around 1810 a series of cruel losses beset the Byer's family. First Edward's wife Hannah, the grandmother, died in 1810 aged around sixty five. That same year, Thomas and Hannah's last child Alice was born at Hill House East and in 1811 her mother, Thomas' wife Hannah, also died. Looking at the birth years of her children I worked out that the poor woman had had a child roughly every two years in her twelve year marriage and so, most probably due to ill health or pure exhaustion, had not survived the birth of her sixth child by very long. Sadly this was also an all too common tale of the time. The cruellest blow fell the next year, 1812, when her husband Thomas, whose occupation was put as miner, succumbed to the gruelling, health robbing demands of this occupation and died, aged thirty nine, a year after his wife. This, shockingly, was well above the life expectancy of a lead miner at the time. It left six orphans at Hill House in the care of a grandfather who had lost a wife, a daughter-in law and a son in three years. How Edward coped, aged sixty seven, is not recorded but presumably some or all of the grandchildren were farmed out to other family members, much as Willy Watson's mother had to do at the end of that century. Perhaps there were older boys in the family, maybe already working in the mine and helping their grandfather on the smallholding? There was no social security for a retired farmer in those days. Or was he retired? Had he also mined as well as farmed? I have seen records of men still doing some mine work at that age. He certainly went on living at Hill House East till his death in 1820, at the age of seventy five, and the house was passed on through the Byers family. The last record I have is of his grandson John Byers living here in 1851, although by 1861 he had moved down the hill to Shallowford.

When we had patched together all the pieces of this story I couldn't stop thinking about the little girl, Hannah, who had died at Hill House East in 1803. Suddenly, like a key finally fitting into the notches of a lock, I remembered something:

We had some very loyal B&B guests from Sunderland who came regularly to stay with us, Kay and David. Sometimes they brought other friends with them for the weekend. One such friend called Les was, Kay confided in me, a medium. Not a medium in the fairground, 'pay as you go', somewhat dodgy sense but a 'sensitive'; carefully trained in spiritual matters who only used his gift with those who came to him with a real need. He never charged money for this.

"I can ask him if you like? If you would like him to do a reading here, tonight, for us all?"

"Well, it seems a bit of a cheek when the poor man is here to relax!"

"Oh, Les won't mind; and it's better than watching telly! Les!......."

Of course John recoiled in horror at the whole idea but I am very open minded about such things. Les very willingly went off upstairs to quietly prepare himself and when he came back I spoke to him first. Most of what was said will remain between him and me but at the end he enquired if there was anything I wished to ask him.

"Yes," I replied, "My inner senses have always told me that this house is a very peaceful and benign place; I would like to know if you sense any spirits here at all?"

"I am aware of two, and yes, both peaceful and benign. One is actually a large dog that seems to go around sniffing under the doors! But there is also is a young girl present in the house; she is not distressed or unsettled, in fact she is very peaceful and happy here."

We have a good friend in the village called John. There are so many people we know called John that, because of his extensive knowledge on many subjects and his cultured accent, we call him 'Posh John' and he takes no offence. I told him about what had taken place with Les and our young girl presence.

"Oh my dear! Of course you have a presence! – I have often sensed her."

"You have? Where!"

"Well, if I go up to the bathroom she is often there at the top of the stairs; close to the bedroom door. Seems quite happy."

Now, with the knowledge of young Hannah Byers having died in the house, I put these clues together and felt as if a bucket of ice cubes was being poured down my back and my skin erupted with goose bumps. Hannah Byers who had died two centuries before? Was it possible?

Of course there was no way to definitively prove this. But then I received a letter from the Johnsons, safely back home. They had refined their searches further. I had found it a remarkable coincidence that they had been led to us in 2010 and found the house where her many times great-grandmother had died in 1810, exactly two hundred years before. Now it seemed we could be making even more remarkable links. It wasn't just the thought that it could be little Hannah Byers whose memories, if not actual spirit, lingered on within our walls that shook me; it was the dates that were contained in the letter:

Hannah had died on the 24th October 1803. I had received the letter on the 23rd October, so the next day would be the anniversary of her death. This was also the date of my mother's birthday, also our wedding anniversary and a few days before 'Halloween' or 'All Hallows Eve' or the ancient Celtic festival of 'Samhain', depending upon which spiritual direction you come from - but all pointing to the time of year when, traditionally, the veil between this world and the world beyond is considered less opaque.

So, the next night, the 24th October, I put a small vase of garden flowers and a lighted candle at the top of the stairs for our small but unseen spirit, whom John and I have decided to think of as little Hannah, as we feel strongly that this is who it must be. The door at the top of the landing leads into a guest double bedroom now but, of course, in the early 19th century there would be no door there and, had there been, it would have led straight into thin air as the extension, which lies beyond, it was not built until the 1960s or 70s. What would have been there in Hannah's time would have been the outside wall of the house, a wall which would undoubtedly have had a window in it at about that point. If Hannah does like to be there, is it to look out of the window I wondered? Perhaps to look up the lane that still winds up the hill to Swinhope and the old lead mine at the top? Perhaps to look for someone coming down the hill, someone returning home from that mine which now, long deserted, still delves wet, cold and dangerous into the hillside?

The candle shed a warm light that picked out what colour was left in the last flowers of summer and threw their shadows against the old wall of the house and all were at peace; the house and its occupants of the present time and those of times long past.

Another couple who stayed with us on the trail of their ancestors locally were American. Stuart was the one linked to the Coulthard family in Weardale, many members of which are here to this day; Evie had no need to search far for her ancestors. When she wrote her surname in the visitors' book I couldn't help but say, "Einstein? That's an unusual surname; I don't suppose you are...?"

"Related? Yup, he was my great grandfather!"

It turned out she was a professor of some highly technical science or other; so I suppose some things do run in families!

Anyway, we helped them explore for their Coulthards over the next few days and what great people they were to be with. They found out everything they needed to and much more. The high points were finding and photographing family graves in St. John's Chapel church yard and visiting the large but semi-derelict house in the ancient hamlet of Swinhopeburn, where Stuart's family had once lived. On the public footpath this is less than a mile from Hill House East, in fact you can nearly see it from here. So it is not a great stretch to think that his Coulthards and the Byers of Hill House East would have at least been on nodding terms.

Our most recent descendants that came and stayed with us to look for their roots were not in fact looking for a Weardale connection; they were looking for his Hetherington descendants and he, Ken, was my heaven knows how many times cousin - though he and his branch of the family had lived in Australia for several generations. He had found me via that fount of genealogical information, the Ancestry site, and, as they were visiting England, decided he would come to meet the person with whom he shared three times great grandparents and look up the area where the family had once lived, just over the Durham border from us in Northumberland and Cumbria. The split between our two branches of the family had occurred exactly two hundred years previously when John Hetherington, 1790 – 1837, and his wife Mary (nee Robson) 1796 – 1857, married in Haltwhistle, Northumberland. They had a large family that included a daughter Margaret, born in 1819, and a son Robert born in 1821. This is where our ancestors split off, as Robert was my second times great grandfather and Margaret went on to found Ken's line. Margaret, quite shockingly for those days (or was it?) had two illegitimate daughters, who were largely brought up by their grandmother as 'Robson

Hetheringtons'. The youngest of these, Dianna, an unusual name for the time, was born in 1841 and married a man surnamed Graham. It was their daughter, Margaret Graham, born 1867, who married a coal miner William Millington and emigrated to Australia. And it was this Margaret Millington (nee Graham) whose granddaughter, Bobette, was Ken's mother. What a ravelled and tangled ball of wool our ancestry was and yet, go back two hundred years and we sprang from the same source. Was Margaret shamed and shunned by her community for her two illegitimate daughters? Or was it of no more consequence then than it is now? Could she have imagined her descendants would live and prosper in Australia in a way they could never have done in the coal mines? What did Robert Hetherington think about his illegitimate nieces? Did he even have the time or energy to care after a long shift digging coal? Could he have imagined that his great granddaughter, Elsie Hetherington, daughter of a pitman, would marry an officer in the Colonial Service and go to live in a splendid house in Nigeria, complete with servants, where she would eventually give birth to me?

A very tangled ball of wool indeed.

I took Ken to see the tiny hamlet of Blagill, just over from Killhope and into Cumbria; Jane Walton, who became the wife of Robert Hetherington (Margaret's brother), came from there. I wondered what our shared ancestor Mary Hetherington (nee Robson) of 1796 would have thought about her descendants - both prosperous and unimaginably wealthy by her standards and now living at opposite ends of the earth - getting out of a motor car to see where her son's wife had lived? Could she have seen us she would most likely be terrified, having no points of reference to the life she lived then at all.

We spent a lot of time discussing those mafia terrorists of the sixteenth century in these parts, the Border Reivers, to which the Hetherington family ignominiously belonged – though they were never as bad as the murdering, pillaging, havoc wreaking Grahams! I recommended all the essential reading on the subject, especially the authoritative work, 'The Steel Bonnets' by George MacDonald Fraser and I told Ken of my frustration that the Reivers didn't quite seem to have made it over the hills into Weardale; an odd thing to want for the poor people then, but they do carry a sort of dastardly romance about them! That the Hetherington family at some point spread this way is undoubted, as witnessed by Ken Heatherington and his brother David from the Weardale Museum. Yes, their name is spelt differently but several variations have developed over the years. The following year we had a request at short notice for Ken's first cousin April and her husband Mario to drop by while they were in England; Ken had simply told them they must see Weardale, they must see Hill House East and they must *meet me* – as I was also her heavens knew what cousin. They were delightful and the bond was quickly forged and the separating generations slipped away when she said on meeting me, "Oh my God! You're Carol? Good Lord, it's like looking at Aunty Pam!! And is that your daughter in that photo? No! She's the image of my niece!"

Then, just when I had given up trying to forge connections between Weardale and the outlaw raids of the Border Reivers, two things sprang before my eyes. While rereading Peter Bowes' 'Clearing the Forest' to learn more of the disastrous end of the lead mining industry, I read something I had not noticed before. He was explaining why, in the later sixteenth century the economy of Weardale had been in a rut for nearly two hundred and fifty years. The explanations for this were disastrous weather, restrictive land policies by the Bishops, the Black Death of 1348 and the 'Border Raids'. So, it would appear that there had been reiving in this part of County Durham. Shortly after this I looked in the local newspaper and there was a property for sale a mile and a half from here, up Harthope, which was advertised as being 'a former bastle house'. The bastle house was the first line of defence against the Reivers that ordinary farming families had; wealthy families had their peel towers to retreat to in the case of a raid but the less fortunate had to rely on their bastle house to protect them. Bastle houses are a type of construction found along the Anglo-Scottish border, in the areas formerly plagued by Border Reivers. They are fortified farmhouses, characterised by security measures against raids, such as extremely strong stone walls up to a metre thick and small or arrow slit type windows. The family would live on the first floor and reach the ground by a ladder, which would be pulled up inside the house at night. Their valuable animals would be herded into the ground floor and kept safe behind massive doors in the event of a raid.

The name 'bastle' is said to derive from the French word 'bastille'.
Was this the confirmation that the animal rustling, the pillaging of goods and the murderous fighting associated with the Reivers had gone on in Upper Weardale?

I chose to think so!
Of course, there is nothing to prove that the Hetheringtons or the Grahams - our own personal family baddies - ever reived around here but one thing I have never been shy about is letting my imagination have a good riot.

Family

21

THE LONG GOODBYE

During the first month of 2002, just after our second Christmas at Hill House East, as the lambs were growing safe inside their mothers preparing to struggle into the world, my mother was preparing to leave it. Everyone thinks their own mother is uniquely irreplaceable and I was no exception to this, though it took me longer than most to realise it.

My mother was in her eighty ninth year and had been in a nursing home in Crook in County Durham for nine years. That in itself was quite a feat, given that the average length of a stay in such establishments is three years. She had been widowed for nearly thirty years, my father having died at sixty eight, which now seems a cruelly early age. Parkinson's disease, brought on I am convinced by the shock of my father's death, had started almost unnoticed and then step by stealthy step had gradually robbed her of all her physical abilities. By the age of eighty she felt she could no longer cope on her own, even in the sheltered accommodation she had moved into seven years previously only a couple of miles from where I lived. So she elected to move into nursing care, still quite near to me.

"I don't want to be a burden dear," she said, in her always understated way.

My mother had lived a quietly remarkable life. Elsie Hetherington was born the daughter of a miner turned publican who came from a very long line of Hetherington miners in the coal fields around Bedlington in Northumberland. She met Norman Turner (who was nine years her senior) when she was just eighteen in the pub my grandfather, Joe Hetherington, managed. My father, and his whole family, had their stars ascending within British Colonial Nigeria and he worked in the Colonial Service as an accountant. His tours of duty were twenty two months long, followed by leave home to England for six months. This was in the early 1930s, when the Crown Agents appointed ten men for every eight vacancies to allow for natural fall out from tropical illness or even death amongst the men they sent out to the tropics.

Their courtship, during most of which he was in Africa, lasted four years and they were married in July 1936. Norman took his bride on a six week honeymoon to Belgium and Switzerland and then they sailed First Class on an Elder Dempster ocean liner to Lagos, where Elsie took over as mistress of a house with a full complement of native servants; before her marriage, the furthest she had ever travelled was to Scarborough in Yorkshire.

It was a new universe, let alone a new world, to a publican's daughter from the north east of England. Bravely she adapted and coped, managing to run the grand house with the sweeping drive that went with my father's final job promotion to Accountant General of Northern Nigeria.

She learnt how to manage the servants and maintained her gentle nature through the endless rounds of dinner and garden parties and the other trivialities of colonial life – including the wives who were social climbers or personal backstabbers. Then, thirteen years into her marriage, there was an even greater adjustment to make; she found she was carrying her first child. And so, with a mother aged thirty six and a father of forty five,

I came into the world just before Christmas 1949. And this is why I am called Carol. I am very thankful I was not a boy, as I would have been called Noel.

Elsie was a very caring mother and a dutiful wife. However, she showed a rare defiance of my father by refusing to send me to boarding school in England when I reached the age of six, as was the norm in colonial circles. Instead, she and I returned to north east England to live near the seaside town of Whitley Bay, where she had lived as a girl. There we lodged with an elderly widower called Mr McCoy, who was an old Masonic friend of the family, and I began attending the local junior school for nine months of the year, with an extended three month summer holiday in the mansion on Racecourse Road in Kaduna with my father and the retinue of household servants. I accepted, as all children do, that mine was a perfectly normal way of life. When a lady once asked me, "And where are you going for your holidays this summer dear?" I had replied with a bored sigh, "Oh, Nigeria as usual."

But the sun was setting fast over the British Empire; the red areas on my father's globe of the world beginning to recede like a fading blush. In 1959 Nigeria achieved independence and we all came, or more accurately were sent, home. It was to a very different way of life, a transition that must have been the hardest for my father. He had lived for over thirty years in Nigeria; now there were no servants, no vast compound, no house with a long sweeping drive. Now there was a detached, compact, modern house on the corner site of a middle class housing estate just north of Newcastle. My mother however, rejoiced in having her first own home in twenty five years of marriage and I was enrolled at an independent girl's school in Newcastle. School days, college days and then teaching days followed in what now seems very long ago. Through them all I was a dutiful daughter, somewhat in awe of my father and never really close to my mother in the very open, affectionate, sharing way I have with my own daughter. It just wasn't the way parents behaved then; they were parents, not friends and they seemed, frankly, so old. I was a teenager in the sixties; an era that really did sweep away many of the social norms of the past. My father was in his own sixties. I would moan the moan of the ages to my friends, "They just don't understand – they are so old fashioned!"

I married stupidly young, probably just in order to get some independence and freedom. The most unexpected thing that came out of that was that, as a married woman, my father stopped treating me as a child and for one wonderful year, I discovered him as a person; a man of great achievement but also of frailties that he had never even disclosed to my mother.

One night, aged sixty eight, he had a massive heart attack and died.

My mother, then fifty nine, had been entirely dependent upon and subservient to him through thirty seven years of marriage.

I was twenty three.

I knelt by his coffin at the chapel of rest weeping, begging him not to leave me with the responsibility of caring for my mother. It felt, at the time, like having Jacob Marley's chains attached to me to drag through life. Later, the selfishness of these thoughts would come back to haunt and shame me. The only excuse I could ever offer up was my youth and my lack of experience of the realities of life. I hope it will, one day go into the right side of the balance sheet of my life that, never once did I ever consider shirking my responsibilities towards my mother. Her independence gradually slipped away during the fifteen years after she gave up her own home. I moved her into a sheltered accommodation' flat only a couple of miles from where I lived.

At first, I was taking her shopping.

Then, doing it for her.

First walking with one stick, then two, then with a walking frame; finally not able to walk at all.

First helping her walk to the car, then taking her in a wheelchair to the car, then using a board to slide her into the car and finally unable to manoeuvre her into it at all.

For about thirteen of those years, I collected my mother on a Saturday or Sunday morning, took her home for the day and returned her in the late evening. When we got back to the nursing home in the evening she used to look at the 'poor old souls' lost in their confused memories, sat dozing in washable, high back chairs arranged around the edges of the lounge and say, 'Dear God, don't ever let me end up like that'. God, for some reason known only to himself did not heed her and the only mercy was that, by the time that she too was propped up in a chair with a rug over her knees in the final, devastating dementia of Parkinson's, she was quite unaware that that she had joined the ranks of those poor, lost souls. No actually, that was not the only mercy; the greatest mercy was that she never lost her recognition of me. To have gone to her and to have been met by unknowing eyes would have been utterly unbearable. As it was, in the last couple of years when it was almost impossible to get her out anywhere, I really began to hate and resent going to see her. Not because I did not want to be with her: I did. But it began to feel more and more pointless to go and sit, chattering about anything I could, most of which meant nothing to her and to which I got no reply, watching her shrinking, dissolving slowly into a bag of bones who stared hopelessly at me. What I really wanted more than anything, quite frankly, was for her to die; quietly, peacefully and with dignity, so that the ordeal would be over for both of us. One day, I felt so utterly hopeless and devastated by it all that, kneeling on the floor in front of her, I put my head on her lap and began to cry bitterly.

"I can't bear this; I feel so useless – there is nothing I can do to help you, nothing. You, of all people, do not deserve this"

I felt a featherweight hand on my head, stroking my hair.

"There, there. Don't upset yourself."

Her voice, though faint, was clear and calm.

"I've got a lot to be thankful for. Had a good life, had such good times, wonderful times. Come on now, don't get upset dear; I'm all right you know, I'm all right."

It was one of the few times we had ever been so physically close and it was the last lucid thing that she said to me and it was immeasurably precious.

At the end of 2001 there had been a couple of scares. The nursing home was under strict instructions to contact me at any hour of the day or night if she was giving cause for concern. They had twice raised the alarm and twice I had gone, sat by her bed, even slept the night there, and the next day she had rallied. I really did not know what was keeping her alive; she was eating practically nothing, her skin was almost translucent and was stretched tautly over her emaciated frame.

"I know this is a hard question," her carer said to me after the second scare, "But if it gets to the point that your mother has to go to hospital and be put onto a fluid drip to be kept alive do you want that to happen? Or do you want her to just have nursing care here?"

"No hospital," I replied at once. "She stays here. Till the end."

"I thought you would say that. And, if it is any help, I would do the same if it was my mother."

I knew at once when the third alarm was sounded at the end of the first week in January that this marked the end. My mother had always been very superstitious about things happening in threes anyway. There was no imminent end in sight, they said, but she was deteriorating rapidly.

A couple of days at the most they said.

When this had stretched into almost a week of my mother in a near comatose state they were disbelieving - how could she be holding on? I looked at the calendar; it was January 12th.

"She is waiting for January 14th," I told them, "Waiting for my father's birthday."

"What do you mean?"

"I'm telling you, she will die on the 14th; it was my father's birthday."

Where this absolute certainty came from I will never know, but it did.

On the 13th January I went straight from school to sit with her. She appeared to be just sleeping calmly but the nurses were very worried by her low blood pressure and pulse. By ten o'clock at night she was settled and the nurses suggested I go home to sleep – there was no great change in her. I promised to call in on my way to school the next morning. It was after 11.00 when I got to bed and I was surprised that I fell straight into a deep sleep. I was awoken by the phone by the bed.

The clock said 12.15am.

It was January 14th.

"Sorry Carol, I know you must have just got home and got to bed but there have been some sudden changes. She is very restless and in a lot of pain. We have given her morphine. Her colour is not good either; her hands and feet are rather blue. It's just that you left instructions to be contacted at once if…"

"I'm on my way."

John sat up and blinked as I was pulling myself back into my clothes.

"I'll get dressed and get the car out."

"No, please don't. I really, really want to do this on my own. Please let me."

"But you must be exhausted; you shouldn't be driving all that way," he protested.

"I'm fine, honestly I am."

And indeed I felt remarkably serene; quite energised and with spirits that were lifting rather than plunging.

John gave me an appraising look and said, "If you are sure?"

"Never surer."

When I got to her room, she was curled up in a foetal position, her breath quite rapid and rasping and making small restless movements with her hands and feet. The nurses made some checks on her and then simply left me in peace. I sat for a long while just holding her almost skeletal hand, feeling my warmth transferring to it.

I had taken my father's Bible with me. It still had the last marker he had ever put in it in place at the twenty third Psalm. I am not a Bible reader as such but the Book of Psalms has often brought me comfort: I can find despair, hope, love, faith, weakness and rage all in there. It gives me great support in times of need to know that nothing has really changed in the human condition in the last five thousand years. Someone, sometime, had told me that people who are dying keep on fighting death because they feel it is their duty to keep going, that others will be needing them to stay even when, in their own soul, they are weary of the fight and want to make their last journey. They need to be told that it is all right to let go, to be free of this world's burdens. I opened my father's Bible and read the twenty third psalm to her. The ancient words 'Yea, though I walk through the valley of death, I will fear no evil' shone from the page, as if my father had put the marker there so many years before just for this very day.

"It's all right Mum," I said when I had finished, "You can go now; I'll be alright, honestly. It would be easier for me to know you were free from all this. I can cope you know."

There was no reaction at all but I continued talking to her.

"It's January 14th today, Daddy's birthday. What better day for you to be with him again?"

Her breathing became less rapid and rasping and she became less restless, otherwise nothing changed.

A great tiredness came over me. I pulled my chair to face the bottom of the bed and put my legs across the bottom of her feet. That way I was in actual contact with her body and would be able to feel any movements she made. As I dozed in the chair I felt like one of the 'foolish virgins' admonished in the Bible because they fell asleep while on watch, who did not keep their lamps alight for the bridegroom coming. I was brought out of my doze by jerking spasms in my mother's legs. She began to moan gently. I pulled the emergency cord for the nurse and looked at the clock; it was 3.30am.

The nurse ran in and checked her pulse. My mother had turned over onto her back and I put my face close to hers. The nurse and I exchanged glances but nothing was said. Then my mother took in a long, deep, slow breath, gently exhaled and was gone. She had always said that she would willingly give me the last breath of her body and had been true to her word. I held her awhile but did not feel the need to cry.

I opened the window in her room to respect the old tradition of letting the soul fly out on its journey. I kissed her and left my father's open Bible on her chest. Then I walked out into clear, chilly January darkness feeling awed and privileged to have been with her at the end rather than grief stricken. I drove home gently down a deserted Weardale road on a clear, starry night and got back into bed.

'She's free" I whispered to John.

"Mrs Graham?" said the undertaker the next day, "I am sorry to tell you we cannot collect your mother's body just yet. She has been taken from the nursing home to Bishop Auckland Hospital for a post mortem. We can do nothing until they release the body; Mrs Graham?"

There was a bursting pain in my chest. I could hardly speak.

"Who gave permission for this?"

"The doctor is just following procedures; he reported her death to the coroner."

"I won't let this happen."

"I understand you are very upset at this time Mrs Graham, but it's a very usual procedure I can assure you and I am afraid there is nothing you can do to stop it."

"But why? This death wasn't unexpected; in fact everyone is astonished she did not die days ago. There is no need for a post mortem; I can't, I just won't let this happen."

As I put the phone down the sobs finally came bursting out of me, the first since my mother's death; not sobs of grief but sobs of rage.

John did his best to console me but I was inconsolable.

"Why?" I raged, "Why are they doing this? There is nothing unexpected, nothing suspicious about my mother's death; good God, the doctor has seen her every day for weeks now! I kept her away from the hospital exactly so that she could be spared any more indignity, any more interference... and now this! Now they want... to cut her up!"

The sobbing had nowhere to go but out and out it all eventually came. When it had finally subdued I repeated once more, "Well, I won't let this happen to her. It will not happen."

"Sweetheart, there is nothing you can do, honestly."

"I won't accept that either."

The phone calls seemed to take most of the morning, ricocheting between the funeral directors, the hospital and the Coroner's Court. Finally I found myself with the name of the relevant coroner and on the line to the morgue at the hospital.

"Hello, can I help you?"

My own nerves were very frayed by now and I had lost all my original bravado. With great effort I held myself together so that I didn't sound either too demanding or slightly deranged.

"I believe you have my mother there; Elsie Turner?"

"Yes, Mrs Turner. That's correct."

"My mother died through the night at her nursing home and they have sent her to you for a post mortem. I am imploring you, begging you, please don't subject my mother to this last indignity. She is in her 89th year and has had Parkinson's disease for nearly thirty years. She has been bedridden for weeks now, not eating and being visited by the doctor all the time. Everyone knew she was going to die. There is no reason to do this to her..."

"Well, I'm sorry Mrs Graham, but I'm afraid if her doctor…"

"Do you have my mother's body there now?"

"Yes, she is quite nearby as a matter of fact."

"Then please, I beg you, go and look carefully at what is left of my mother. Surely to God the question is not, 'What did she die of?' but 'How was this woman alive?'"

I heard a few steps, then there was a pause and the footsteps returned and the phone was picked up again.

"Yes; I do understand what you are saying. I will get in touch with her doctor and see if he feels this is really necessary."

"Oh, thank you. Thank you with all my heart."

I had no qualms about the ceremony at the church; I wanted it to be a celebration of her life, an opportunity for as many of her friends and family as possible to say goodbye. While she lay peacefully in the little chapel of rest in Stanhope I informed all the far flung Hetherington and Turner clans, organised places to stay for those travelling from a long way, began baking, cooking and freezing food, organised for members of a local choir she had loved to hear to sing at the service and organised flowers for the church. I took a picture of her on her wedding day over sixty years previously to the florist and asked her if she could copy her wedding bouquet. The only thing that was troubling me was the thought of going to the crematorium; I knew that this was the point, as she was finally taken from me, when I would find it hard to cope and I wanted to be as private as possible with my grief.

I confided this to Philip, our good friend and wonderful vicar.

"I know the usual form is to have the funeral service and then all go to the crematorium but I don't want that. It might sound selfish but I want it to be just us – John, Megan and I. But I can't say to all the others, 'You can all go home now.' For once, I really do not know what to do."

"What if," Philip said gently, "We have your mother's service, more of a memorial service than a funeral service, in the church on the Sunday afternoon and then you can take the family and friends home for some time with you. Your mother can lie in the church overnight and on the Monday morning we can go to the crematorium; just your Mum, Megan, John and I. How would that be?"

"That would be perfect Philip. Perfect; thank you."

Although it was mid January - and in Weardale that could have easily meant ice, snow, freezing winds or all three - the weather was calm and benign. Saint Andrew's church Westgate was half full; which was amazing, as it seated over 200. The coffin, adorned with a 1930s style bouquet of huge cream lilies and trailing, green foliage, preceded John and me up the church aisle. Megan followed us on her father's arm. Our marriage may have been long over but he had never lost his fondness for his mother-in-law and had wanted to attend. Despite it being so early in the year, I had managed to decorate the church with daffodils, the spring flower that my mother had always called 'Hope'. The singing was wonderful; the combined voices of the church choir and the Crook and Weardale Singers doing real justice to 'Guide me, Oh Thou Great Jehovah'. I kept my composure and did not cry through 'The Day Though Gavest Lord is Ended', nor through the delivery of my eulogy.

But I gave way to tears when Megan gave her reading; she was so poised, so calm, so completely grown up. She was twenty three, exactly the age I had been when my father had died. The service was everything I had wanted it to be in terms of a joyful farewell. Family and close friends came back to the house and were there till well into the evening, eating, drinking and remembering.

"I will be holding a vigil for your mother here later tonight, about nine," Philip had said as we left the Church, "Would you or anyone else want to come?"

Megan and I had to negotiate our way up the pitch black Church drive by the dim light of a torch. I thought Philip must have changed his mind as the church appeared to be all in darkness. But the door was open, we went in and he greeted us draped in his long, black woollen, clerical cloak. The church was icy, the heat of the afternoon service long gone. But it was not in darkness; there was a crescent of candles burning around my mother's coffin where it lay in front of the altar, their glow reflected in her lilies. The air was heavy with perfume – more than the scent of the flowers?

Incense.

Philip said prayers so ancient, so beautiful and so powerful that, though the words are lost to me, their effect never will be. It was as if all pain, suffering and indignity of age were stripped away from my mother; she could have indeed been the bride she once had been, lying there with her bouquet. Mostly we sat in utter stillness and in utter silence, as if the church itself was breathing for us, time itself stopped. Finally we realised that we were chilled through and that it must be very late. We got up and left in silence. Philip was still sitting in prayer and I will never know how long he stayed with my mother that night. Next morning, at the crematorium I had no dread of the last farewells. As the curtains finally concealed my mother's coffin from me I felt only peace and closure:

It was just an empty box.

My mother had no presence within it anymore.

Yes, she had been a worry, a responsibility and even, at times, a burden for so many years. But never as much as the worry and despair I must have burdened her with for most of my adult life, as I lurched from one medical and relationship crisis to another. She had never wavered in giving support, refuge, loyalty and love. I decided that there had been purpose in her long goodbye; it had given me time to move on from sheer loyal duty to genuine heartfelt love for my mother. When she was only fifty nine years old, the only man she had ever loved was suddenly, cruelly gone. It had been a long and very lonely twenty nine years, becoming even crueller as it passed. It would have been very easy for me to be angry or bitter or even despairing of any hope or purpose to life having witnessed her decline. In the end though, what I found myself filled with was admiration that, in journeying through those long, lonely years, my mother had shown such faith, patience and courage. She was never angry, never bitter and only occasionally despairing; her body gave up on her long before her spirit. She accepted bravely and even with humour each discomfort and disability. Her later life, apparently futile, had in fact a wonderful purpose to it as a focus and shining example of endless, selfless, unconditional love for both Megan and myself.

We both had a lot to live up to.

22

A COUNTRY WEDDING

We were in our fourth year at Hill House East. Four years of very hard work, restoration and renovation: all to create a home that we would love to live in and a house which guests would love to stay in. At last, by the summer of 2004, we were ready to open our doors and welcome guests.

Technically.

But something much more important was happening in the July of that year; Megan, my only child, was marrying her beloved Bernie. This was a once in a lifetime occasion for me (and I hoped for her) and I wanted it to be perfect; something really special. They agreed, or perhaps didn't dare say no for fear of breaking my heart, to be married in our church in the village; St Andrew. On the plus side for Megan, this meant the ceremony would be performed by Philip, our wonderful vicar who was a great friend and of whom Megan was very fond. We agreed on a day that would be traditional but not stuffy, relaxed rather than formal. We were renting the fields around the house at that time and there was a large area, just off the garden, that was flat enough to accommodate a marquee. As far as possible, we wanted a wedding that all of those who wished to contribute their talents to the event could do so, to make it very personalised. So a lovely neighbour who was an accomplished cake decorator, did fantastic things with sugar on the three tiers of cake that I baked. One tier had to be chocolate and nuts, my daughter having had a gag reaction all her life to all things that could be described as fruit, including the dried variety! In a style that Megan later described as a cross between a quartermaster and a sergeant major, I organised tables and chairs, crockery and cutlery, table decorations and flowers, invitations and menus, the wine and champagne and fridges to put it all in and all the other minutiae needed for a wedding reception in a field.

Ah yes, the Portaloos, I did not forget them.

The theme, perhaps surprisingly, was to be Scottish. Well, there is nothing quite like a swirl and a skirl and a glimpse of hairy thigh to make a wedding is there? Though a bit of a stretch from true Highland origins, seeing he was born and bred in Kent, as a lecturer at St Andrew's University Bernie was fully entitled to get married in the university tartan. So was his best man; so far, so good.

John? Well, of course, he is a Graham so that was his entitlement, though we found hiring a true Graham tartan proved difficult but it is actually much like Black Watch with a pale blue line running through, so that was the next best thing. Megan's cousins who were to be ushers were called Angus and Alexander, which was Scottish enough for me and her father's side had a Robinson line which provided a tartan for her halfbrothers. Her father however, though even closer to Scottish blood, insisted on wearing a grey tail coat. I think his formative years at a Colditz-like grey, granite boarding school in the Highlands, where he had to wear a kilt all the time, take cold showers and eat an awful lot of porridge had probably given him an allergy to them.

Think of Scotland and what colours come to mind? A palette of greys and blues and purples? Hopefully, as that was what we chose. I was truly blessed in having a friend who was the catering lecturer at a further education college and he offered to do all the cooking and to provide all the waiting-on staff; it would be, he said, a perfect opportunity for some real life experience for his students. I hired a local village hall in which he could do all the preparation work with them. More cogs fell into place; a friend who was a professional photographer, the local pub happy to run the bar, a live group from Newcastle that we were particularly fond to play their mix of folk/ modern/Cajun music throughout the evening. Doug and Judy, my old friends from New England accepted an invite to the wedding. Judy, amongst her many other talents, had once worked in a florist shop and, in her gruff, practical way she wrote and said, "We're coming. Order your flowers; I'll arrange them." Perhaps the cherry on the top – or the aged, single malt of great price – was to find that here, in Upper Weardale, there resided a retired regimental piper, who had been a piper for the Royal Family and who had apparently piped at the wedding of Prince Andrew and Sarah Ferguson, as well as at the funeral of the Queen Mother. He still had all his magnificent regalia and was available for a 'wee fee' not only to pipe at the wedding but to act as a Master of Ceremony at the reception.

The months since their engagement the previous spring passed increasingly swiftly. The next big decision was the wedding dress. We were recommended to go to a bridal shop in the Northumbrian Market town of Morpeth and we were not disappointed. Flouncy things, lacy things, far too low at the back dresses, dresses that looked more like a full pavlova than just a meringue were tried on, paraded, rejected.

And then…

Megan came through the dressing room curtains in a simple satin skirt and a tight fitting bodice, beaded with panels of seed pearls, and a plain satin edged long veil.

I began to cry.

Before me was the sight that many mothers I am sure, consciously or unconsciously, imagine from the day they hold a damp warm bundle in their arms and are told 'You have a daughter'; the sight of that little thing, grown, happy, sure, and ready to become a wife herself.

And the mother of the bride?

I chose a two piece in harebell blue silk; a mid calf straight skirt and a short, mandarin style jacket, both embroidered, just here and there, with the outline of a dragon fly in blue. It cost a lot of money but I didn't give a toot. My hat was straw, very plain and boater style; it cost eighteen pounds and I didn't give a toot about that either; I liked it.

Suddenly July was terrifyingly near. We had made the date for one week after the end of my school term; I thought that would give me ample time for all the last minute things like seating plans and having the garden perfectly manicured for the guests to swan around in after the wedding with their glass of fizz and their 'can-o-peas'. But it was as if time had diarrhoea and suddenly it was the Thursday and huge trucks appeared bearing the marquee, the tables the chairs, the Portaloos and all the other paraphernalia that had been hired. We had been cutting a patch in the field the size of the marquee with the lawnmower for weeks before thinking, "That doesn't look very large – will it hold a hundred people?" After hours of mighty tent pegs being driven onto the ground by a squad of brawny young men and much heaving on canvas with ropes, suddenly there it was in 3D, and it was huge! The floor was covered in matting, the walls & roof draped with billowing fabric, two chandeliers hung from the roof; if this was a tent, it was from the Arabian Nights. John went to Newcastle airport to pick up Doug and Judy arriving from New England and, en route, stopped off in town to pick up his kilt. There was no time for them to have the luxury of jetlag; Doug was up a ladder cleaning the house windows within a couple of hours of arriving and Judy was counting her vases and planning her flower arrangements. Well into the evening we hauled tables and chairs around to where we wanted them and began counting out boxes of cutlery and glassware for each table. We went to bed shattered but too excited to sleep.

I will never know how we did all we did the next day; there were points when my courage flickered and I thought, 'We'll never do it; simple country wedding my foot – why didn't we just go to a hotel?' But I had underestimated the army of family, friends and neighbours who pitched in and worked flat out all day and well into the evening.

Somehow it all came together.

The florist delivered a van load of flowers and Judy and her 'flower helpers' transformed them into forty four arrangements to grace the church, the house and the marquee. They scoured the lanes for foxgloves and cornflowers and tiny blue forget-me-not, which made their efforts fresh and natural rather than stiff and formal.

"Say Carol, this is supposed to be a Scottish wedding isn't it?" said Judy in her floristry department (John's workshop), "Well, I reckon we need some thistles for the table decorations; any chance?"

"I can only think of one! Leave it with me"

I made a phone call and half an hour later Denty's quadbike pulled onto the drive, throbbing and sputtering.

"Wilt these do ye?"

He pointed at a plastic crate on the front of his bike which was stuffed with very prickly thistles of green and imperial purple. His forearms were bloody and lacerated with scratches and his hands not much better.

"Denty! They are perfect! Where did you get so many – and what have you done to your hands and arms?"

He grinned, "Ah went up ont' top o' fell; I knew there were some grand uns there; 'cause, silly sod, ah were in such a hurry ah' forgot me gloves, but ah' had me penknife. Bye, they're prickly beggars is thistles."

And of all the vases and buckets of flowers that were used to beautify that day, the only ones I shall ever really remember were those green leaved, purple thistles sitting proudly and defiant in the centre of each table; symbolising Scotland but actually pure, wild, Weardale.

Another symbolic arrangement for the wedding day was a bridal arch over the gate where the bride and groom would go into the garden on their return for the reception. Philip, who amidst all his other talents was a gifted basket weaver, plaited together an arch with long, supple willow branches. I then wove into this arch greenery and flowers and, most importantly, thin branches of hawthorn leaves. The hawthorn is a tree which has long been held in respect in ways that could be considered either sacred or superstitious, depending on one's personal interpretation of these things. On the one hand it is a tree associated with death because the flowers have an odour akin to the sickly sweet smell of decomposition and because of its association with the Crown of Thorns worn by Jesus of Nazareth at his crucifixion. This is why it is considered extreme bad luck to ever bring hawthorn blossom into a house, in case it brings death with it. My mother stressed this to me at an early age, remembering only too well the trouble she had got into as a little girl when she brought some of the small, pretty flowers home for her own mother one day. On the other hand, the hawthorn is a symbol of fertility and the riotous fecundity of spring and so is also known as May blossom and linked to May Day rituals and used at weddings to bless unions and the hope of them being fruitful. Of course, I divulged none of this to Megan – nor Philip! – as she would have probably said, 'Silly old superstitious bat!' So, to most of those present at the wedding it was just a pretty floral arch; for me it was rather more.

They say true friends do things they know you need without having to be asked. The rough and ready mountain of sandwiches I'd made for our small army of helpers were quickly dispatched at lunch time and, by late afternoon, when there was still much to do, I was wondering how on earth I was going to feed everyone again. Then through the tent door marched Dhun, my Pakistani teaching assistant at school who, given my state of hyperactive state of panic at the end of term, had clearly thought, 'What is this woman's problem? Only one hundred guests coming to the wedding? All over in one day? She should come to Pakistan – I'll show her a wedding!'

Though, of course, she was far too polite to say so.

She strode into the tent with an enormous platter in each hand.

"Hello my friend! Oh! You are all so busy! I thought you might be hungry by now so I brought a little food. Megan! Oh no! She cannot be making you work? You should be resting, having a massage, having your nails done; this is no way to treat a bride!"

She placed the earthenware platters on the table and took the lids off to reveal several pounds of fluffy, saffron coloured vegetable rice and a huge pile of chicken pieces, dripping with a sauce that smelled divine.

"Just a little chicken and rice," she shrugged modestly, "I'll go and get the rest out of the car."

So we all sat gratefully and licked and chewed our way through a glorious feast that was much needed; friendship manifested in food. By late evening I was finally satisfied that everything was done and, other than those staying overnight, people slipped away. It had been a lovely day and it was a glorious evening; I couldn't stay away from the tent, I kept going back for just one more look. The sun filtered gold through the canvas and glinted off the gleaming white tablecloths, the silverware and the glassware. The chairs looked like little girls at a party, clustering round the tables, their party dresses tied back with a big bow sash, the scent of flowers was everywhere and the seating plan was propped on a tripod by the door like a head waiter, full of his own importance. I tried to imagine the next day

when the long, empty tables would be groaning with food, the plates would be being filled and wine would be gurgling into glasses. There would be chatter, excitement, speeches, kilts and sporrans and it would be a day unlike any other I would ever know again. If we were blessed with a repeat of the weather that day we could all stroll out on the hillside in the late evening sun, gaze at the glory of the Dale around us and the hills above, see the tent lit up and throbbing with light and music, feel utter happiness – and no small measure of relief. Sleeping with so much adrenalin coursing round had been an erratic affair, so it was very early when I slid out of bed and peeked through the curtains at a Weardale day that was as drear and grey as it was possible to be, with a wind that was giving everything a good shaking, including the marquee.

"No! No, no!" was all I could keep repeating, as if that would make the sun shine.

It's true that it did not actually rain, but that was the thought that was uppermost in everyone's mind throughout the morning: throughout the arrival of the caterers, the hairdresser, the bridesmaids, the bouquets, the family. The plan was, sorry, had been, for guests to circulate around the lovingly tended garden after the Church ceremony, drinking something bubbly, eating interesting nibbles and taking lovely photos. I loved Weardale with a passion and knew just how temperamental the weather could be but, today of all days, it was letting me down badly.

Very badly.

In summer frocks the lady guests would be blue with cold and their hats would be blown all the way to Eastgate. What the climate would be like up the chaps' kilts didn't bear thinking about. However, I hadn't been a Queen's Guide for nothing and 'Be Prepared' had remained my motto. Although considering really horrid weather most unlikely at the end of July I had, when ordering all the paraphernalia that goes with a wedding reception in a tent, decided it was worth the extra expense to order a hot air heater; by doing so I thought it would ensure we had a glorious day. The minutes and the hours of the morning passed with a speed I didn't believe possible. Suddenly the time had gone; suddenly this was it. My normally unshakeable reserves of energy for ordering everyone and everything around suddenly deserted me as I helped Megan to get ready. I was useless; shaky, truly overwhelmed by the sight of this... this... woman, my only child, standing there in her wedding gown, so excited, so nervous, so beautiful. Everyone expects the mother of the bride to shed a few tears as the bride stands at the altar but I had not expected this. The moment was shattered by a bellow from John, who was also trying to get dressed, so I handed the bride over to the chief bridesmaid. I soon sorted John's problem out; he had his kilt on back to front.

John was not Megan's father but he had been, since she was aged twelve, her very much loved 'Dad' figure. It was not his place, in the traditional ritual that was about to take place, to take her to the altar and yet, it was important that he too had a role. It was actually Megan's father who suggested a solution; he borrowed a Bentley from a chum to use as the bridal car. So it was, with John at the driving wheel and with her father sitting beside her, Megan went to her wedding with them both.

In the church, an expectant calm settled. The age old ritual began. The organ sounded, the doors opened, a father walked his daughter up the aisle to the arm of the man who was to be her husband. Vows were exchanged and then kisses. The congregation smiled and clapped and the couple and their witnesses disappeared to the vestry to do the legal bit. But they did not reappear when the rest came out.

"Family, friends," Philip said, "I always think that, after nerves and pressure of the ceremony, it is important to give the new couple a little time together just quietly on their own, to gather their thoughts and to realise that they are, from this moment, man and wife. I would ask that we too sit in quiet and reflect on today and pray for Megan and Bernie and the vows they have just exchanged."

We all sat in silence with our thoughts in that large, Victorian church perched above the village, the only sound that of the wind beating on the windows, until a new sound was carried in by that same wind; the sound of our piper playing outside the Church porch - surprisingly softly and gently, a hauntingly beautiful air that mesmerised us all. Then that quiet moment of reflection gave way to Alex the organist giving it full throttle as, relaxed and beaming with smiles, the newlyweds made their way back down the aisle. At their appearance at the church door, our piper puffed out his cheeks and they were greeted with a rousing reel.

"You never pipe a bride into the Church," he had told me earlier, "You pipe her out of the Church, once she's a wife."

There was a small custom observed at the church gates, which may be peculiar to Westgate and which had been told to me by the village living treasure and fount of all local knowledge, Elsie Fairless. The gates have to be tied together so the couple cannot get out; the children of the village gather in front of the gates and demand pennies from the bridegroom and, once these are thrown on the ground and scrambled for eagerly, the gates are cut open and the couple free to go. I like old customs; they should be honoured and preserved as, once lost, they are lost forever. So the gates were tied. But, so small is the population of the village since Elsie was a girl and smaller still the number of children, that it was only three or four prearranged children that searched, rather indifferently, for the shower of coins that Bernie produced from his sporran. The wind was strong and quite chilly and Megan's bare shoulders were exposed to the elements. Gallantly, Bernie removed his warm highland jacket and draped it around his new wife's shoulders as they walked down the church drive. The photographer caught the moment and took what was to become the most special photo of the whole wedding.

Of course, there was no promenading around the garden when we got back, nor taking of any lovely photos there; the sky had assumed the hue of an old lead roof and the wind was worse than ever. There was instead a rather undignified dash through the bridal arch - on which the ribbons were flapping wildly and the foliage was being sucked off into the air - for the shelter of the marquee. Inside the marquee the huge hot air blower, powered by Calor gas, was stuck like a mammoth's trunk under the canvas; it seemed to be doing the trick as the ambient temperature was quite pleasant, though the thing was noisy and those nearest to it must have felt they were in front of a giant hair dryer. Our piper deserved every one of the drams he was given by the guests. He led in the happy couple to the head of the table looking fiercely magnificent in his full highland regalia. He conducted a small ceremony with the bride and groom, who shared whisky from a two handled, shallow silver bowl known as a quaich, or a love cup to seal the marriage and he proffered a scarily real and sharp sword, with which the cake was cut.

He also announced the speeches.

My daughter's father, a diehard member of the hunting fraternity couldn't resist using the occasion to berate the recent legislation on blood sports and to promote the Country Sports League. He did wittily question whether her new husband's receding hairline was due to the size of his brain or all the stress his daughter had already caused him. He also spoke ruefully about Megan failing to live up to family standards in the horse riding department - having bought her a pony when she was three, which she promptly fell off and badly broke her elbow. This, he said, had caused an inexplicable reluctance to get into the saddle again, but, he assured the guests, he had had her mounted on several occasions. That certainly was a showstopper, resulting in a stunned silence from the assembled throng; as a wedding speech line though, it gained a sort of immortality in many peoples' memories of that day.

As the reception was really warming up, the skies finally unleashed their bursting clouds upon Upper Weardale. The wind truly battered the marquee and the rain hammered on the roof and sides. The canvas bent and buckled, then sucked out again. The chandeliers swung wildly from side to side, clinking and tinkling. Ropes creaked and timbers groaned. We were, in fact, pinned down in a field on a Weardale hillside but the overriding sensation was of being at sea at the height of some life-imperilling storm, just about to be smashed onto the rocks. Actually, it all felt rather exciting and exhilarating – but that could have been simply the adrenalin and alcohol. Certainly venturing out to the Portaloos took on a whole new dimension when you didn't know if you would be plucked from the ground and hurled, like Dorothy in the Wizard of Oz, into the void of the sky. The dancing, the drinking and the eating were all thoroughly enjoyed and went on till nearly midnight. I had to gently point out to the happy couple that the guests would be expecting them to leave; they clearly were all set to party till dawn but the older guests were clearly flagging – as indeed was I! They were only going three miles down the road for the night to a lovely country hotel and so the borrowed Bentley was brought round for them. As I went out of the marquee into the dark country night I found that the skies had cleared, the wind had dropped and the stars were pinpoints of light above us. It was still, calm and lovely.

The car doors closed, everyone waved and smiled and, at a signal from Megan's father, he and her halfbrothers and cousins took hunting horns from their jacket pockets and blew the long warbling notes of 'Gone Away' into the night air, over and over. With my entire body literally vibrating to the sound I entirely forgave him for his somewhat unconventional wedding speech for his daughter: this was his way of showing his love for her. The car moved slowly down the hill and then, in the total darkness at the crossroads, the piper stepped out and played a long lament as they drove away.

Then the dam burst, then the tears came.

Then I knew what was truly meant, when a daughter is married, that she is 'given away'.

263

23

TWO THISTLES AND A LEEK

I received a card from Megan just after their first wedding anniversary. I was puzzled, as there was no particular event or celebration at that time. There was a short message inside with an impact that briefly stopped my breath.

'Start knitting for February 2006!'

I was about to become a grandmother; I was ecstatic, overjoyed, over-emotional, slightly scared – all the usual female emotions. I had never had any grandparents, the last potential one having died ten days before I was born, so they were unnamed, unknown to me. But now... I was going to be a ... what? A Grandma? A Gran? A Nan? No, no; suddenly I knew I wanted to be a Granny; 'Granny Graham' – that sounded right. But I was still a full time teacher, I was only fifty six; was I old enough to be a 'Granny'?

Yes, of course I was ready to embark on this wondrous new role.

The due date for our first grandchild up there in St Andrews came and went, which was not unusual for a first baby and actually pleased me, as every day late was a day nearer my halfterm school holiday and the chance of being there for the event. On the day Megan went into very gentle labour I went into gentle anxiety. I had a desperate longing to be there with her, for her, as mothers throughout the ages have been.

"Sorry," my head teacher had informed me, "I can't give you any leave of absence to be with your daughter; you see she is not a dependant."

"So, if she was a sixteen year old, unmarried mother I could go?"

"Certainly."

Twenty four hours later she was in strong labour and all her careful preparations for her desired home birth swung into place; the birthing pool was filled and heated, oxygen and nitrous oxide cylinders were brought out, the candles were lit and preselected soft music was played. I had grave misgivings over the wisdom of a first birth at home but there were things over which even I had to give way. I needed more tranquillising than just a candle and soft music when I went to bed that night, convinced that by early next morning I would awake a Granny; but the phone remained ominously silent. Telling myself that no news was good news I drove anxiously to school, only to receive a phone call that sent me straight back home again; Meg, Bernie and the bump were off to Kirkcaldy Hospital, a thirty three mile journey, as even the midwife was beginning to feel anxious. This effectively marked the end of Meg's home birth dream but, nevertheless, Bernie assured me that a normal delivery was expected during the morning.

"Sorry," I informed the school office, "My daughter has just been admitted to hospital; sounds like there are problems, so I am going. I am more than happy to lose pay and I will face any consequences, but I have to go."

John and I made good progress towards the Scottish border on a February day of bright sun, brilliant blue skies and crisp air. I kept thinking what a beautiful day it was to come into this world. We were well past Otterburn, when the mobile rang and Bernie announced we were now grandparents - to one 'Fergus John'.

But –

'But' in that context is a small but very alarming word.

The baby had weighed in at only five pounds two ounces, despite being overdue, and had been delivered by an emergency Caesarean section after his heart rate had suddenly plummeted on their arrival at the hospital. Just how 'emergency' an emergency Caesarean it had been was measured by the mere fifteen minutes that elapsed from Megan being examined to having her baby in her arms. *BUT* – mother and child were fine. The unexpected and worrying news of the manner of my grandson's arrival was all that filled my head for the next few miles of the journey. Finally other thoughts surfaced.

I had a grandson.

A boy; that was going to be different.

Megan had kept chiding me throughout her pregnancy with, "It'll probably be a boy you realise; then what will you do? You only like girls!" In truth I did have a preference for small girls over small boys but had to admit that this was probably based on the fact I only had experience of being an only daughter and having an only daughter myself. This was going to be a steep, and I hoped unprejudiced, learning curve. Then there was the name, a closely guarded secret till the birth.

Fergus.

Certainly Scottish. Certainly unusual out of Scotland. Did I like it? I rolled it around my tongue a few times. Probably. But Fergus John? Those names sounded so good together and what a deeply touching honour for John, Megan's stepfather, that her firstborn should be given his name.

Yes, I decided, it was a wonderful name.

Fergus John would be about three hours old when we first saw him. More translucent blue than pink, wrapped in a fluffy towel he lay like a small, exhausted, hairless rabbit on his mother's breast, seeming stunned and astonished by his sudden emergence into the world of air and light. He was unbelievably tiny with long fine fingers that looked almost transparent and ears that were crumpled over at the top, like those of a newborn kitten. His face was faerie rather than baby; tiny features and high cheekbones over a sharp jaw line. He had none of the rounded, peach softness his mother had when I had gazed at her for the first time. My first reactions were not of joy or love but of a gnawing concern; was he really all right? I had never seen a premature baby close up but this tiny post-mature baby seemed ill equipped to deal with the demands of feeding, keeping warm, even breathing on his own.

Megan was astonishing; serene, calm, happy, fully engrossed in her little newborn son. Bernie looked drained with worry and exhaustion and almost reeling on his feet. Neither had had any real sleep for forty eight hours. When the hugs, the kisses and the congratulations had been exchanged weariness began to win over excitement and I suggested that John took Bernie back home and that I would stay with Meg and the baby until they threw me out. A nurse came to check Meg, who was still attached to several tubes, and she picked up the towel wrapped bundle and placed him in my arms.

"Here ye are Granny, could ye nurse him a wee while?"

A featherweight in my arms, I sat in the armchair by the bed and peered into the folds of the towel. A tiny mouth moved in search of something to suck and his eyelids, so fine I could clearly see the veins in them, fluttered open. Two shining pools of indigo fixed me with a solemn stare. I know all the stuff about babies cannot focus, I know that all they see at first is a blur beyond a few inches away but for long quiet minutes we gazed at each other, weighed each other up and then favourably accepted each the other.

The nurse had finished with Meg and drew back the curtain.

"Are ye all right there Granny?"

"I couldn't be happier."

"What your daughter needs the most now is sleep and what the wee laddie needs more than anything now is warmth; a bit of 'Kangaroo Care'. Would you like to oblige?"

She had quite lost me and I had no idea what she meant.

"Sorry?"

"Body heat! Preferably skin on skin; better than any incubator!"

"Of course."

"Right then; up wi' yer jumper!"

Removed from his towel wrappings the baby looked even more tiny and frail.

"Is he – alright?" I asked quietly but urgently.

"He's fine; just cold and very tired," she assured me as she pushed the baby gently up my front, "But he'll be lovely and warm soon."

We rearranged my clothes so that his head and face popped out of the top of my jumper.

"If I have a nap now can you stay and hold him?" asked a weary, anxious Megan.

"Relax and go to sleep my darling. He's safe and warm and I can stay here as long as you need me to."

"Thanks Mum," she mumbled, already allowing herself to drift into her first real sleep in over two days.

There have been few times in my life when I felt so privileged. I sat in the chair in the quiet twilight of the ward and watched over my daughter, now a mother herself, and her baby, who was now my grandson and realised that this little span of time was very precious, unrepeatable and mine alone.

Of course, eventually the nurse had to come and wake Megan, check her drip and check the baby. I reunited a now much warmer and pinker baby with his mother and quietly left to let them get to know each other properly for the first time. I set off on the thirty three mile drive back to John and Bernie, suddenly feeling very tired and still beset with little nagging anxieties about the baby. As the span of the Tay Bridge came into view the sky was lit by a brilliant shooting star, which trailed a silver tail across the Tay estuary. It was so sudden and so brief that had I not been looking at exactly that piece of sky I would never have seen it.

'That's for Fergus,' I said to myself, 'To tell us that all will be well.'

When I told John about my reassuring portent he simply said, "It could have been a coincidence." However, the next morning as we set off for the hospital again, a beautiful rainbow arched across the Tay, just where the star had fallen the night before.

"Well, does *that* count as a celestial greetings for Fergus?" I asked, "Or do you want a cloud formation saying, 'Welcome to the world'?"

John just gave one of his, 'It's best to humour her' smiles.

The best thing actually was that it was now officially half term, so I had a whole week to be where I most wanted to be.

But the next weeks weren't the easiest for the new parents or the new grandparents. Fergus' weight dropped to an alarming four pounds twelve ounces and he was struggling to feed well. He spent some time in the special baby unit at the hospital being fed through a tube up his nose before he was finally allowed to go home. At five weeks old, he made his first journey south to Hill House East; he was fretful, still seemed weak and cried a lot.

Megan was in much the same state.

"He is being sick so much Mum; he takes ages for even a small feed then, more often than not, he brings it back up again."

She had just nursed him in the big armchair by the fire and sat him up to gently rub his back. A projectile of vomit was ejected at great speed for a great distance by the tiny person on her knee; if I hadn't seen it for myself I would not have believed it possible.

"Now that cannot be normal; I am going to phone the surgery."

Our local GP practice in the Dale was magnificent. Within an hour Fergus was in the children's unit at Bishop Auckland Hospital. Shortly after being examined, Meg and Bernie were told he had 'Pyloric Stenosis'; this meant the valve from his stomach into his intestine wasn't functioning correctly, so he couldn't digest his food. He would need an operation to correct this and the best place possible to have this done in the north east was the Royal Victoria Infirmary in Newcastle.

"Shall we take him there now?" they asked.

"No, he needs to go in an ambulance to be on the safe side. You follow in your car."

Not only did this tiny scrap get an ambulance all to himself but two paediatric nurses travelled with him on the journey.

Thank God for the NHS.

We were all frantic with worry but the nurse on the childrens' ward at the RVI was almost blasé.

"Oh don't worry; we get at least two 'Py Babies', as we call them, on the ward each week. These days the operation is very straightforward and, in a few days, you'll see a much happier, hungrier baby!"

And, thank God and the NHS again, we did.

Fergus John grew and thrived and we were all filled with relief; and amazement at how much love the 'wee laddie' had brought into the world with him.

When he was less than two years old Fergus made his first solo trip to Hill House East. I was determined that being away from his parents for a day or two shouldn't become a huge drama at some future point when it may be useful, or even needful for him to stay with us. He happily carried his little dinosaur bag, specially bought for his 'holiday', out to the car. Of course, he had no idea what a holiday was but he toddled about saying 'Oliday, oliday!'

Of course, there were tears – after all, he was still tiny.

As I pulled off the drive they were running freely down Megan's face and Bernie looked quite bereft whilst Fergus, grinning happily from his baby seat waved, 'Bye!! Bye!!' We all benefitted from those couple of days; Megan and Bernie got their first weekend alone since his birth and I got to deepen my relationship with my grandson. How ashamed I was of my initial disappointment at learning Megan had had a boy; my love for him was so fierce that it shocked me. And, as Megan's best friend had said to her when she had confided my misgivings, "Nonsense! She will be glad of a strapping grandson when she is old to carry her to her commode!"

We had a family celebration for his second birthday up at St Andrews. A double celebration as Megan was now safely over four months pregnant with her second child. I say 'safely' as she had gone through two devastating miscarriages in the previous year. The little birthday party had been a delight, as had Fergus who kept running up to Megan, patting her tummy and saying 'Baby!' When he then came up to me and patted my middle and said 'Baby!' I had to put him right.

"No darling, not baby; fat Granny!"

He found this hugely amusing and toddled round chanting, 'Fat Granny! Fat Granny!'

This second baby was due in mid June and, of course in the middle of a school term again. I didn't even bother asking for leave of absence. Wisely Megan opted for a hospital delivery this time but rejected all suggestions of a second Caesarean section; this time she was determined to do it on her own. And she did; though it was very tough.

"You have a very healthy granddaughter," Bernie told me on the phone, wearily but proudly, "Megan has named her 'Rose Madeline'."

Of course I cried.

A granddaughter; a Scottish Rose with my own middle name.

How blessed and honoured could any Granny be?

John and I drove up to Scotland in a serene state the day after her birth. Megan was holding Rose in her arms in the living room and as I walked in this pink, strong baby, who was in fact of average weight but seemed so large after Fergus, swung her head round and looked me long and hard in the eye, appraising me.

I felt her gaze so physically that my first words to her were. "Oh! And who are you? You are an old soul I think!"

This one had definitely been here before.

And she proved to live up to her name; she was strong and determined, thorny and prickly when challenged but petal soft in her loving, caring heart, only growing more beautiful as she blossomed through girlhood. She could be summarised at age two by the following: when reaching for a biscuit on the table without asking I said sternly, "Rose! What is the magic word?"

She thought about this for a second or two.

"Mine!" she replied.

Though, having secured possession, she would have shared the last crumb if asked to.

I thought my happiness as a Granny utterly complete.

When Rose was two the family left one coastal university town on the east coast of Scotland and moved to another coastal university town on the west coast of Wales: Aberystwyth. My initial reaction was childish and selfish in the extreme; I wept buckets! Driving to St Andrews could be achieved in less than four hours, driving to Aberystwyth was going to take six hours or more.

"Mother! For heaven's sake! We are not going to the moon! And you haven't said a word of congratulations over Bernie's new job at the university. It could have been a lot worse – we did look at a post in Canada!"

I thought of my mother's sometimes twenty two month gaps away from my father when he had worked in Nigeria and felt rather ashamed of myself. So, they moved to Wales and into a perfect family home; a three storey Victorian terrace house within walking distance of the university. In fact, walking was something one did an awful lot of in Aberystwyth I was to discover; most of it up and down rather steep hills! The move however had also meant Megan having to leave her job teaching French at a school in St Andrews and the opportunities to do so in Aber were limited by her not speaking Welsh. But this opened up a new opportunity; she had always wanted to do her PhD in St Andrews but the cost would have been prohibitive if she had left her teaching post to do so. When she applied for, and was awarded, funding at Aberystwyth to pursue her doctorate it seemed as if all the jigsaw pieces of their family life had fallen into place; Fergus was about to start school in the September and there was a super day nursery for Rose at the end of their road. So – bish, bash, bosh; she could begin her PhD part time then go full time when Rose started school. Three or four years of hard work and study ahead and a PhD could be in Meg's grasp so she leapt at the opportunity. By 2012 Fergus was seven and Rose, at four and a half, was about to start school. At last Megan could now pursue her studies full rather than part time as so carefully planned.

"Mum."

The tone of her voice immediately alerted me to something important going to be said.

"Are you all right?"

A pause.

"Yes; I'm absolutely fine. But I am pregnant."

Suddenly the jigsaw of life was rearranged. The sensible thing would have been to just give up on the whole academic endeavour and concentrate on her pregnancy and then on being Mum to three small children as a full time occupation.

But this was my daughter.

So she carried on.

There were many setbacks along the way; health, time, energy, morning sickness, and reaching deadlines being the least of them. The most devastating was when her professor, who was supervising her PhD and who was the inspiration behind her doing it in the first place, died quite suddenly of cancer at a cruelly early age. She was rudderless for a long while and had thoughts of quitting.

But she carried on.

My own career was coming to an end at this time. I could have retired from teaching at age sixty but instead went back part time for three years. Though I could have carried on doing this till I was sixty five, as I approached sixty four I realised that I was weary and needing to say goodbye to the school where I had worked for the last eighteen years. It wasn't the teaching itself or the demands of my students that led to this decision, though working with young adults with severe learning needs and often social and behavioural problems as well required a great deal of energy. It was the constantly changing goal posts, the endless policy documentation, living almost in terror of the next Ofsted Inspection and jumping through ever higher hoops to justify what you were doing that finished me. After forty two years as a teacher the prime imperative now seemed to be ticking boxes. When I had started as a teacher in 1971 it was very much a profession that was viewed with respect by the pupils, their parents and society in general. Professional judgement was something you acquired in the course of your teaching and this would be listened to and also respected; it was expected that an experienced teacher would know what a particular pupil needed and how best to provide it. By 2013 this was no longer true; it was impossible to make any independent decisions or to act on experience or use one's initiative. Once, if my students had worked well and it was a day of good weather I would occasionally say, "I think you deserve a lesson off this afternoon as a reward; we will take some balls and some juice and biscuits and go out and enjoy this lovely weather!" A quick phone call to the office to say my class and its staff would be out for an hour or so, and exactly where we would be, and off we would go to the nearby police playing fields, with a first aid kit, any medications needed and a mobile phone. There the students could enjoy some much needed outdoor activity, something many of them did not get in their home situation. Forward a few years and in order to set foot outside the school perimeter with the students I had to put in an application three weeks in advance, provide a full risk assessment and get written permission from the parents.

It was the red tape that strangled me in the end.

But my final school summer holiday, in 2012, was to be my most memorable ever; my third grandchild had graciously decided to make an entry into the world slap bang in the middle of it and Megan and Bernie expressed their wish to have me there with them for the birth.

Nothing this time could prevent me from being there for this astonishing privilege.

I was in residence down in Wales soon after school ended. Megan was large, hot and fed up; she became even more fed up when the due date passed, then more days passed and still no baby. The baby was lying in a way that put pressure on a nerve in her pelvis and Megan was having shooting, stabbing pains in her leg because of this. Between this pain and heartburn, sleeping was extremely difficult. The maternity unit at the hospital told her she just had to say the word and they would induce the baby. The hospital in Aberystwyth actually lay directly behind their house. To get there took literally two minutes, up the very steep hill they lived on and just around the corner.

But... she carried on.

After a week she finally cracked.

"Right," she announced, "I have had enough of this; I have had a terrible night, no sleep at all for the pain. So; induction? I'm going to tell them to bring it on!"

"Then I'll run you up in the car; John will look after Fergus and Rose."

"Don't be silly! It's just round the corner; I'm pregnant, not an invalid. I'll be back soon."

And off she went, puffing and heaving herself up the steep hill.

Half an hour later the phone rang.

"Mum?"

"Yes!"

"Apparently I am five centimetres dilated already; that's why I could not sleep last night! So they won't let me out. Can you phone Bernie at work? And then can you come? And bring me something to eat? I'm starving!"

The only thing I could find in the fridge to make sandwiches with was garlic sausage, which I urgently stuffed into buttered bread, grabbed a packet of biscuits and my spinning stick and wool, then I was off up the hill.

That morning was quite surreal and completely unforgettable.

Megan, seemingly no different than when she had left home, was in a large, comfortable delivery room munching ravenously on pungent garlic sausage sandwiches while I sat in a chair beside her unravelling and pulling soft, curly wool that had come from my Teeswater ewe, Teasel, wrapping it round and round a rotating spinning stick to form a yarn that was destined to become a Christening blanket for the baby we were now all waiting for.

There was a calm excitement pervading the room in that very special time.

The midwife came in; after the mother, she is the most important person at any birth and Meg had been understandably anxious that it be someone who she could feel not just comfortable with but could also trust in. She sniffed the air suspiciously and wrinkled her nose at the contents of the lunch box and gave a bemused look at the weird older woman tugging away at her wool like some French Revolution knitter, spectating at the guillotine.

"Hello Megan; I'm Sue, your midwife – just popping in to see how things are coming along."

"Good I think; this is my Mum Carol – oh! And this is my husband Bernie just coming in now."

Had she had her choice of any midwife in Wales – or anywhere actually – Megan could not have picked better than Sue. She was a very experienced ex Army midwife, who had delivered babies all over the world, sometimes in the most harrowing of situations. She was the completely perfect mix that Megan needed; a more mature woman, sensible, comforting and yet absolutely taking no nonsense. And, as she told us, she would be with Megan till she went off duty at three pm, which should be plenty of time. Actually, it wasn't quite enough time, and as three pm approached Meg's only worry was that she would leave her.

"Don't worry; I'm not going anywhere till this little one is safely here. However long it takes."

With that reassurance and her very expert hands it did not in fact take that much longer and, with one final heroic effort, baby arrived. Bernie was so busy encouraging Megan that I was actually the first one to see their new child enter the world. Sue picked her up, examined her and pronounced, "You have a lovely daughter, Megan!"

"Daughter?" she seemed truly surprised, as she had convinced herself this was another boy.

"Yes! Definitely!"

"It's 'Eve' then! Oh! It's Eve!"

"Who is going to cut this young lady's cord?" Sue asked.

"Your honour this time Granny," Bernie insisted

So, with a snip of the scissors Eve began her first day of independent life; 'Eve Maria' to be exact; middle name for Megan's godmother, my friend since childhood. Cleaned up, swaddled and in her mother's arms I kissed them both and left the parents to get to know their new daughter.

Twenty four hours after she had struggled up the hill, Megan came back down with her husband and new daughter, who was ready to meet her brother, sister and granddad.

"Mummy?" Rose asked, after looking at her new sister and thinking deeply, "Will Eve have a leek on her bit of paper?"

"What bit of paper?"

"You know – like the one that Fergus and I got in Scotland to say we had been born."

"Oh! Your birth certificates?"

"Yes, well, ours have a thistle on because we are Scottish aren't we?" Rose liked to tell people she was Scottish because she had been born in Scotland and had a thistle on her birth certificate to prove it – "Well, Eve will be Welsh won't she? So will she have a leek on hers?"

In June 2017, after nearly seven years of mostly part time study, the whole of my wonderful family rose to their feet in the gallery of the Great Hall of Aberystwyth University to cheer and clap as Megan, in robes of vibrant emerald and scarlet, the colours of the Welsh flag, walked towards the Chancellor of the University and received her Doctorate in Modern Languages. I was, and am, so proud of her that it is at times overwhelming; I feel she also deserved a PhD in sheer determination.

As for my grandchildren, with two of them already at secondary school and the third well into primary, time has passed scarily quickly. They are completely different from each other in many ways but the one thing they do have in common is their love of coming to Hill House East. The girls love to feed the sheep, look after the hens and collect the eggs. Fergus enjoys working on projects in Grandad's garage, Eve is developing a love of gardening. They enjoy paddling in the River Wear in summer and sledging down our hill in the winter. All of them enjoy me passing on my cookery skills to them. Christmas is always special with the time honoured pastimes of eating too much together, singing at the carol service, snoozing in front of a roaring log fire and playing silly board games; sometimes snow is thrown in as an extra bonus. The hawthorn boughs in Megan's bridal arch have certainly borne the most cherished of fruit and I have been deeply blessed by my two thistles - and the leek.

24

SOLSTICE

The nucleus of our family was very small; it comprised just John and me living out our life in a way familiar to most - dictated by work, health, income and responsibilities. Around this central point, like spokes in a cartwheel, were our wider family; parents, children, grandchildren, close friends and our dependent animals. This wheel was driven round by cycles of the year such as school terms, school holidays and annual celebrations. But I realised quite quickly after coming to live on The Hill that above all our life was now dependent on and turned by the seasons in a way it had not been when we had lived more divorced from the forces of nature, protected by suburban living from the full effects of the weather. I soon learned to recognise why, from ancient times, people had an awareness of and expectations of the four cardinal points of the solar year; the spring and autumn equinoxes and the summer and winter solstices. The solstices, in June and December, marked the time of the most daylight and the least daylight; times of change. Times to realise that the plenty and light of summer would slowly end after June and that the harshness, darkness and deprivations of winter would not go on forever; they too would come to an end.

Perhaps painfully slowly – but the light and new life would come.

The winter solstice was, above all else, about hope.

As time passed this yearly cycle was something we came to accept and cope with, in fact something I highly valued and looked forward to. Although no twelve month period ever passed in exactly the same way and, like everywhere else, there were some bad winters, some good summers, some very late springs, some very early autumns and everything in between. But there were seasons, real seasons that weren't always necessarily all about the weather but about the land, the animals and the people who worked with them.

Let me dwell on winter.

Of course, we had first moved into Hill House East late one December and by the January we had thick snow and bitter temperatures. The shock to the system in a cold, draughty house was simply awful and nearly caused us to deeply regret moving there at all. But, year on year we learnt how best to keep the house and ourselves warm and to recognise, at some point each year that 'winter is coming' and it was prudent to be ready. Stock up on fuel, on animal feed, on human feed, on winter tyres, on oil for lamps and check through our winter wardrobe; on with the thermals, the flannelette nightwear, thick hats and gloves and warm socks for wellies.

Turning out into a frigid, black-dark morning to drive to school and returning to find conditions just as bad was, I must admit, tough. But it was always balanced and compensated for by summer evenings of six hours to enjoy after my day's work. In retirement I have learnt to embrace winter, even enjoy it. The short days are now gentle in their demands; there is no need to get up in the dark and I can drink tea in bed and watch the first light fall on the hillside opposite. There is no need to keep on top of the garden in winter, nor the lengthy daily rounds of watering it that hot weather brings. There are no flies or midges. As night closes in before 4.00 pm in December the animals are all put to bed, the log fire lit, the thick winter curtains drawn and the sofa pulled nearer the stove. We, like so much else around us, simply hibernate. Our primeval cravings for hearty nourishment are satiated with comfort food such as dollops of creamy mashed potato, fat sausages and onion gravy, followed perhaps by my ultimate winter comfort pudding; spicy ginger sponge covered in thick, hot custard. After such a meal John and I waddle to the beckoning sofa by the fire like two well fattened dormice, and utter contented sighs for several hours.

Utter bliss.

Although winter is technically a season that runs for the months of December, January and February, the high North Pennines take a more flexible approach; snow can arrive as early as November, and keep arriving till the end of April. Once we had a winter where there was some snowfall in five consecutive months. Increasingly, it may not arrive at all. Instead, also increasingly often, it can be replaced by endless cold, heavy deluges of rain and gales, which are much more unhealthy and unpleasant than snow for the land, animals and farmers alike. Our winter came early in 2008; we had our first snows in November, and then it remained bitterly cold up until Christmas, when we had a further seasonal sprinkle. The first really serious snow however waited until the night before I was due to go back to school in January and I awoke to a blizzard that obliterated from sight the house just across the field from us and banked snow in huge drifts at the end of the drive. The Zwartbles ewes in our bottom field were more like crabs than sheep, as they were all encrusted in a hard shell of frozen snow. Actually they were not taking any hurt from it; in fact it was beneficial as it served to insulate them from the wind. There was no question of going to school, which I confess I was delighted about. However, I did as duty required and phoned the primary school in St John's Chapel and prepared myself mentally for the mile and a half trudge through the wind and snow to reach it. It had been stressed to all the teachers at our school by the Local Education Authority that, in the event of bad weather or other disaster preventing us from getting to our own school, we had to, if humanly possible, report to our nearest educational establishment.

"Hello – St John's Primary? This is Carol Graham at Westgate; I am snowed out of my own school that I teach at in Durham and I am supposed to report instead to my nearest school – which would be you."

Someone chuckled at the other end of the phone, in the way that people do when they think the person they are talking to has lost the plot.

"Well, if you do you'll be the only person here! We are closed too; have you not been listening to Radio Newcastle? I live just across the road from the school and I've popped in to see if everything is all right, then I'm off back home to a cup of hot tea and a nice warm fire – I would suggest you do the same!"

And there were glories to winter too.

The bright, intense blue of winter skies and the pale lemon of the sunlight would light up the hills and fields on cloudless days, piecing through the bare skeletons of trees and bushes in a pure clearness so unlike the warm richness of summer. On just such a day, I walked down Swinhope from the old barn near a field called Camp Lot towards home. It was one of my favourite walks and I loved the history and stories of the naming of fields and places all around me; this field had got its name from being the place where, over two hundred years previously while walking from Teesdale to Weardale to preach his Methodist message, John Wesley had paused and made 'camp' for several days and was joined by people from all over the region who came to hear him preach in the open air. Weardale has a long history of strong, early Methodism; in fact John Wesley made as astonishing thirteen visits to Weardale, the first of these in1748, when he preached under a thorn tree near Ireshopeburn. There was obviously a need for Methodism in Weardale in Wesley's day, when harsh working and living conditions and little support from the established Church - other than to take taxes from the hard won lead - resulted in recourse to drunkenness and its accompanying social evils. Westgate, our quiet little village, was renowned as the centre of a particularly cruel social evil of the time: cock fighting. Simon Jenkins in his book, 'England's Thousand Best Churches' says of Weardale, 'This is the country where the fires of Methodism took hold, fanned by an absentee Anglicanism'. Wesley's visit led to the founding of the High House Chapel at Ireshopeburn and by 1772, when he returned to preach there, the Methodist Society in Weardale had 266 members. Methodism in the Dale continued to grow long after John Wesley's death, with Chapels in virtually every village. So flourishing was the movement that in 1842 a local historian Jacob Ralph Featherstone wrote; 'The High House (Chapel) on a Sunday afternoon is a spectacle worthy of beholding: here you may see from six hundred to one thousand good looking, fresh coloured and well dressed persons of both sexes.'

As late as June 1790, aged eighty seven and only a few months before his death, Wesley was back in Weardale preaching in Stanhope, a place he had described on his first visit there as, '... eminent for nothing in this age but a very uncommon degree of wickedness!'

The decline of the Chapels began with the catastrophe of the lead mining industry collapse of 1882, which led to a dramatic fall in the local population and thus Chapel attendance. This decline was something that was to continue into the twenty first century; in the last two decades I had seen Wearhead, Ireshopeburn, St John's Chapel, Westgate, Eastgate and Frosterley Chapels all close. The greatest loss was that of the birthplace of Methodism in Weardale, High House Chapel, as recently as 2019. It is no longer a place of worship but is, thankfully, under the ownership and care of the Weardale Museum, to which it is attached in every sense of the word. The 'Fires of Methodism' that burned so fiercely here two hundred and seventy years ago are perhaps the reason that George Fox's Quaker message never took root locally and why there is no Quaker Meeting House in Weardale. Yet, Meeting Houses were established, and still function, on all four sides of Weardale at Allendale, Cotherstone, Durham – and at Alston; the Meeting which I attend in the tiny stone building of the 'Society of Friends', built in 1732. So, though it would be 'unquakerly' to even think such a thing, perhaps George Fox was more tenacious in the end. On the three hundredth anniversary of John Wesley's birth, a special service was held at High House Chapel at Ireshopeburn, the place where Wesley himself had once preached. The Bishop of Durham, no less, read a passage from Wesley's journal of that time in which he described how, having laboured up a 'great hill' from Newbiggin (in Teesdale) he finally began to descend into Westgate and how he had been heartened by the sight of the cottages and farms below him, where he knew that his words had begun to take root. Somewhat stunned, I realised that the road he had walked that day was the road down Swinhope; the road which still passes Hill House East.

On my walk down that very road on that winter day I did not bump into Charles Wesley, nor was I menaced by any of the wild boar for which the valley was once named; they were all hunted out many centuries ago. Instead, I was rewarded  with the sight of a group of black grouse, scratching in the powdery snow on the fellside in search of food. These glorious birds, also known as blackcock in the Dale, have not yet met the fate of the wild boar but there are apparently only about 5,000 of them left in Britain. Denty reckoned he had seen up to forty or fifty of them at 'lekking' time; that meant about one percent of the whole population of the country was on the Swinhope fells. The 'lek' is the annual courtship ritual where the males strut their stuff, fanning their distinctive lyre-shaped tails to attract the female birds and uttering their gurgling song, whilst posturing and fighting. It is an amazing sight, usually occurring very early in the morning, but it had been a privilege and not a hardship to get up at Denty's bidding on the 'right' morning to be at the 'lekking ground', where the birds return year on year to perform their ritual dance - as they have no doubt done since before the Romans hunted up the Swinhope valley.

That day, mating and breeding were the last things on the birds' minds; finding enough food to survive till the spring was all that mattered. The winter was hitting harder than it had in many years with snowfalls interspersed with sub zero temperatures. It was certainly very cold; it had been well below freezing for days and the vegetation was stiff and brittle with crystals of hoar frost. The day was completely calm however, a rarity in Weardale, and the sun shone brightly, though with little warmth. Had there been a wind it would have been far from pleasant; the wind chill factor would have dropped the temperature many degrees more and would have whipped the icy crystals into my face till it was reddened and sore. As it was all was still, calm, very silent and very beautiful. The sunlight reflected from the hoar frost on the grass, making it glint and shimmer as I passed and here and there ditch water had overflown its boundaries and frozen into a stream of uneven glass down the side of the road where I walked. The silence seemed absolute. The road, which was gated, virtually single track and which led over into Teesdale, was reputedly the highest minor road in England, reaching 2,000 feet at the 'Top Gate', where Weardale turned into Teesdale. In this weather the route was impassable by even the most intrepid of four wheeled drives and so not a single vehicle passed me on my walk. The snow completely muffled any noise from the Dale road down in the valley below and not a bird flew, not a sheep blared. It was as if everything was held in suspended animation, asleep, waiting for the light and life of the spring to come. I stopped, the better to enjoy the peace, and considered the rarity of such a place, free from the noise of the modern world yet so close to communities. Gradually I realised the silence was not in fact absolute; I could hear a quiet burbling, murmuring noise of water running. I couldn't think what it could be when all the water around appeared frozen solid until, peering through the glassy surface of the ice on the side of the road, I saw tiny lines of moving water. These flowed slower or faster according to the gradient of the hill and where two or more rivulets bumped into each other they gathered force and momentum and flowed stronger, trickling audibly and merrily. I watched and listened quite mesmerised; that which I had thought asleep was very much alive. Beneath its winter coat, life was still flowing gently through the veins of Swinhope.

By 2009, with our tenth Christmas at Hill House East approaching, the changes to the old house and to our lives during that decade were so many that I had to actually make myself sit down and go through them in my head. Our first Christmas we had been still living out of packing cases and in chaos in a house which had been empty for over two years with no heating, hot water or a proper cooker. A decade on and the house was transformed, warm and welcoming; it had doors that fitted and the winter was where it should be, outside. Logs flamed in the stove, both ovens on the range cooker were going full blast and we were snug and safe and utterly content. If the first winter had been a trial by freezing cold then it had been well worth enduring. The most precious gifts of the past decade arrived for Christmas that year tired but very excited; my two grandchildren. Christmas meant little to Rose as yet but this was to be Fergus' fourth and he was bursting with it all. They were all there waiting for me when I got back from school on the last evening of term.

"Granny, Granny!"

Fergus ran, slithering and slipping on the flattened snow outside the house when he heard the car pull up. As it had done ten years before the snow had arrived to stay and a white Christmas was almost guaranteed.

"I have told Santa I am going to be here for Christmas! And I have brought my stocking to hang up!"

They had arrived that evening to be with me for the next day, which was my sixtieth birthday.

My sixtieth birthday! It was hard to realise that I had reached such a milestone along life's road.   It sounded, well, so old.   The realisation was driven home however when I received a letter saying my 'Old Age Pension – sorry, my 'State Pension' – would begin the next week and that I would not be required to pay any more National Insurance contributions.   I was also able to pick up a prescription at the chemist without paying and was informed how I could apply for my bus pass. So, becoming such a matriarch did not seem so bad after all, though I was not quite so enthusiastic when I received my DIY bowel cancer screening kit from the NHS in the post.   Megan had taken charge of my birthday treat; she, Fergus and I were going to Newcastle to the Theatre Royal to see the pantomime Cinderella. We had fabulous seats in that beautiful old theatre and, as much as the costumes, the music, the laughs and the well worn story the greatest joy was to share it with Fergus, who was seeing all of this through very young eyes for the first time.   We booed and hissed at the baddies, shouted 'Behind you!' and 'Oh no he isn't!' at the top of our voices and gasped when the magician made a real horse appear out of an empty box. It made me feel six again rather than sixty and it was the perfect gift.

Of course, I am called Carol because I had been born so near Christmas; a child of the winter solstice, which is maybe why it is so significant to me. So, no sooner was my birthday over than we were full steam ahead preparing for that event. There were small, never to be repeated gems from Fergus which gave the celebration a whole new perspective. I told him we were going to visit a very old friend of mine called Mary, who would love to meet him; "Oh good," he replied, "Will Joseph be there?" He watched his daddy stuffing onions up the backside of a bird whilst preparing it for supper and asked, "Is that to stop the eggs falling out daddy?" On Christmas Eve, he came into the kitchen alight with excitement having really seen Santa's sledge from the front porch pull up the dark hill far, far above him, complete with flashing lights on either side. It had of course been Denty, on a late night feeding round in the field with his tractor and trailer, but to him it was magical. Then he found me crawling round the kitchen floor searching for the infant Jesus, who had mysteriously disappeared from the crib scene on the dresser, shortly after Rose had been playing in the vicinity.
"What are you looking for Granny?" he enquired.
"I am looking for the baby Jesus."
"Oh, have you looked in the fridge? That's where mummy keeps them."
I was completely baffled, "Sorry Fergus, I don't understand."
"Mummy buys those for me for my lunch box. They are round and red Granny - you know, baby cheeses."
The Holy Infant did finally reappear the following month when, struggling to put my walking boots on, I found an obstruction; Rose had obviously thought the Christ Child would be much snugger in the toe of a boot than in a wooden box filled with straw.
All the ritual preparations for Christmas were finally performed; the tree was up and decorated - with Rose trying to pull things off as quickly as

we put them on- the presents were wrapped and well hidden and on Christmas Eve a mince pie and glass of ginger wine were solemnly put out by the hearth for Santa, along with a large juicy carrot for the reindeers, then the stockings were hung and 'T'was the night before Christmas' read aloud. On Christmas morning, after mountains of ripped paper had been gathered up and we had all eaten a hearty breakfast, the children went out with daddy, grandad and the sledge. Sledging was something they did not get the chance to enjoy in their seaside home and I hoped they would retain childhood memories of hurtling down the steep hillside in our field, falling off into drifts of icy, powdery, white crystals and then trudging uphill to repeat the process over and over till they were exhausted, frozen and famished and needed mugs of hot chocolate to warm their hands and defrost their red noses. For our Christmas meal Megan and I applied ourselves to a yard long piece of pork loin, stuffing, roast parsnip and all the trimmings. I always cooked a loin of pork at Christmas; my mother had done so and her mother before that and Megan had taken a solemn oath to carry on the tradition. Boned and rolled it was so easy to carve, the crackling was sumptuous and it sliced perfectly for sandwiches when cold with absolutely no bones or waste. And, of course, there could be nothing more appropriate for the celebration living as we did at the foot of Swinhope, the 'wild boar' valley. Despite finding the mashed and buttered turnip in the oven after we had finished the Christmas pudding the meal was wonderful, not just because of the food but because of having all my family gathered around the table to enjoy it. I must have warmed the brandy for the pudding too well though and driven all the alcohol off because, having amply doused it, it simply refused to ignite. Determined to set fire to it I poured another very generous amount straight from the bottle and this time it went 'whoosh'. Actually, it was a bit too much 'whoosh' because, by the time it got to the table, blue flames were licking up and over the top and had set fire to the holly! We managed to extinguish the pudding before it cremated itself and it was just as Christmas pudding should be; rich fruity, moist and alcoholic without being at all heavy. Rose thought it was delicious while Fergus preferred the fascination of the flames to actually eating it. On Boxing Day the family left for home and we were left to celebrate the remainder of the twelve days of Christmas on our own. The forecasters were beginning to move their predictions from 'worst winter in ten years' to 'worst winter in thirty years'. Certainly it was the most severe winter we had known since we came to Westgate. The snow and the sub zero temperatures did not abate even slightly which meant that, festive season or no festive season, it got harder day by day to get out on the fell and to see to the flock. Battered and bruised, Denty sat nursing a mug of hot tea in our kitchen having been nearly flattened under four hundred sheep. He had been trying to shake out a bag of sheep nuts when he slipped and fell in the snow and landed on top of the feedbag. He had been quickly engulfed by a tide of famished sheep, desperate to get to the food underneath him. As much as anything I think the shock had been that, whereas once he could have shaken off the sheep like a dog annoyed with its fleas, now, also approaching sixty, it had taken him all his strength to even get back on his feet. After that, and for the many weeks of that bitter winter that were to follow, John went with him up on the fell most days to help feed round. Every day it snowed and every night the temperature plunged lower and lower. The weather was more like Austria than the north east of England. During each short day, when the sun crept above our hillside at 10.30 am and then sank beneath the far fell top by 2.30 pm, the sky was an intense, clear blue and the warmth of the sun was just sufficient to slightly melt the snow on the roofs so that it dripped from the gutters and formed very beautiful icicles that froze every night and grew again the next day. The largest of a row of icicles outside our bedroom window gained in length and girth this way until it we had a transparent unicorn's horn hanging there. When, at over three foot long – a metre in 'new speak' – it threatened to pull the guttering down, John had to get his ladder and dislodge it. But we kept it intact, stuck in a snow drift near the front door; an icy finger pointing up at the winter skies.

The time came to go back to school and I managed to do so with not only great reluctance but with great difficulty; on the second day of school, forced by snow to come the long way round, it took me two and half hours to travel what would normally take me fifty minutes. On the third day of the new term the unthinkable happened; the head teacher closed the school till the following Monday; in fifteen years there I had never known this to happen. It was like being given the best possible belated Christmas present; five whole days to be snowbound at home. It mattered not a jot to me that we could not get out anywhere; selfishly, with all the food and drink we could possibly want and enough wood to burn until the spring if need be, there was nowhere I wanted to go. I dug out all the cold weather clothing and footwear, made vast pans of soup, finally got round to using the fruit that had been patiently waiting in the freezer since the autumn to make blackberry jelly and spiced apple butter and was utterly content. I put on layer after layer of clothing, topped it off with a fur lined leather helmet of obscure eastern European origin and a pair of goggles, grabbed my walking poles and ploughed for miles through the brilliant, blue-white, powdery snow with my nose covered by a scarf against air that was so cold it almost hurt to breathe. The outside thermometer had not been above freezing in over two weeks and read 'minus 11' one morning. At that level of cold, beautiful though the Dale was to my eyes, real suffering began to set in for animal kind.

The flock had been totally dependent on Denty to bring them food for many weeks, but now in the unending bitter cold and biting wind their appetites were even keener and the daily feeding round took on a greater urgency; getting the food out through the snow in sufficient quantity whilst there was daylight. Each day, after breakfast until the afternoon light was failing, John was up at Glenwhelt and out on the fell. Denty would descend from Glenwhelt, appearing out of the grey swirling snow on the hill driving the huge blue tractor with an enormous round bale of hay impaled on the spike at the front; like some prehistoric carnivore tossing its prey in the air.

"Are ye ready?" he would shout to John.

"I've just finished feeding round down here" John would reply.

"Aye, well divven't forget yer hat and gloves; an' yer fur lined long johns if you've got any!"

A couple of minutes later they were away, the blue mechanical monster roaring and lurching up the hill, John standing behind Denty's seat in the cab. I knew they would have a hard morning ahead of them reaching the 'out-bye', checking the flock, distributing the hay and feed, going on foot in places where even the tractor could not go. But for Ray Dent and his father George before him, for whom this snow would have seemed like a mere sprinkling, the whole journey would have had to be covered on foot, leading a horse pulling a sled laden with hay. Once on the fells, Denty and John would drop off the big round bale, open it and allow it to unwind down the hill like some long, stair carpet of hay. As is nature's way, the weaker, smaller or older sheep suffered the worst and the first fatalities of the winter began; sheep who had got crushed or trampled in the mad stampede for food, sheep who had somehow got separated from the main flock and had perished alone in the night conditions, sheep with poor or damaged fleeces that could not insulate them from the cruel cold. Any sufferers found still alive were brought back down to the farm to recover; their ambulance the back of the tractor, their paramedic John. Quite a few were blind or lame, many just exhausted and famished. Denty came down to collect John one morning grumbling loudly that one of the sheep they had rescued the day before, with a lot of walking, digging and dragging involved, had come running up the barn door when he went in, promptly stopped breathing and fallen dead at his feet.

"When ah opened her mouth there was a geet thistle stalk stuck int' throat; it must hev been in the bale of hay ah'd put out last neet. Why could the daft bugger not just have deed on't hill yesterday and saved us aall that bother?"

I thought it defied possibility that sheep could live up there at all but then these were Swaledales, bred generation after generation to live out all year on the fell tops in all conditions and to not only survive but to thrive and grow their crop of lambs while the winter raged around them. All they needed to do this was hay, a handful of sheep nuts and a reasonable wall to shelter behind from the worst of the wind.

There were other casualties of the cold. Denty found an owl lying on its back in the barn, its feet still curled as if it had frozen and fallen while perched.

"It's these modern round hay bales ye knaa," he said sadly, as though he were personally guilty, "There's nee space in them for the mice to scamper through, an' nee spaces in the stacks for the owls to hunt. Feel him; there's not a scrap of flesh on't poor bugger; just skin an' bone. Death by starvation ah reckon."

Another unexpected winter event that year was to find myself caught up in a protection racket with the local rabbit population. Maddened with hunger, when every blade of grass was under thick snow, they descended on our garden like locusts. The casualties were not the rabbits but my trees and shrubs. At first I did not believe my eyes when I saw two long eared furry bodies half way up my carefully trimmed evergreen bushes but it was true; there they were, stripping the leaves with their teeth as they clung precariously to the branches. That was bad enough but then I realised that they were systematically stripping off the bark as well, which meant the bushes would be unlikely to survive after the winter. Desperate for some way to protect what remained of my garden, and given that I had not access to a firearm, all I could do was to put out a bribe of hay for them to eat and hope that this would be more palatable than the bark. The result was quite comical really as, twice a day, there was a row of rabbits with white cottontail bottoms up in the air and heads down munching hay - and of course we had put yet one more livestock feeding round on the day's agenda. It was a bleak midwinter indeed and the efforts it took for John and Denty to see to the livestock and for me to battle to and from school each day were exhausting and took their toll; we felt that winter was draining the life out of us and that it was never going to end. But, of course, the cogs in the year's wheel kept turning and with each turn, in tiny increments, the daylight got longer, the bulbs in the garden somehow pierced the frozen soil and, with February upon us, the ewes' bellies were beginning to visibly swell and our thoughts were turning to new life, not death. The hope given at the Winter Solstice finally prevailed.

25

EQUINOX

Denty had his own way of classifying weather in Upper Weardale. Clashy roughly translated as 'windy' - but windy in the hard, gusty sense, probably at a low temperature and usually with rain. It rendered anyone out on the fells soaked, cold and probably exhausted and miserable. A 'clarty' spell often followed on from clashy weather and basically meant it was so wet and muddy that it sucked the wellies off your feet. Both of these types of weather could occur at any time of year. 'Claggy' or 'clouty' weather occurred less frequently, usually in the summer or early autumn; it was oppressively warm and humid weather, which caused men and sheep alike to sweat and pant, thus attracting squadrons of 'flying teeth' (the breed of particularly voracious and sadistic midge peculiar to Weardale) to increase the misery further.

There were other types of weather. Warm but not hot weather in spring after a spell of long, gentle rain showers was declared to be 'growy', (the 'ow' pronounced as in 'cow' rather than as in 'grow'), simply because he said, if you listened closely, you could hear the grass growing.

The most feared of weathers, in terms of the work and worry it brought, was wind-driven snow and the best was the days when the wind dropped, the sky was clear and the sun lit up the Dale. These were the days when Denty would lean over our wall, survey the world and pronounce: "Bye; i'nt it grand!"

We lived in the North Pennine hills at over eleven hundred feet above sea level; Glenwhelt was at fifteen hundred feet, the 'top gate' at two thousand. We did not expect – nor want – endless hot, blue-skied sunny days with an unchanging view.

If we had, we should have gone to live on a Greek island.

The changing skies and temperatures, the unpredictability of the weather was one of my many joys of living where I did. We had real seasons, that changed our views and the way we had to live and dress throughout the cycle of the year. Not all of it was good, nor easy, particularly for those who had to make a living from the hill farms, but coming in chilly, wet and windblown to a warm, welcoming fireside and being able to watch the weather rage on the outside of strong stone walls was, certainly for me, a joy. If the balance of weather conditions throughout the year tended heavily towards the colder, greyer and wetter, it served to make the streams and springs flow and the grass grow. It also ensured that every 'grand' day was a gift to be treasured. Sometimes, surveying the panorama around me from the garden, the fells to the west climbing up to Burnhope Seat in the far distance, the moors to the north rising steeply up towards Rookhope and the River Wear forging its way between tall trees in the valley bottom I would wonder, if there was a paradise, how it could possibly be any more beautiful than Upper Weardale?

I was always grateful when we got through January and the calendar flipped over to February. The first day of February was Imbolg, the Celtic festival of lambs, milk and fecundity and technically the last month of winter and, yes, we would have delicate but fiercely brave snowdrops in their virginal white skirts dancing in the garden. However, whilst there may have been lambs, milk and fecundity in some parts of the country by early February, the North Pennine weather kept the land in a harsh, cold grip. The hill lambs, as if aware of the grim conditions outside, very wisely continued to grow safe and deep inside the ewes. Each year we could only hope that, by the time they were ready to enter the world, things would have improved but there were never any guarantees. One of my annual beacons of hope was the arrival of the lapwings; they would just suddenly fall out of the sky, uttering their piercing and distinctive call of 'peewit! peewit!', which gives them their common name. They would wheel and swoop over our top field, looking for a suitable nest site in which to lay their precious eggs. The sight and sound of those first arrivals would fill me with a joy that was irrational as I knew that, far from heralding the end of winter, often the worst could still be to come.

This was the time of year when the 'scanner man' arrived at Glenwhelt to scan all the ewes with his mobile machine. This was a practice not around in Ray Dent's day and Ray, I suspected, had always thought it a waste of time and money when one could use a practised eye fairly well to determine how many lambs a ewe was carrying. However, scanning them gave a more accurate picture of whether a ewe was having a single lamb, twins or was 'empty' or 'geld' and so Denty could adjust their feed accordingly. Often, John's job was to daub the relevant number of spots of green paint on their backs as each ewe passed through the scanner and the pronouncement was made; one, two or sometimes even three green dots. The geld ewes carried the red dot of shame, that could mean they would be got rid of at the next sheep sale to take place. The harsh economic facts of hill farming took no pity on a ewe that failed to produce lambs; without them she was just a financial liability requiring feed, care, clipping, dipping, worming and of course time, all without profit at the end. Only 'soft fools' like ourselves kept ewes that did not lamb year after year and castrated wedders that would never father lambs.

Of course, we did breed from our ewes when they – and we – were younger and they too would go for their scans up at Glenwhelt, though of course they did not come back clutching a grainy photo of their foetuses! Usually the scanner man would pronounce that they would be due from around March 20th onwards. This would delight me as the spring equinox, celebrated in the Celtic calendar as 'Ostara', occurred at that time; the time in the earth's annual journey around the sun when the light and darkness were held momentarily in balance, day and night of equal length. From that day onwards light would have supremacy over the dark and the days would lengthen and lengthen until mid June and the summer solstice, or 'Litha', – the longest day. After that day darkness would slowly take the lead once more in the northern hemisphere in the eternal dance around the sun, until the autumn equinox.

So the daylight would slowly grow throughout the short month that is February and, unless there were meetings after school to attend, I would no longer have to travel in darkness to or from work. When March, the first of the spring months, arrived, it rarely took notice of the rules set down in the old rhyme about its weather; The 'lambs and lions' would chase each other in an endless circle throughout the month. A couple of days would be still, warm and sunny, then a few with howling gales and bitter cold; then a return to the spring sunshine for a while. You might even wake up to a covering of snow. Denty's phraseology for March weather, apart from the expletives, were 'Bye! It's caad!' and 'Ah wish it would mek its bloody mind up wat it's ganna dee!' I soon abandoned all thoughts of ever discarding my vest before the end of May; 'Never cast a clout till May's right out' as the old saying went. Denty's take on the saying was, 'Aye, but what div they mean by 'May', eh? Now't te dee with the month; ah reckon it's when the May's out!' And thus he would tenaciously hold onto his winter underwear until the hawthorn trees were in full bloom, often a date in early June up here rather than them blossoming in the month that gives them their pseudonym, May trees.

But the greatest gift of March, a month when our daffodils were still making a brave attempt to create buds, was the day when something would prickle my hearing and I would rush to the front door and scan the horizon.

"Ssshh! Listen!"

"I can't hear anything but the wind," John would usually say, or, "No! You are imagining things."

"No! Listen – there it is again!"

295

High, high above us, from the edge of the fell, a pure, clear song would drift through the rain, the mist and the wind, rising and falling in a crescendo and then beginning again. I could not see the bird but it was unmistakably the first curlew of the year. Soon the pairs of large, brown speckled birds with their exceptionally long, graceful curved beaks would be wheeling and dancing in the sky, cementing their relationship before the hazardous duties of parenthood began. The lapwings were the advance guard but the curlews, the glorious, beautiful curlews, with their goosebump-raising, haunting cry, were the heralds of spring. We might yet have to endure weeks of hard, miserable weather with driving rain, biting winds, sleet and snow. But the curlews screamed defiantly at it all; spring was coming and nothing could stop it now.

Throughout my teaching years, I had always found the optimistically but erroneously called spring term, the longest, toughest and most gruelling of the round of three. Easter was always the longed for goal at the end of it but, being such an erratic moveable feast in the Christian calendar, the term length could vary by three weeks or more. So sometimes our lambs would arrive before Easter and sometimes after; one memorable year a gimmer lamb arrived actually on Easter Sunday and was promptly christened… Easter. It was so much easier to keep an eye on the expectant ewes and to be with them for the lambing when I was on school holiday. However, Mother Nature did not consult my timetables! So, if I had to spend half a night in the sheep shed, waiting anxiously while one of our ladies paced round and round but did not get down to actual lambing, well, then I would just have to go into school bleary with lack of sleep. Or, if a very early morning found me with my arm inserted in a sheep and groping round inside for little legs, then I would wash well before I set off, hoping that noses did not twitch too much! Yes, of course, Denty could always be relied on to come if there was a problem and, of course, John kept an eye on things during schooldays but I really, really wanted to be there myself. It was a miracle, a privilege that never ceased to amaze me, to witness and sometimes even help a warm, wet bundle, all slime and legs, out into the world of air and light; to see it take its first breath, clear the mucous from a tiny mouth and hear a tremulous bleat, hear the mother reply softly and coaxingly while the lamb struggled up onto uncoordinated, wobbly legs and watch it move unerringly towards a fat, pink teat and the promise of warm, sweet milk.

Yes, a privilege indeed.

Easter, that festival of rebirth and new life was always a special time of celebration with the family and, as the years passed, Easter had become as special as the Christmas celebration of mid winter. Our family had grown with the arrival of first Fergus, then Rose and finally Eve. Our celebrations at Easter always had certain activities and rituals; there would be an Easter egg hunt around the garden and in all the outbuildings and the children would fly around with little buckets searching for chocolate eggs in the most unlikely places we could think of. When the girls were very small, hiding chocolate eggs in the hens' nesting boxes always brought squeals of delight. Then we would all have an 'Egg Booling' competition with 'paste eggs' – hard boiled eggs that the children decorated beforehand – which were 'booled', or bowled, down the steep hill in our field. Quite simply, the egg that rolled the furthest won and many came to grief on the journey down; smashing on rocks, getting stuck in the grass, falling in the stream. Few survived the journey unscathed! After the paste egg race we would apply ourselves to a breakfast of soft boiled eggs, buttery toast and a heap of homemade hot cross buns. Our main meal of the day always kept the family tradition of roast lamb and the gaps between meals were filled in with chocolate. Weather permitting we would fit in a bracing walk; although one white Easter the children enjoyed the thrills and spills of sledging in the field. One event that seemed to elude me year after year was for a lamb to be born while the children were there. Often we did have lambs by the time Easter came and sometimes there would be 'special needs' cases, or one of a set of triplets, that they thoroughly enjoyed bottle feeding. They learnt young that lambs were not always the dazzling white, adorable infants of Easter cards and children's books. True, most of ours were black anyway, but they would lie in the field and get caked in mud or lie in the sheep shed in a pile of recent poo. A few days after birth, when mother's rich milk was being constantly guzzled, it often began to come out the other end as something that resembled a thick mustard plaster; this would then congeal around their backside and tail, like cooling lava that got deeper and harder with each new eruption, until there was barely room to poo at all. Denty called this condition 'clarty arse' and the solution, if it got too bad, was to cut off the solidified lumps and wash the sticky, still liquid bits off with warm water. If the children pulled faces at having to hold a small, very wriggly lamb while I attended to its sore bottom I would point out that their poo was only solidified milk – a sort of cheese really – and that I had had far more odoriferous bottoms to deal with when they were in nappies. Having thus accustomed them to the less glamorous sides of sheep keeping, and the realities of mucking out heaps of poo and pee sodden bedding from an early age, I did not think they would be traumatised by watching a lamb being born; in fact I hoped it would fill them with amazement.

One Easter holiday, when Fergus was about ten and Rose around eight, it finally augured well; the family were due to arrive and so were Custard's lambs. Custard was the daughter of our original amazing Zwartbles ewe Crumpet, and of that noble tup Zulu. She had been one of triplets that Crumpet had caught us out with, giving birth prematurely and very early one morning on a cold wet hillside. Her two gimmer lambs, Crumble and Custard, had fared remarkably well, but Crumpet had wandered off leaving a tiny, cold, damp, tup lamb lying on the hillside. It was only when John nearly stood on him, that the little tup was found. He was in a pitiable state. Intensive care, living on a hot pack in the bottom of the kitchen dresser and bottle feeding were called for. We called him Zeeb and he actually went on to become even broader and taller than his very impressive father. Not needing any more ewes to breed from, we gave Crumble to Denty, who had a shortage of ewes in his Zwartbles flock at that time. Custard, who remained with us, was a good mother, never had problems lambing and invariably had twins, so I had no worries whatsoever about her producing her latest crop of lambs and she had been really well throughout her pregnancy. She was well 'bagged up', her swollen udder producing globules of waxy milk when squeezed. My early morning check found her pacing around her pen and not long after that she began a restless getting up then lying down again routine. The family were all finishing off their breakfast at this point.

"I am as sure as I can be that Custard will produce her lambs within the next hour; is there anyone who would like to be there to see them born?"

"Me! Me!" Fergus and Rose shouted in unison, followed by "And me!" from Megan.

Bernie obligingly offered to look after Eve, who was very young at this point.

I donned my usual lambing attire of waterproof trousers, short welly boots and a tatty fleece jacket, collected a pile of old towels and off we went to see how Custard was coming along. She was certainly near to lambing; getting up and down with increasing frequency and rubbing up against the walls of the sheep shed. There was certainly plenty of fluid trickling out of her rear end but, despite much heaving and stoic grunting, there was no sign of the awaited two little cloven feet. When about a quarter of an hour had passed with no sign of progress, I began to get a bit anxious; Denty's advice was always 'Divven't wait too lang te find out if summit is up!', so I rolled up my right sleeve up and gently inserted my hand into the birth canal.

That certainly made her grunt a lot louder and Rose enquired anxiously, "Is she all right, Granny?"

"Yes sweetheart, she's fine; I am just checking to see if everything is alright with the lamb."

The strange thing was that everything did seem all right; the lamb was not lying with a leg back nor in the breech position. All I could feel were two perfectly normal front legs poised in the correct position to enter the world. With her next contraction I inserted my middle finger between the forelegs, just above the ankle joint, then grasped both legs firmly. As

Custard pushed, I gave a steady pull and soon the lamb was sliding out into the world.

"Here it comes!" I told the wide eyed children.

But even as the lamb slid out onto the straw there was something wrong about it; it was leaden and very limp. I had delivered several lambs which plopped out seemingly lifeless but responded quickly once the mucous membrane around their mouth was cleared and their lungs gently pummelled into life. I grabbed a towel and vigorously rubbed the face clear, then the body and even shook it to see if I could get it to breathe. As a last resort I opened its little mouth to try and blow some of my breath into its lungs but what I saw was not a healthy pink mouth; the tongue was very pale, the mouth tinged blue. Throughout this process, having given her lamb one perfunctory sniff, Custard turned away, as if she had no further interest in it. It was a perfectly formed, good sized, full term gimmer lamb; there was nothing about it that was abnormal, in fact it was a beautiful little thing.

It had just failed to make the perilous journey from womb to world.

Sensing something was wrong the children had gone very quiet.

"I am so sorry my darlings but this little lamb just didn't make it."

"Why?" asked Rose sorrowfully.

"I really don't know; it's just something that happens sometimes."

My own sorrow at the loss of the lamb was overlaid with guilt that the children had had to witness what had happened. What was meant to be a revelation of the marvel of birth had instead been their first encounter with death. Megan put her arm gently around them to take them back to the house but Rose asked,

"Can I see the lamb Granny?"

"Yes, of course you can."

I wrapped the small, black body in a clean towel and passed it over the gate to Megan; it was limp and still warm from the heat of its mother's body. Rose stroked the damp black wool on its forehead thoughtfully.

"It just looks as if it is asleep Granny! Just asleep! But is it dead?"

"Yes; it is dead."

"But it doesn't look scary."

"Why should it? Death is as natural as birth; one is the beginning of life and one the end; in a way this lamb was never alive – it never took a breath of its own."

Fergus gave a tug on my coat, "Look Granny, Custard is doing that pushing thing again!"

And with no drama and seemingly little effort another slimy, black bundle slid out of Custard onto the straw. I quickly knelt to check its mouth was clear of membranes and this time Custard was helping me by nudging and vigorously licking the lamb, which shook its head a few times and then began a wailing bleat. Within a couple of minutes it was struggling to its feet and, after a few trial attempts at coordinating its legs, was firmly latched onto its mother's plump udder. The children watched in pure amazement.

"It can walk already! It took Eve ages to do that!"

Had Denty been there he would have looked at the first lamb, shaken his head and said, 'Just not meant to be.' Then he would have looked at the second, nodded and said, 'Aye, footed and tekkin suck; it'll be reet.'

I waited until the placenta was delivered – 'Ugh! What's that?' – tidied up the straw, gave fresh hay and water to Custard and then we all left the mother and new lamb in peace. The experience had not been the one I had hoped for and yet, in some ways, it might have been an even more profound lesson for the children. In the midst of life there is always death, each as natural and necessary as the other; on this occasion they had witnessed them hand in hand.

Life and death.

Light and darkness.

Joy and sorrow.

In their lifetimes they would come to know them all.

That Easter holiday also gifted us with a few perfect April days; bright sun in a cloudless blue sky yet still with a hint of chill in the air. The blue tits were busy building in the tiny hole in the wall above the front door to which they returned every year. One blue tit must have caught sight of himself in the wing mirror of John's car on the drive as it flew past with a beak full of moss. Enraged, it forgot all about domestic bliss and set about knocking seven bells out of the image in the mirror - an imagined intruder on his patch - like a tiny, demented budgerigar. The starlings were also busy moving into their annual nesting quarters under the metal curves of John's workshop roof - which we referred to as 'Corrugation Street' - where they all got on very amicably, with heads poking out of their terrace row of nest sites all afternoon. The children were in the field, petting the sheep and trying to keep up with the lambs, which by now had formed into gangs and were racing around like demented, jet-black imps. They were leaping across the water in the ditch in the middle of the field like horses taking Becher's Brook, ricocheting off the stone walls then racing back again. Once they had finally exhausted themselves they suckled their mothers briefly before stretching full length to snooze in the warm afternoon sun. The children, equally exhausted, straggled back to seek succour themselves with tea and scones.

As the sun gradually lowered in the sky the air became more hazy, the light more golden and diffused. The sheep were settled with their lambs while the cattle in the fields opposite, recently released from their long winter captivity indoors, were making the most of their freedom, ripping at the spring grass with relish. Above Swinhope curlews circled over the fell, their liquid call rippling through the air and in the very top of our tall pine tree a blackbird sang evensong. The year was now several weeks past spring equinox and each week the sunset reached further and further towards the other side of the Dale. In the darkest days of winter the sun only struggled above the hill behind us on the southern side of the Dale by mid morning and by mid afternoon sank back weakly again. By summer solstice, the longest day, it rose and set on the opposite side, barely sinking behind the hills before a glow appeared and it rose again. This 'sun-ometer' was the feature that most marked our seasons at Hill House East, making us aware of them and attuned to them in a way that has been lost to those unable to see horizons. A local saying about Westgate is: 'sunny-side and money-side' - the sunny-side being the northern side and the 'money-side' the southern. The sunny-side reference is easy to understand; in spring, autumn and particularly summer it enjoys almost uninterrupted sunlight on bright days and thus is favoured for hay fields. The 'money-side' had me puzzled for a long while though; being deprived of sunlight in the stygian days of winter can hardly be an indicator of wealth can it? Finally I decided that it must be because the longer winter hours of gloom and therefore cold means we have to have our fires lit or heating on far earlier than the other side. The 'money' therefore referring not to wealth but the need to spend more of it!

May can be a glorious month in the Dale but in June there is a full, joyous, riot of growth that only comes in that month. My Rose was well suited to the month of her birth; mercurial, extravert, full-on with joy and energy.
Beautiful and loving but prone to showers, or even storms.
Of course, one never gets constant good weather here and June can be still cruelly cold and the steady rain equally chilling; sheep huddled miserably in the lee of walls and the hens reluctant to leave the shelter of their house.
But on a 'grand' day...

On such a June day, after a morning of steady gardening, I sit on a garden bench with a cool drink under a true sky-blue sky, with only a few wisps of high, cirrus clouds. The sunshine is hot and brilliant, making the new season's leaves an impossible glowing green. The sunlight makes me feel translucent too; the light energy flowing in, through and out of me. But the air is not still or heavy; there is a true breeze. It moves gently, erratically, stirring the ends of the honeysuckle tendrils and making a soft rustle in the trees, a light, air-stirring breath keeping people, animals and plants cool in what would otherwise have been fierce heat. Mid June, mid afternoon on a bright, warm day is indeed paradise at Hill House East. June is the month when the garden had all the brashness of youth; by July it is maturing to middle age and by August already preparing wistfully for autumn. The autumn equinox in September readied us for the death of the year in mid winter, marked by the Celts as Yule and morphing into the celebration of Christmas. But the dark and the cold were far away on that June day. John was away for the day, which meant I was alone; a quite rare state of affairs. There is a state of mind, which I think may be peculiar to women, in relishing having the house and garden all to oneself, just for a while, with no real agenda; doing what you want, when you want, eating and drinking what you want, when you want and looking like a tramp and not giving a fig. I had that almost girlish sense of freedom that day but was deeply aware that it was only possible in the sure and certain knowledge that it would be just for a limited period of time; John would return and with him, security, comfort, companionship. It was one of those 'let there be spaces in your togetherness' times, as recommended for long and happy relationships by Kahlil Gibran in The Prophet; a passage that was actually used as a reading at our wedding – to the consternation of some guests and wry smiles from the friends that truly knew me. I thought about being really reckless and having a lunchtime glass of white wine but realised my sense of wellbeing and contentment could not be greater and wine would only serve to dull my senses.

And I really did not want that to happen.

I had long dreamt of such a day when, the pressures of working in school being over, I would just sit in my garden on a June afternoon and do nothing but let the beauty of it and of the hills around saturate me. I would gaze on all we had done, all we had achieved with this old stone house and count all the blessings it had brought into our lives since we had found it, empty and unloved.

Well, this was that day; a rare and precious jewel of a day.

Gemstones are only precious because they are rare and hard won; if I turned over a shovelful every time I stuck a spade in the ground they would become common place, of little value.

I settled into a sitting silence; a silence only broken by the splashing of water as a blackbird cooled himself in the bird bath, the bleat of lambs up the field and the bubbling, haunting crescendo of a curlew's call on the hill top. My Quaker journey was teaching me the value of silence, the joys of sitting in stillness and just letting go, letting the mind seek and ponder on all that really mattered. What mattered to me in that moment was to be me; to be alive in that place and time and to be grateful for it.

Retirement and age were bringing the things that we all come to; painful hips, stiff joints, aches and pains, grey hair, less energy. In the silence and stillness I was learning to accept these things as being as much a part of the natural order as the vivid recklessness of youth. Another development was an increasing appreciation of so many small aspects of my life, as I realised that time for me was now a precious, diminishing resource that was not to be wasted. 'Do small things with great love': thus reads a plaque in our porch. I am increasingly quite happy, as the Quakers advise, to 'seek new light from whatever source it may come.' Mind you, one of the things I do miss from church services is the chance to sing a good hymn. Not a new or trendy hymn but a good, weighty, solid hymn; one that I have known all of my life and probably sang in school assemblies. Lines, scraps and tunes of hymns often pop into my head at the most unexpected moments. Alone in the garden that special day the lines that come are –

Praise to the Lord, the Almighty, the king of creation,

Oh my soul praise him for he is thy health and salvation…

…Hast thou not seen? All that is needful hath been

Granted in what he ordaineth.

Amen to that; I must remember to tell Megan that I want it sung at my funeral - she already knows I want people to leave the service to the theme music from 'The Archers'! I hear the throb of a quad bike, the engine is switched off and Denty comes through the garden gate.

"Bye! En't it grand?"

"Tea?"

"Aye – gan on. Mind, nowt to eat; ah've just had me dinner. D'ye know I found a pack o' bread buns reduced to 10p at the Coop and ah've just had two wi' fried eggs and salad cream – gorgeous!"

So I leave my thoughts and the garden bench to go to put the kettle on. But one thought remains: indeed, all that is needful has been more than granted.

26

THE TAIL END

I thought that all the memorable events, the visitors and the animals that had played their part over the last twenty years had been committed to paper and my stories were at an end – but I was wrong; life and Mother Nature always seem to have yet another trick up their sleeve!

I do not loathe cats, nor am I allergic to them. However, I would never actively seek to own a cat - if such a thing is even possible. They are far too independent, unbiddable and unreliable for my liking. I am more of a dog or horse person when it comes to animals as 'pets'. Actually, for years now we have had only hens and sheep to be responsible for and at least they can be reasonably expected to come to you when you offer food and not to leave the confines of a field. No, I would never choose to live with a cat - though, in the course of the last forty five years, eight cats have chosen to live with me. Each one has brought me companionship, aggravation, amusement, worry and happiness in equal measure. The last cat John and I shared our life with moved here with us to Hill House East. I got her as a kitten that was going to be put down because she was not thriving, was puny and sickly for her ten weeks of age and no one wanted to adopt her. As it was a few days before Christmas, I agreed to take her and give her a chance.

I named her Holly and she lived into her twentieth year.

We were both sixty when she died and thought, 'If we get another cat that lives that long we could be dead before it is.' So we introduced a strict no pets rule and avoided all attempts to introduce anything small, cute and with big eyes into our lives or hearts.

Ten years on and we are both seventy.

There had been a feral cat living on the hillside for over a year. She was very wary, rarely seen and, when she was, often had a raggle-taggle of kittens trailing behind her. Then mother and kittens would just disappear into the fellside again. We had a rare sighting of her in the October of 2019 prowling up our hill, thin and slack bellied through feeding the two kittens that followed her. About a week later we had just sat down in the late afternoon when I heard a faint and desperate mewling outside in the garden. John, of course, heard nothing; forty five years of working with printing presses had long since robbed him of being able to hear high pitched sounds.

"Did you hear that?"

What a stupid question!

"There it is again!"

And again... and again.

Curiosity got the better of me and I went out to investigate. It was an awful afternoon; cold, wet and windy.

Clashy, Denty would have called it.

Sitting beside the garden gate I found the source of the plaintive cries; a very small, very damp and thoroughly miserable kitten looked at me, shaking the cold raindrops off its ears and shivering with each gust of the chilly wind. I got within about three feet of it before it hissed loudly and shot off across the lawn and under the dubious shelter of the deck in front of the summer house.

"Oh dear," I reported to John, "It looks like one of those feral kittens has got separated from its mother. Still, I am sure she will come back for it."

"I hope so," was the reply, "You remember our solemn vow? No more pets."

"John, this animal is not pet material; it is feral - wild - just like its mother. I would never get within an arm's length of it and, even if I did, it would scratch and bite me and run off again."

The next morning it was sadly apparent that the mother had abandoned the kitten and had no intention of returning. Once more it cried pitifully at the gate and once more it ran off under the deck when I approached. We decided that the last time it had seen its mother must have been by the gate, which was why it kept vigil there. I was conscience stricken; did I let it just die of exposure or did I intervene in some way?

"I can't just let it die; I am going to put some food out and we will see what happens."

"Here we go!"

"Here we don't go anywhere! I'm just going to let it fill its belly, then it might have the strength to move on."

"Uh huh?"

"John! Honestly! I – we – don't want another cat!"

Though I never saw it take the food, as it ran off as I put the dish of tuna fish down, the food was gone by the time I went out. The next time I offered food I watched from a window in the house and, sure enough, after a safe pause, the kitten crept from under the deck, ate the food and then shot back in.

"You know," I said by the second day, "It would be all right if it stayed here as an outdoor cat; it could live in the sheep shed or hay shed and it might keep the rodent population down?"

"Uh huh?" was the only response I got, yet again.

The next day I came downstairs to find Denty in the kitchen supping his customary large mug of tea.

"Ah, Denty have you seen anything of that feral cat on the hillside?"

"Aye, aah did see her a day or two since, slinkin' about; she seems to hev' shook off them kittens though."

"We know; she has shook off one of them in our garden!"

"Aye an' that's the second or third lot she's dropped this year. Poor little beggars."

We returned late afternoon from a Sunday lunch out with friends, to find the kitten once more keeping its hopeless vigil by the gate. The cries were quieter now, its dash to the safety of the summer house slower and more of an effort; it was getting weaker.

"Right!" I announced in a decisive voice, "I can't stand anymore of this; I am just going to have to catch it!"

John did not even bother to say 'Uh huh?' this time, he just raised a somewhat incredulous eyebrow.

Out of my Sunday best and into jeans and a jumper, I donned wellies and thick leather pruning gauntlets and found the children's fishing net. The kitten had not had any food all day so would be very hungry by now. Each time I had fed it I had put the food a little further away from the deck and each time I had stood there till it came and fed, so it was now not entirely unused to my presence. It was in fact looking at me from under the deck when I put the dish down and I backed off and stood stock still, the fishing net raised above my head. I made what I hoped sounded like encouraging maternal cat noises and the little thing crept out, mewing softly back at me. I raised my eyes heavenward and uttered a rather demanding prayer.

"Right, you up there! If you want me to help this kitten, I have got this one chance. When I bring this net down if it doesn't go over it I will never get near it again. So, it's up to you really!"

I brought the net down with a mighty swoosh when the kitten's head was in the food dish – and it was caught. Lifting the net up I grabbed it by the scruff of its neck with my gauntleted hand and disentangled it. I was braced for the teeth, the claws and the hissing and spitting. What I actually got was a small, cold body desperately burrowing into my jumper, purring loudly.

"Well, thank you very much," I shot heavenward, "That's a rotten trick! What am I supposed to do now?"

Once back in the house I rather nervously took off my gauntlets and stroked the little creature. It was a beauty; a classic tabby with huge, blue-grey eyes that just gazed at me, not fearful, not wild; just calm, serene and I think relieved. It purred and rubbed itself against me, seeking the warmth of my jumper. I knew in that instant that this kitten was going nowhere, that this kitten had found its home.

"It would appear," I told John as I handed him the small, now warmer bundle, "That we have been adopted."

The look John gave me was inscrutable but I read it as, "I knew this was going to happen".

But any resistance that he might have had quickly evaporated when I placed the very young, damp kitten into his arms. It immediately climbed up his jumper and buried its head into the safe woollen warmth of his arm pit, where it began purring loudly and kneading the wool with its front paws, the way kittens do when suckling from their mother.

"It is very feral and wild," I warned him.

"What a little sweetheart! Do you know if it is a boy or a girl?"

I plucked the kitten from his jumper and examined the nether regions carefully.

"I am pretty sure that it is a girl. But it seems to have sticky lumps on its fur; what can that be?"

John had a careful look; "I think it is pine resin; look, there are one or two pine needles stuck in it too."

"I expect that's from the pine tree that overhangs the deck where it, sorry, she, has been living. So, the next thing we need is a name?"

"I take it that means we are keeping it?"

"What do you think?"

The kitten gazed at John with huge, fathomless blue-grey eyes and I knew he was sunk.

"Well, she is very sweet and very sticky; how about Fudge?"

"I thought my days of fireguards and nappies were over!" John mock-grumbled, as we hunted around for things to make provision for the kitten. All our previous cat items were long gone, so a cardboard box with an old towel in became a bed and a paint roller tray with some sawdust from under John's workbench became an improvised litter tray. To our amazement and delight she hopped straight in, had a little tinkle and then took great care to cover it up with sawdust with her tiny paws before hopping out.

"How does she know how to do that? Toilet trained in half an hour!" Feeding and drinking from the little dishes I provided also posed no problem. All I had that was remotely suitable for a cat was tinned tuna but she ate it with relish, had a drink of water and then sauntered into her cardboard box, curled up and went straight to sleep cuddled into the warm wheat bag I had put in for her. Fed, warm and obviously feeling safe and content, Fudge was staking her claim on our home and our hearts, both of which it would appear, had been ordained that we should share with her from now on.

Next morning, being responsible animal owners, I rang the vet and made an appointment for her to be checked over. A wicker basket with a wire cake cooling tray over the top served as a cat carrier. When we entered the surgery the vet was wearing long, claw-proof gauntlets.

"Ah, a feral kitten I believe; where did you find it?" I related the story while removing said kitten from the box and cuddling her. She rumbled loudly with pleasure.

"Oh my goodness! It is tiny and beautiful and – are you sure it is feral?" "Completely sure," I told her and placed the kitten onto the examination table, where she sat calmly, taking in the new surroundings, "I just think it knows it is onto a good thing."

With gloves removed, the vet examined the kitten carefully, confirmed 'it' was a girl and cut off some of the resinous lumps from its coat. Fudge behaved impeccably throughout.

"Well, I would say she is only about four weeks old, though obviously weaned. She is remarkably healthy actually; no ticks or fleas. But I would like to worm her, as she has been living outside and eating heaven knows what."

Like a saint, Fudge swallowed the worm pill in one gulp with no fuss at all. Our last cat, Holly, would have been spread out like a freefall parachute jumper whilst, at the same time, foaming copiously from her mouth.

"She's gorgeous; I could keep her myself! But that's all she needs for now, we need to look at injections and another worming in a month or so. One lucky little cat."

All afternoon the kitten snoozed in her box. She did not even respond to the sound of her bowl of food being put down, which was strange, as this little thing loved her grub.

By teatime I lifted her out and put her on John's knee.

"She seems very dopey; perhaps it is the effect of the worm pill?"

Round about five o'clock John said she must be having a very exciting dream as she was twitching in her sleep. But these muscular spasms were no dream; they were more like someone going into an epileptic fit. Frantically I tried to get a response from the kitten but she could not stand, nor open her eyes, while spasm after spasm shook her body.

"That's very strange," a worried vet said, "Can you get her to the surgery as quickly as possible? Only I am not in Stanhope now, I am in Alston about to do evening surgery."

I had acquired both of the only two speeding offences of my entire life on the road to Alston, both doing over thirty miles per hour, but under forty miles an hour, a hundred yards or so into a thirty mile an hour zone. I think I could have acquired enough speeding offences to ban me from driving for life on the dash to Alston that evening. I kept slipping my hand into the box beside me to feel the small, furry body and see if it was alive; its breathing seemed shallower each time. I was taken straight in to find the vet examining a print out from the computer.

She looked worried.

"I have done a check on the worming product and it would appear that one in ten thousand kittens can have a toxic reaction to it. That, I am afraid, is what has happened. The trouble is you can't ask an animal if it is allergic to anything."

"And? What can be done?"

She sighed, "Not a lot I am afraid. The drug will have been completely absorbed into her system by now. It is just a question of whether she is strong enough to survive the affects. But it has affected her so badly that, I have to say, the outlook is not good. If she continues to go downhill over the next two hours then, well, the kindest thing would be to put her sleep."

I could hardly believe my ears. It was roughly twenty four hours since I had first brought Fudge into our lives and now I was being told we would probably lose her. I nodded dumbly, fighting back tears.

"I'll ring shall I? In two hours?"

"Yes, do. And I am so sorry."

Sat in the car in the carpark outside I broke down and wept. Stupid, stupid woman I kept saying to myself; you didn't want the damn kitten in the first place – it will just be a bloody nuisance.

But still I wept.

I cursed myself for my weakness, my sentimentality.

I cursed God for having let me capture it when it could have just run off. I cursed the providence which, through doing something to keep the animal healthy, may in fact have killed it. I wept because there was simply nothing else to do. Finally I composed myself enough to start the engine and to drive home; slowly this time, as there was no need to hurry when the next two hours stretched in front and seemed agonisingly long. I had only been home about an hour and a half when the phone rang and the display came up 'vet'. I lifted the receiver, heart banging in my chest and barely able to breathe. The two hours were not yet up; she obviously hadn't even made it that far.

"Hello? Mrs Graham? Don't worry; she is still with us. She is no better I am afraid but she has not deteriorated any more. If it is all right with you I would like to put her on a drip and keep her in overnight? She might have a chance that way."

I began to breathe again, "Yes, yes! Please, do that; do anything – anything that will help at all."

"Fine. I will come in and check her again at ten tonight and then first thing in the morning. Then I will give you a ring."

"Thank you; thank you so much."

"Well, we are not out of the woods yet."

We slept, or partly slept, very badly and at seven o'clock on the dot the phone rang and John answered it. There was a long silence on our end of the phone, other than John saying, 'Ah,' occasionally. I could have sworn my heart actually stopped as well as my breathing this time. Then, after an endless pause he said, "Okay, I'll do that. Thank you."

I was braced, I was ready; I was trying to be brave.

"She says we can pick her up at ten thirty this morning and that she is bright eyed and bushy tailed; apparently all the staff are taking selfies with her!"

So here we are; aged seventy and with a kitten who flies round like a Tornado jet, who is utterly fearless and climbs everything and everywhere. She gave us two heart attacks within the first week by disappearing altogether and making us search the entire house, garden and all the outbuildings. On the first occasion she had squeezed into a space where the central heating pipes are boxed in, fallen to the bottom and couldn't get out again. On the second she had got into the wine rack inside a cupboard and the door had then been closed. Only when we went to get a bottle, to drown our

sorrows at having finally lost her, did she appear huge-eyed and inquisitive and in need of her tea. Of course, she has all the best necessities of life; a tweed fur lined cat basket, a very swish ensuite toilet, top quality cat litter and ditto kitten food. Oh, and the vet recommended goat's milk. All in all, her first few weeks cost a pretty penny and we still have inoculations, chipping and spaying to look forward to. So has this unexpected addition to Hill House East been a curse or a blessing? I think, without doubt, the latter. We are like a couple who think their family is complete and, after a long gap, find they are to be parents again. Yes, there are the sleepless nights and nappies – and thank goodness we do not actually have those – but also the joy of watching new life, watching growth and all the little developmental steps to adulthood. And, oh that final and unexpected time, how young you become yourself, how precious, how important each of those steps become when you realise you may never witness them again.

Thank you Fudge, for coming into our lives and keeping us young at heart for a little while longer.

GATHERIN' UP...

A ll life is a circle; birth, then death, then new life to take its place and to also die in turn.

That is the large circle.

Within the circle of our own little lives there are smaller circles; we all live our days to the tune of hours, weeks, months and years.

The years pass to the rhythm of the turning seasons.

Throughout my life, it has seemed to me that moving around these circles we find we have our own personal circles. These often bring us back to where we may have been before, or to people we thought we had lost, who can pop up in the most unexpected places; aged, changed, but still sharing memories with you. It took me over a quarter of a century to complete one of these circles, from buying the first house I ever owned and lived in here in Weardale, to returning to buy what I hope may be my last home – though not for a good while yet!

My husband John's 'Weardale Circle' took even longer to go round. When he moved here, he had no idea just how deep his roots go into the local soil; some four hundred years in fact. His mother was a Westgarth and a direct descendant of the Westgarth family in Weardale. They were important landowners, living in Unthank Hall in Stanhope from around 1600; an historic house that dates back to before Elizabethan times. His two times great grandfather left Weardale a hundred and eighty years ago (not far – just thirteen miles to Tow Law!) and John is the first descendant to return. His middle name, Westgarth, is proof that he is no incomer and his forefathers lie beneath their graves in Stanhope churchyard as further evidence of his lineage.

I was also astonished to find out that he has roots much nearer to our home here in Westgate. His eight times Westgarth great grandfather, in 1656, married a young woman called Margaret from the equally renowned Bainbridge family here in Weardale. She was born and lived at Fieldstyle, Westgate; less than a direct mile from our door.

So, although my association with Weardale stretches back a paltry half century and I was the one so desperate to return, it is indeed John who has truly come back home. I wanted, very deeply, to find some ancestors of my own who had lived in Weardale before me but they are all Hetheringtons, from the turbulent border between Scotland and England. Cumbrians and Northumbrians all, right down to my mother's day, they were once a Border Reiver family whose claim to fame was to invent blackmail; the extortion of money from tenants on top of their normal rent, or 'mail', to 'protect' them from being pillaged by a Reiver band – possibly one of their own. One of the ironic twists of history was that one of their bitterest feuds was with the neighbouring Graham family, who were the Super Reivers of the era, unmatched for their violence, cattle thieving, murder and duplicity. Having acquired this once feared name through John's father's line, I hope, in some small way to have brought a degree of reconciliation between the two families. The nearest I have come in my quest for some roots of my own in Weardale, was to discover that my two times great grandmother, Jane Walton, lived in the tiny village of Blagill, just east of Alston. She certainly had a very local surname before marrying Robert Hetherington and moving near to Haltwhistle in Northumberland. But, although Blagill is only ten miles in a direct line from Westgate, it is over the border line into Cumbria – or as it would have been in her day, Cumberland – and not part of County Durham or Weardale.

I was a young teacher when I first lived in the Dale in the 1970s. However, when I left, I had a lot of years out of that profession. I was mostly involved with horses and particularly carriage driving for a decade or more. That circle completed when I returned to the Dale and I was once more teaching. One of the most amazing things when I returned, after more than a quarter of a century, was the number of people who had been in the Dale all that time that not only recognised me but greeted me casually by name, as if I had just been away on an extended holiday.

Or perhaps a lengthy prison sentence.

Yet just how much time had actually passed was brought home to me by one middle aged lady in Stanhope saying to me, "Ee! You used to be my cookery teacher!" before introducing me to her grandchildren.

It is twenty years on from 'openin' the gate' and stepping, not just into this property, but into a life rich with friends, community and animals situated – as it says on the logo for Upper Weardale – in an Area of Outstanding Natural Beauty. I am grateful for every day we have lived here and hope we will be blessed with many more before having to finally face west, other than to marvel at the glorious sunsets from the deck of the summerhouse, where a lot of this book has been written. Thanks to John's endless labours of love here, all is now as we would want it to be. The front gaff, once a churned up paddock of mud and rubble, is now a pretty little garden space with a small rill running through a stone walled channel. The house stands transformed – warm, cosy, relaxing – and always ready to receive friends and family. Our wooden summer house stands in a garden in which, over the years, I have come to understand the plants that will tolerate life at this altitude and the ones which just curl up their toes and die. The Hemmel, once so derelict and lost, has been one of John's greatest projects; it is now refurbished with an insulated roof, a beautiful pine floor and a large wood burning stove. It is put to many uses; as a workshop for myself and friends to have craft days, a place for me to card and spin my wool, a peaceful place where some Quaker friends and I gather for some quiet reflection and at other times a joyful, noisy place where we can gather with family and friends to eat and drink at seasonal celebrations. Best of all, in the roof space, John has created a floored area where the grandchildren can have their own special place to play, to create and retreat to. They all love coming here and know they are privileged to have a place where they can play in fields and streams or swing on a rope, feed hens and collect eggs, plant beans in the spring and eat them in the summer. After a summer week here someone asked Rose what she had done on her holiday; what trips out she had had.

"Well, none really - we were just at the house."

"Wasn't that boring?"

She gave them a withering look.

"Bored? There is always something to do at Hill House East!"

Of course, in no way do I wish to create the illusion that we live in some enchanted place where there are no problems, no pain and no setbacks in life. As with everyone, we have had our fair share of worries, ill health and sadness over the last two decades. But the peace, the tenacity, the sheer solidity of this house, which has kept it upright over the centuries, is what has always somehow given us the strength to get through and move forward again.

We once had an Irish gay couple who stayed here for a few days. They were here looking for a place to rent to live in because this looked such a beautiful, quiet area. Their story was tragic and they were both visibly ground down by it, almost to hopelessness. The elder of the two had been a teacher but relentless stress had forced him to leave because he simply couldn't cope. His younger partner was tense, nervous and anxious when they arrived, as if he lived daily in dread. They, their clothes, the old car they arrived in and the little dog that slept in it all seemed somehow shabby; as if there was really nothing much worth making an effort about. After a day or two here, a thawing occurred; they no longer jumped if we knocked and entered the room, they visibly enjoyed their food and relished evenings in front of the log stove just sitting quietly.

Peacefully.

Each day they went out to look at properties available to rent.

On the day they left the younger man asked hesitatingly if I would show him round the garden.

"Of course! It's there for guests to enjoy as well as us!"

"I love gardens," he told me as we strolled, "I would really love to find a place where we could have a proper garden; we live in a terrace house you see. I have tried planting pots outside the door and window boxes and things but... well; they just get smashed... or dug up and thrown in the street."

"I am truly so sorry."

"That's just part of the harassment; we get eggs thrown at the windows, awful things through the letter box. We thought if we could get away, right away, to somewhere peaceful in the countryside, things might be better for us."

"And have you found anywhere?"

He made a sound between derision and despair.

"Oh yes; several places. We would have been happy to take any of them."

"But?"

"But everyone wants a guarantor to lay down money for us. No one will do that."

He stood and quietly, looking at the far hillside and its chequerboard pattern of grey stone walls, the sheep grazing, the moors rising behind and the constantly shifting clouds above and I knew he was seeing exactly what I had seen the very first time I had stood in that spot.

"You know," he said resignedly, "You live in heaven: I live in hell."

I have never forgotten that couple, even though we were never to know the final outcome of their quest for a quiet life. I carry his words with me as a reminder to never take for granted the privilege of living here, nor the fulfilment and healing it has brought to my life.

Alas, even here there is no fountain of eternal youth! Since retirement, the years are passing quicker than I thought possible, or wanted them to. Here I am, a septuagenarian with a new hip, orthotics in my shoes, cataracts removed from my eyes, just about managing to hang onto my own teeth and with the threat of a knee replacement looming over me. However, my daughter was right about one thing; modern hip replacements are wonderful!

Fearing that if we bred more lambs recently then they could outlive us, our little flock of sheep is now down to four beloved pets: Zeeb (now even bigger than his fabled dad Zulu!), his sister Custard and two incomers Teasel and her son Tussock, who are of the rare Teeswater breed. But theirs is another story! The time for planning, building, expanding is over. Now is the time to reflect, to gather up the memories against the day when they may be all we have left of this amazing place, which we have been blessed to live in and to share with those - human, woollen and feathered - who have all been as family and taught me so much.

Twenty years on, almost exactly to the day that we first saw Hill House East on a glorious May afternoon, I sit writing in the summer house on an equally glorious May evening, overlooking the familiar and much-loved patchwork of grey stone walls flowing down the hillside opposite. This year's lambs in our field are well up now and, having exhausted themselves racing around the field and are settling down beside their mothers for the night. The trees along the banks of the river Wear below me seem to be turning up their volume on green with each day and the hens are having one last rake about, purely for pleasure, as they know their supper awaits them in the hen house. Fudge, the feral kitten, has now grown into a long, sleek and very characterful cat and she has been with me as I write, stretched out on the sofa in here, basking in a sunbeam. Now, as the sun begins to dip, with a last yawn and a stretch, she has decided to go into the house to see if her supper has been served yet. John has spent the afternoon renovating an old hand operated sheep clipping machine, that Denty had found heaven knows where, but is now also winding down on the day in the garden with a glass of red wine in his hand.

And with one for me when I finish writing this.

All is peaceful and more idyllic than we could have ever dreamt of. Yet...

Shortly after we moved here in 2000, a dark, malignant cloud hung over this country as the plague that was foot and mouth disease raged across it. The people, and all the animals, in Upper Weardale were miraculously spared its ravages. Well, now an even more terrifying threat is hanging over the whole world, called Covid 19. John and I have been in self-isolation for nearly three months now and there is no end in sight. We find it darkly amusing that we are in the Elderly Vulnerable category. Since lockdown began I have dug and planted a large vegetable garden and brought on tubs of peas, beans, salads and tomatoes in the greenhouse. John has daily embarked on a programme of repair and renovation of just about everything he has laid his eyes on. He has put a new wall and window into a large shed and painted hundreds of yards of fencing and gates with preservative. Jointly we have embarked on a new hobby; brewing our own wine. So far there are thirty bottles of Pinot Grigio and thirty of Merlot in the storeroom – though weekly this tally falls because it is, dare I say it, rather good. We go to bed each night tired out but happy and, frankly, missing very little of the outside world, other than not being able to see our family and friends. We acknowledge with gratitude just how fortunate we are to be here while the disease accelerates across a world which has no barriers against it. In fact, I feel very guilty a lot of the time; we want for nothing, we are content and know that we are safe as long as we stay put in this beautiful place until normality returns – though what that word will mean in the future remains to be seen. Mine is not to question how this pandemic began or why, but, as the skies clear, the air we breathe gets less polluted and marine life has improved across the planet during the pandemic, I cannot help but wonder if this world, that we all share, has just had enough of our greed and mistreatment.

So, the journey within this book began with a plague and, as I end it, we are living through another one. Something else is ending too; another circle has been completed – though we have only come to realise it very recently, during our time in lockdown. After sixteen years of at times hard but thoroughly enjoyable effort, and having met the most wonderful, eclectic mix of people, we will be taking down the signs for Hill House East Country Bed and Breakfast at the end of this year. We have of course been closed because of the virus for months now and probably wouldn't be allowed to open again till near the end of the year anyway. We have had such a sense of achievement, of adventure, of satisfaction through the B&B that we want to finish while it has all been a joy – and while we are number 1 locally in the hallowed Tripadvisor ratings!

And we are thinking of it as retiring rather than closing, as it is much more positive.

Being quietly here on our own all these weeks has made us realise that the time has come to have the house and our hillside just to ourselves for a while: no agendas, no deadlines, no getting up at 6.00 am to prepare breakfasts. Just being here and living here in the fullest sense of those words for as long as I can bake a batch of scones and John can push the lawnmower. When I told John recently that he had so many jobs planned that, if he wasn't careful, he was going to run out of lockdown he was genuinely horrified and said, "It's not going to END is it?"

Thus speaks a man who is truly happy in his space and time.

As am I.

May it continue for both of us until we are called – as Denty would say – to that 'Top Pen' in life's mart.

But what an incredibly rich time it has been here, in every sense of the word, on our Shoulder on the Hill.

Carol Madeline Graham   May 2020

A SHOULDER ON THE HILL

There's a shoulder on the hill; a house sits on the shoulder,
Watching the years turn in the Dale below,
The stone slabs of its roof and the old walls straight and firm
Are all washed by the endless seasons' flow.

When the winds of Winter howl and the valley fills with snow,
A fire in the hearth will keep me warm,
And when my breath is turned to ice and the shepherd's ewes are lost
Within its hold, I cannot come to harm.

Here, the Spring winds still blow chill yet days they slowly lengthen
Till green shoots push up through the sleeping ground,
And the glory of the Curlew's cry echoes through these hills,
While lambs suck from the ewes the Shepherd found.

When the Summer days are come, it seems night has almost gone
As grass is cut in long, warm evenings' balm,
And backs bend to the shears as the sheep are shorn of fleece,
While hay fills up each empty, waiting barn.

But when the curlews' cry is gone and swallows have all flown,
The leaves change hue to Autumn shades of gold,
Then new life begins to grow safe, deep inside each ewe,
As the circle of the year is growing old.

There's a shoulder on the hill; a house sits on the shoulder,
Watching the years turn in the Dale below,
The stone slabs of its roof and the old walls straight and firm
Are all washed by the endless seasons' flow.

Carol Madeline Graham   2002

ACKNOWLEDGEMENTS

Without the help of so many people these stories would never have appeared in print. My thanks go to all the people and animals that played a part in creating the stories in the first place and to the friends, neighbours and family who constantly encouraged me to keep writing them down and to later tackle the difficult task of turning them all into a book. I suppose I also need to thank dear old Hill House East for being the root out of which all these stories have grown. There are however individuals that I must acknowledge with particular gratitude for their specific role in creating 'A Shoulder on the Hill':

Hilary Kristensen of Wagtail Press, who took the ultimate step of having enough faith in the book to publish it.
Gill Whatmough, who put in so much work to edit the book on a tight timeline and was very patient with me altering things nearly every day!
Jennie Henderson, an artist and friend who created the majority of the sketches in the book so beautifully and who also put me in touch with her sister-in-law --
Christine Barnicoat, who painstakingly proofread the whole book, probably several times!
Christine Stark, my dear friend over our hill in Teesdale, who paginated a manuscript that was a real tangle and her husband –
Stuart Stark, who gave unstintingly of his help and advice, gleaned from his lifetime in the printing world.
Tony Graham, my brother-in-law, who has photocopied tirelessly for me on a photocopier much cleverer than mine!
Anisa Jameson, who created the distinctive Hill House East logo for the B&B, which is now used throughout the book.
Peter Bowes, author of the seminal book on the history of Weardale, *'Clearing the Forest'*, who so kindly allowed me to draw on historical research and facts from that book.

David Heatherington, of the Weardale Museum and High House Chapel who allowed me to draw on historical facts from those sources about early Methodism in Weardale.

Christine Ruskin, whose books and photos of a Weardale rapidly being lost – The Disappearing Farms of Weardale and The Disappearing Mills and Bread Ovens – were such a source of information and inspiration to me.

All those who acted as readers as the book progressed and fed back opinions and suggestions, especially *Jenny Spooner,* who appears in the book and was a writer herself, but who very sadly died before this book was published.

Ian Dent and his wife Lynne, without whom, quite frankly it would be a very thin and boring book! Their friendship, constant support and endless depths of local information are quite simply essential to our life here 'On the hill'.

Lastly, but never least, my husband *John.* He has lived the whole of this book with me; his atmospheric watercolour of Weardale made the perfect cover picture; he also created beautiful sketches to put in it, took many of the photographs used in it and advised me on so many technical things gleaned from his many years of experience in the printing trade He has also supported me through my constant doubts and worries about writing it *at all* and, in the final push towards publication, supplied me with encouragement and endless cups of tea and coffee - and more than the odd glass of wine - to keep me going..